LEAVING THE HIGHWAY

Leaving the Highway:
Six Contemporary New Zealand Novelists

MARK WILLIAMS

AUCKLAND UNIVERSITY PRESS

First published 1990
Reprinted 1992
Auckland University Press
University of Auckland
Private Bag 92019
Auckland, New Zealand

© Mark Williams 1990

ISBN 1 86940 044 5

Publication is assisted
by the Literature Committee of the Queen Elizabeth II Arts
Council.

Typeset in Palatino
by University Printing Services, Auckland.
Printed by SRM Production Services

Distributed outside New Zealand
by Oxford University Press

For my parents, Cliff and Eileen

Leave the highway just past a store
almost opposite this shortcut through the gorge.
You want to bear west beyond the store,
back of the district high school. As you go
you raise an abandoned church (which is here)
with a small marae. Shortly, the river.
Follow its bank for a bit, until
a farmer's yard, between the cowbail and pigpens.
So drive slowly. You'll need to.
The map says the road ends there. Not true.

KENDRICK SMITHYMAN, 'Reading the Maps An Academic
    Exercise'

Contents

Preface

This book is a critical study of six major contemporary New Zealand novelists: Janet Frame, C. K. Stead, Maurice Gee, Witi Ihimaera, Ian Wedde, and Keri Hulme. Primarily it is a study of the current formal directions of fiction in this country. But it also seeks to understand the ways in which a deep-seated unease about New Zealand's cultural situation is finding expression in the novel.

The book consists of an introductory chapter sketching the literary-cultural context of the late 1970s and 1980s; six chapters on the individual novelists each focusing on one or two major novels; a conclusion which attempts some generalisations about the condition of and directions for New Zealand literature in terms of those particular novelists.

It might be asked why these six novelists were chosen and not a number of other prominent New Zealand novelists. To many readers Maurice Shadbolt, Patricia Grace, and Fiona Kidman have as great a claim to being considered 'major' as those who have been selected. I settled on Frame, Stead, Gee, Ihimaera, Wedde and Hulme because they seemed to me the main forces in the field in whose work the range of possibilities of contemporary New Zealand fiction was best concentrated. These novelists seemed to me to have extended the tradition of New Zealand fiction. All had moved beyond realism without abandoning it altogether; all had struggled to forge a more complex realism. Moreover, these were the novelists to whose works I found myself returning again and again with the sense that they had not been exhausted by my previous readings. Even the flaws I found in their performances as writers seemed part of the scope and ambition of their undertakings. Above all, their work was pertinent to several related questions which lie at the centre of this book's attention:

What are the relations of contemporary novelists to their significant New Zealand precursors?

9

What does it mean to talk about a New Zealand 'tradition' in the novel?

Has there been over the last decade a 'break' with the longstanding tradition of social realism derived from Frank Sargeson?

If so, where are the 'transforming energies' of current New Zealand fiction to be found?

What bearing do the current cultural disputes about race, language and belonging have on contemporary New Zealand novelists?

Since the middle of the nineteenth century the question of national identity has been a continual problem to which New Zealand writers from Thomas Bracken to Keri Hulme have offered various solutions, both affirmative and negative. But at no time since the 1930s has fiction in this country been so directly involved with crucial and unresolved questions of national self-definition and evaluation as was the case in the late 1980s. In the various and vigorous engagements of these writers with previous New Zealand writers, with the English language in the forms it has taken in this country, with the two main cultural traditions that have taken root here, and with the general literary inheritance of the English-speaking peoples, we find the extent and the limits of our common world as citizens of a country still in the making.

A number of people were helpful in the writing of this book. Elizabeth Caffin at Auckland University Press gave invaluable guidance on its scope and shape. Ken Arvidson, John Jowett, and Kirsty Cochrane, my colleagues in the English Department at the University of Waikato, and Susan Ash at Auckland University read parts of the work and offered encouragement and advice. Alan Riach, who was visiting Fellow in the English Department, and Trevor Burnard, who lectured in the History Department during 1989, read early drafts and made detailed comments. Gregory O'Brien, as always, was a source of ideas and encouragement. My wife, Kathryn Rountree, once again, supported, advised, and encouraged me.

I also wish to thank the University of Waikato Research Committee, which generously supported the work with a grant.

Some of the ideas in the book were developed in a number of articles published during 1988 and '89. I wish to thank the editors of *Journal of New Zealand Literature, Island* (Tasmania), *Meridian, Span,* and *Kunapipi* for permission to adapt the material.

INTRODUCTION

The Cultural Context

... it was all very well for the Empire's dairy farm to be momentarily annihilated, but I could not help being suspicious of the involuntary romantic images of tropical islands and palms that it was immediately replaced by.

FRANK SARGESON, *Once Is Enough*[1]

IN a now famous review of the 1985 *Penguin Book of New Zealand Verse* edited by Ian Wedde and Harvey McQueen, C. K. Stead takes Wedde to task for claiming in his introduction that the book is '"the first Penguin anthology anywhere in the 'post-colonial world' to include quantities of poetry in an indigenous language"'.[2] By that inclusion, Wedde means to encourage the acceptance by white New Zealanders of their Pacific location and to signal the anthologists' recognition of the priority of the Maori presence in that place. At the same time, Wedde offers a kind of belated homecoming for white New Zealanders by setting out to show how the development of New Zealand poetry into a distinctive tradition in its own right has made it possible to set poetry in the New Zealand-English idiom alongside poetry in Maori.[3]

Stead's response to this is to assert the centrality of the British and European culture, 'which is my particular inheritance and which has become also a part of the inheritance of most who are of Maori blood'. Moreover, he adds, 'the idea that our hold [on that inheritance] is secure, or that we go on possessing it without effort and vigilance, seems to me false and dangerous'. When Stead points out that the English tradition 'includes Shakespeare, the English Bible, the Romantic poets, Dickens, Melville, Henry James, and so on up to the great moderns',[4] he draws on T. S. Eliot's view that tradition constitutes the essential background to literary activity provided by the continuous civilisation of which the individual writer is a part. For Eliot, that continuity is more thoroughly grounded in the classics of Greece, Rome and the general European inheritance than it is for Stead, and

11

Eliot lays a much greater stress on the force of Christianity in that heritage than Stead does. But for both, 'tradition' means the primal allegiance owed by writers in all those countries that have come under European influence to the general European high-cultural legacy.

We find here a difference about the meaning of the term 'tradition' which goes to the heart of a current debate about the condition, direction, and priorities of New Zealand culture. Much of the argument about cultural identity in this country rests on a conflict between a sense of tradition which would preserve the essential links of white culture to its European past and an opposing 'post-colonial' sense which would purge local writing habits of Eurocentrism and privilege the indigenous tradition that is considered more appropriate to a Pacific country.

The trouble is that *both* these understandings of tradition, in the terms in which they have generally been advanced in this country, are limiting because they restrict the sources of knowledge that are available to writers. In the Introduction to his *Six Plays* the Nigerian writer, Wole Soyinka, states:

> There's no way at all that I will ever preach the cutting off of *any* source of knowledge: Oriental, European, African, Polynesian, or whatever. There's no way anyone can ever legislate that, once knowledge comes to one, that knowledge should be forever excised as if it never existed.[5]

Soyinka's words are particularly pertinent wherever the legacy of colonialism remains a shaping force in the national culture. He implies that this is an ambivalent legacy. Colonialism caused loss and humiliation. It mutilated the cultures of subject peoples. But it also brought with it other kinds of knowledge, knowledge that can be cast aside now only at the cost of further impoverishment. The danger in the effort to redirect a culture whose habitual forms and judgements have been determined elsewhere is that decolonisation will mean no more than the attempt to expunge all traces of the colonising presence. In countries trying to assert a special national character where identity has traditionally been granted in terms of some colonial power, the urge to cut off the distracting sources of knowledge which accompanied that power is understandable, but it is nevertheless regrettable. For the descendants of the colonisers as well as those of the colonised, the history of the colonial encounter is an ineradicable and a formative experience. It must be confronted, not denied; met in its complexity, not forced into manichaean oppositions; understood, not simply resisted. This is especially true in New Zealand now that a new nationalism is developing around the rhetoric of post-colonialism.

Over the last decade, many Pakeha have become dissatisfied with their lingering 'colonial' status, anxious to find some means of self-definition that does not categorise them as displaced Britons. Many have come to see themselves as actors in the politics of decolonisation rather than as distant observers of it. At the same time, Maori people have shown themselves increasingly determined to identify themselves as the victims of colonial dispossession rather than as partners in a benevolent social project aimed at establishing a model country in the Antipodes. Inevitably, this process has encouraged a reaction against the stubbornly English elements in New Zealand culture. Along with this reaction there have emerged signs of that wish, which Soyinka fiercely castigates, to cut off objectionable sources of knowledge because of their colonial associations.

One result of this is that the former colonials transpose the desire for 'home' from the lost European origin to the world immediately to hand and seek to identify with Maori religious beliefs and with the indigenous features of the country. Now the 'native', which had for so long reminded the settlers of their distance from England, is made to speak of a new sense of belonging. The danger here is that identifying with the native will serve the purposes of an ancient but psychologically devious need among the descendants of the settlers to validate their appropriation of the original inhabitants' land by a further act of appropriation. To claim that one has come 'home' by virtue of having turned away from the European origin to discover the unique values of indigenous culture is in the interests of the claimants more than it is in those of the native peoples themselves.

As far back as his introduction to his *A Book of New Zealand Verse* (1945), Allen Curnow suggested a way of seeing the traditions available to writers in this country which is neither narrowly Eurocentric nor predatory on the indigenous culture. There Curnow quotes a poem by Charles Brasch, 'The Islands':

> Remindingly beside the quays, the white
> Ships lie smoking; and from their haunted bay
> The godwits vanish towards another summer.

Everywhere in light and calm the murmuring
Shadow of departure; distance looks our way;
And none knows where he will lie down at night.

Curnow glosses these lines by noting that it may be by way of the white New Zealanders' disquieting sense of the Pacific as a sign of distance and isolation that we may 'draw nearer the imagination of the Polynesian peoples, islanders and inveterate voyagers; at least in the powers with which we seem to credit the sea. We are closer to them in this, and in what it may imply, than by the direct allusion to Maori myth and chant which some New Zealand writers favour.' In other words, it is not by throwing into their writing the ransacked material of an oral culture that the white New Zealanders will come to understand their place in the world but by 'some identity of vision' that will allow them at last to enter *their own* history.[6]

Tradition, for Curnow, is the debt a people owes to the cultural achievements of its forebears, and the white New Zealanders naturally owe the major part of their debt to the British from whom they sprang. But that recognition of tradition must be modified by a respect for the new and special environment in which the transplanted Europeans find themselves and for the distinctive culture of the people already there.

We glimpse here an understanding of our place in the world as not penalised by its remoteness. For Curnow, even in the 1930s, distance and isolation did not condemn New Zealanders to mediocrity in all their endeavours, as they did for Quentin Pope, editor of *Kowhai Gold*, a 1930 poetry anthology. 'Islanded twelve hundred miles from that other great province of the intellect, Australia, the New Zealanders have heard few of the echoes of modern thought', wrote Pope.[7] They were, for Curnow, the marks both of limit and possibility. The literary nationalism which Curnow began to articulate in the mid 1930s asserted that the white New Zealanders must come to terms with their location and condition; citizens of a small and young country at the bottom of the world, they could nevertheless create a national culture by taking what they needed from other places, including Britain, and shaping it to the peculiar needs and pressures of the new place. The task was to remain responsive to the particular realities to hand, to learn intelligently from other similarly placed peoples, and to avoid self-aggrandisement. In such terms they might come slowly but surely to self-knowledge and, doing so, might exert their own weight in the larger world. But there must be no cutting off of the available sources of knowledge, no retreat into the literary equivalent of protectionist trade barriers.

Fifty years later, the fortress New Zealand option is even less credible than it was in the 1930s. Throughout the post-war period popular culture in New Zealand, as in every other Western country, has been saturated by the prevailing Western fashions, with an American influence progressively replacing the British one since the 1960s. It is true that the efforts of Charles Brasch through *Landfall* and to some extent also those of literary 'nationalists' like Keith Sinclair, Stead, and Curnow himself to promote a New Zealand literary tradition tended up to the 1970s to insulate New Zealand high culture against the encroachment of too much American influence. Even where they responded to American writers, Curnow and Stead were vigorously opposed to the importation of literary theory. Right into the eighties, in fact, there was a correspondence between the efforts to protect local manufacturing against foreign competition and those to promote a distinctive national literature. As Simon During has noted, '[c]ultural sanctuaries flourish behind trade barriers'. [8] Like the economy, however, the literary scene in New Zealand in the middle eighties was radically exposed to the advanced 'technology' of literary theory imported from Europe and America. After the Labour Government came to power in 1984, the longstanding barriers and tariffs protecting local manufacturing were phased out and the process by which New Zealand society became assimilated into the prevailing forms, cultural as well as economic, of Western capitalism was accelerated.

Yet in the late 1980s, in spite of the concern to be up to date and international shown by the appearance of postmodernist fiction and theory in the literary magazines, the arguments of the 1920s and '30s about the cultural situation of the white New Zealanders persisted in thinly disguised forms. Jonathan Lamb has described as a recurring cultural nightmare for the Pakeha the possibility 'that the past might be forgotten or that it might have to be confronted'.[9] The problem is that if it is not confronted it will return and we shall be condemned to repeat in parody the mistakes of the past, such as *Kowhai Gold*. If we are 'to know [our]selves least blindly', as During has stated the problem, we shall need to look to the past for the meaning it holds about the present.[10]

What does it mean in the late 1980s to say that there is a New

Zealand tradition in fiction? For in spite of the constant process of assimilation and change, there *is* such a thing, as the attentions paid by contemporary writers to earlier ones clearly show. A tradition does not mean something closed, exclusive, and final — a body of canonised texts. It means the way in which writing in the present is shaped by writing in the past and itself changes those existing works. It means the way in which people writing in a common language in a given place over time build up familiar patterns of reference. In New Zealand the problem of tradition is complicated by a great deal of confusion about what the past means for the cultural preoccupations of the present. To ask what the past means, what bearing it has on the present, is to ask what kind of country New Zealanders (and *which* New Zealanders) wish to inhabit; and that question remains recalcitrantly unresolved.

*   *   *

In a survey of recent trends in New Zealand fiction published in the Australian quarterly, *Meanjin*, in 1985, Lydia Wevers depicted a writing scene undergoing a remarkable process of transformation. The strong currents in contemporary New Zealand fiction, she announced, offer a challenge to the tradition of social realism so long entrenched in this country, a tradition fatally associated with the outlook of Pakeha men. Women and Maori writers, she said, 'have little use for the apparent literary connection between (white) maleness and New Zealandness'. While these groups, according to Wevers, are extending the kinds of experience realist fiction can include, countering its monocultural habits, the postmodernists are engaged in directly challenging the governing assumptions of realism itself. This leads Wevers to her large claim: '[t]he transforming energy in New Zealand writing at the present time', she asserts, 'is located in those groups of writers who are outside inherited, Pakeha traditions'.[11]

It is true that the realist tradition associated with Frank Sargeson came increasingly under challenge in the 1980s; it is also true that a great deal of energetic, adventurous and significant fiction has issued from the groups which Wevers singles out. Since the mid 1970s in prose fiction as in poetry a body of 'women's writing' has emerged, laying stress on and giving new value to the experience common to women. This process has extended and enriched New Zealand fiction. It means that a more complex and extensive picture of New Zealand life is offered by our writers. But we need to distinguish between writing by women that is significant as writing and writing which is significant as 'women's writing'. Janet Frame's novels certainly represent the condition and outlook of women in a society in which men hold most of the power. They offer a trenchant criticism of male power. But to read them exclusively in these terms is to lose sight of their force and interest as works of fiction. The central and permanent feature of her art as a novelist is her preoccupation with language itself. The criticism of New Zealand life in Frame's novels is directed at the linguistic forms in which the culture embodies its repressions, prejudices and fears. Her novels are valuable not merely because they are formally and linguistically experimental nor because they represent memorably a particular variety of social experience, but because they refuse to allow a separation between language and experience.

The same kind of distinction needs to be applied to writing by Maori. In 1969 Bill Pearson confidently predicted the emergence of a distinctive and distinguished body of fiction by Maori. Maori writing, he suggested, 'will be distinct in its passion, its lyricism and unforced celebration of living'. Provided that relations between Maori and Pakeha became more cordial, Pearson felt that Maori writing, when it appeared, was 'likely to be free of the doubt and hesitancy and self-interrogation that can inhibit a Pakeha writer'.[12] By the close of the eighties Pearson's prediction had been amply fulfilled. A significant body of Maori fiction had been published and Maori novelists of stature — Ihimaera, Hulme and Grace — had emerged. It is true that their writing was characterised as much by 'doubt and hesitancy' as by 'lyricism and unforced celebration of living'. But then, relations between the races had not developed steadily 'towards a cordial inter-cultural adjustment', as Pearson had hoped they might.

The overwhelming effect of the emergence of this body of writing was positive in social as well as literary terms. It made possible a more complex and accommodating cultural picture, a greater degree of self-understanding among New Zealanders. Pearson had written that 'New Zealand life will be greatly enriched when we can learn to see ourselves and the country through the eyes of a number of Maori writers and it may well be that Maoris can help us find ways we wouldn't have found for ourselves'.[13] To some extent this has occurred, although the process is far from complete. Moreover, the 'sympathetic hearing' Pearson hoped that Maori writers would receive — allowing for notable exceptions — has been granted. Reviews of books by Maori in the *Listener* have generally been favourable and culturally sympathetic. Maori writers have figured prominently in local literary awards.

In 1990, twenty years after Pearson had made his prediction, with a secure body of Maori writing in print, it is time to begin the task of making distinctions and discriminations rather than simply welcoming the writing. Essentially, a distinction needs to be made between fiction which is valuable because it speaks for some area of social experience, hitherto neglected, and that which is important because it finds new ways of expressing and giving form to that experience. Short story writers like Apirana Taylor and Bruce Stewart write from a strongly Maori perspective and vividly express the broken lives of dispossessed people. Witi Ihimaera also speaks of and for the Maori experience, but he has struggled to find appropriate forms in which to convey that experience. His novel *The Matriarch* is a vast, ambitious, although flawed, attempt to stretch the novel form to accommodate the Maori world view, Maori mythology and Maori history. The same can be said of Hulme's *the bone people*. It is time now to sort out the ambition from the achievement in such major works.

The 'transforming energy' Wevers identifies is more difficult to locate amid the dispersed activity of current New Zealand fiction than she allows. Moreover, the desire to place that energy 'outside' inherited Pakeha traditions is a curious form of what Australians used to call 'the cultural cringe',[14] except that where the Australian term meant the habit among white Australians of deferring to a colonial centre, the New Zealand variety characteristically involves the display by anxious Pakeha of deference towards the indigenous people of New Zealand.

The desire among Pakeha to throw off the colonial taint of a European heritage is an understandable cultural wish. The problem arises where this wish becomes caught up with the desire of many white New Zealanders to say, we belong in this place and possess a unique identity as New Zealanders by virtue of our sympathetic identification with the original inhabitants. Here Maori culture becomes a decorative sign of difference which displays to the world, like native flora or Maori myth in *Kowhai Gold* poetry, the peculiar tone of New Zealand life and landscape.[15] The literary nationalism that appeared in New Zealand during the 1930s in opposition to *Kowhai Gold* was considerably less self-deceiving than that fashionable in the late 1980s, which attempted to overcome the Pakeha sense of homelessness by using Maori culture to signal the distinctiveness of the national character — the equivalent of celebrating the sesquicentenary of the Treaty of Waitangi by placing 'a thousand poi dancers on Auckland's wharf', as Trixie Te Arama Menzies has put it. [16]

The nationalism of the 1980s rested on the wish to feel utterly unique in the world. The need to break with European values and European origins was stressed. European culture generally was denigrated as materialistic, alienating, scientific, commercial ('Europe' here stands not for Europe itself but Anglo-Saxon industrial civilisation most visibly expressed today by the United States). In opposition to this the Maori qualities of New Zealand were emphasised. The values of spirituality, community, and love were seen as peculiarly Maori. Maori culture here figures as a link with pre-capitalist social life and serves to remind the Pakeha of the pastoral dream of New Zealand as a South Seas Eden. The irony is that the separation of head and heart, reason and feeling, was foisted on the Maori people by the dualism inherent in Pauline Christianity. The way in which Maori writing often stresses feeling rather than reason confirms the dualistic habit of thought that came with the missionaries at the time of European colonisation.

At the basis of the nationalism that emerged in New Zealand in the middle eighties and was expressed by the reception of *the bone people* was the aim to weed the exotics out of the local garden and make the Pakeha into genuinely 'native' New Zealanders. This would realise the vision of Eden at the heart of Christian mythology which came with the settlers to New Zealand and which stubbornly remains. Once they had truly embraced their Pacific location (and remade their culture in deference to a romantically interpreted image of the Maori), the Pakeha would be able to feel truly at home. A prevalent rhetoric in the 1980s stressed the *difference* of contemporary New Zealand writing from that which preceded it on the grounds that the latter was overly dependent on foreign models. This assumes that a literature decolonises itself simply by turning away from European models. It is the attitude which responds rapturously to a new novel in proportion to the signals that book gives of its 'indigenousness'. Thus Joy

Cowley in the *Listener* greeted *the bone people* as though the novel had sprung straight out of the earth of Aotearoa like some hardy native plant:

> I have been waiting for this novel, watching the earth, knowing it had to come. We all knew it. Some day there would be a flowering of talent which had not been transported from the northern hemisphere, which owed nothing to the literary landscapes of Europe or the film sets of California, but which would grow — seeds, shoots, roots and all — from the breast of Papa. Now we welcome it with a glad cry of recognition.[17]

In other words, the novel realises the collective Pakeha wish (whom else does that inclusive 'we all knew' refer to?) to belong in New Zealand without the sense of being cut off from origins overseas, forever looking back to a plenitude left behind in Britain. Here is a novel written in English, so steeped in Maori spirituality, so confidently attuned to the landscape of Aotearoa, that it confers on responsive Pakeha readers the right to belong in the place as unselfconsciously as the Maori people. What 'we all' have been waiting for, then, is precisely this sign of acceptance, this rooting of ourselves in the place effected by a 'talent which ha[s] not been transported'. Hulme's novel comes out of the ground because it has no other possible origins, most prior New Zealand *literature* being corrupted by the European consciousness — male, monocultural, foreign — which has for so long inhabited it.

Yet what is being transformed in the most significant recent fiction produced in this country is the realist tradition itself, not into some other thing, as Wevers would have it, but into a richer version of its own possibilities. This process of transformation and enrichment is being accomplished not by Cowley's desire to immerse the novel in the natural world, but by the 'transportation' of literary influence from, among other places, the corruptly cosmopolitan northern hemisphere. These literary influences are then accommodated to the peculiar stresses and urgencies of the New Zealand writing scene. In other words, they become part of a recognisable 'tradition', one which flows through the major texts of New Zealand social realism from the 1930s and '40s under attack in the 1980s as masculine, exclusive, even racist.

This is not to say that a specifically New Zealand tradition in fiction was founded by Sargeson in the 1930s in the way that the American tradition in the novel was established by the great works of the 1850s, by Melville and Hawthorne. Sargeson himself, not surprisingly, saw his own efforts to forge a literary language appropriate to the New Zealand experience as analogous to those of Mark Twain or Henry Lawson to break with the genteel 'English' writing of an earlier generation of dilettante lady novelists and colonial poets. For Sargeson, even Katherine Mansfield was of no real use to subsequent New Zealand writers. Her influence was discernible chiefly in what he called the 'minor' line of 'feminine' writing that his own writing opposed.[18] It was not simply that he found her international style and her modernism uncongenial; he had himself tried unsuccessfully to master both. The problem was chiefly that 'she spent much of her life in a state of suspension between two hemispheres' and thereby removed herself from a 'sense of social tradition'.[19] For Sargeson, Mansfield was a dangerous influence on New Zealand writers struggling to develop in New Zealand itself a separate national literature.

The very force with which Sargeson denied any influence on his writing by Mansfield suggests the presence of resistance. For Sargeson, Mansfield was dangerous because she stood in the way of his desire to present himself (as Curnow presented himself in respect of New Zealand poetry) as the Abrahamic figure with whom the true lineage of New Zealand fiction begins. It is the authority which invests Sargeson's statements on how fiction is to be practised in New Zealand and his impatience with predecessors, particularly female ones, rather than any acts of self-promotion that announce this desire. Sargeson asserted that there are in fact two separate lines of New Zealand fiction, the feminine impressionist and the masculine realist. By insisting that the masculine line, because of its 'sense of social tradition', is superior to the feminine one, with its stress on sensibility and 'the isolated details and moments of life',[20] Sargeson was staking his claim as against Mansfield's to be the true initiator of a properly New Zealand kind of fiction: realist, masculine, socially significant, linguistically nationalist. He was, after all, the first to record the peculiar dialect of the Pakeha tribe in a way that, while acknowledging all its limitations as speech, made it a flexible literary medium and the vehicle of a powerful negative criticism of the society.

The view of Sargeson as founder of the true national line in fiction[21] not only misrepresents and undervalues fiction by women in New Zealand but also oversimplifies Sargeson's and Mansfield's own writing; the complexity and contradictions in both are more important than any tendencies towards realism or impressionism which may be isolated to show the debts owed them by other New Zealand writers. To characterise Mansfield as an 'impressionistic' writer, as Sargeson does slightingly, is to ignore her concern with the ways in which social experience is registered within the consciousness of the individual. The hard force of precise social observation is present everywhere in her work, not only in isolated stories like 'The Woman at the Store' or 'Millie'. Mansfield's sense of the minute details of which life is composed, grasped as epiphanic moments of consciousness, is always controlled by her acute awareness of life as *social* being, by her awareness of the immersion of humans in the codes and rules and determinants of social existence. Her 'attendance upon the world'[22] involves a continual traffic between those external conditions and the individual consciousnesses on which they impinge.

Conversely, to characterise Sargeson, even the early Sargeson of a secularised moral fable like 'Conversation with My Uncle', as a social realist writer, as though he is unconcerned with interior life, is to simplify his work. In reading Sargeson we sometimes feel that he sees New Zealanders as the inarticulate, almost blank, puppets through which the powerful negations of the culture speak. It is as though his characters have no inner lives, so that their occasional minimal and baffled gestures towards self-disclosure echo over the terrifying absences that lie within. Yet Sargeson's stories are as resonant with sensibility as Mansfield's. The difference is that he works expressionistically, allowing the shapes of lack and desire to spill into a fictional world from the minds of characters whose blandness is superficial and misleading, while she works as a symbolist, using objects as correlatives to states of feeling.

The fiction of Sargeson and of John Mulgan, another major thirties writer unfashionable in the eighties because of his precoccupation with Pakeha males, has not been made redundant by subsequent literary history, but it has been changed by that history. It has been made more capacious in the sense that new ways of reading it have appeared. This is why the real struggle in contemporary literary history is not to identify transforming departures but to find more generous ways of reading our *whole* literary inheritance. Wevers acknowledges this when she says that the social realist tradition is still 'alive and relevant within our literary history and consciousness'.[23] What she does not sufficiently acknowledge is the extent to which fiction writers in the 1980s not only build on the major texts of that tradition but also alter our understanding of those texts.

Take for example, the 'snooks' (a 1930s slang term for children) that turn up in Wedde's 1988 novel, *Survival Arts*.[24] These 'snooks', part of the novel's word-hoard of slang, idiolect, and literary borrowings, derive from Sargeson's famous 1945 story, 'The Hole that Jack Dug': 'Of course, Jack knows that to run the house, with the snooks growing up fast, his missis could have always done with considerably more money than he's able to let her have'.[25] Wedde is signalling by the borrowing that he feels able to take for granted the whole long effort begun by Sargeson to naturalise New Zealand-English as a literary medium.

Sargeson in the 1930s set about defining a distinctive national form of the language by concentrating on the speech of working men, often itinerant, rural, generally poor, much as Australian nationalist writers in the 1890s turned to the speech of the swaggies and bullockies of the outback as embodying the most characteristic, and therefore distinctively Australian, language use. When Wedde talks in the Introduction to *The Penguin Book of New Zealand Verse* about the growth of the English language 'into its location',[26] he means that after more than 150 years of habitation in New Zealand the English language as it has developed here is no longer foreign. Hence the ease of that borrowing from Sargeson. In 'The Hole that Jack Dug' the chief sign of falseness is Jack's wife's preference for the 'English' novels of Hugh Walpole, while the narrator's unqualified approval is conferred upon the inarticulate but obdurately masculine, unpretentious, and 'New Zealand' Jack (one of the hidden ironies here is that Walpole was in fact born in New Zealand, though he later became a successful English novelist). Wedde works by accretion in contrast to Sargeson's rigorous pruning. His novel proliferates with different kinds of language use: the vernacular rhythms of post-sixties American poetry coming by way of his own poetry directly into the prose, contemporary urbanised lingo, traditional New Zealand working-class speech with its heavy residues of thirties slang. But all the language, literary and colloquial, has been invested with Wedde's quick sense of the peculiar, lithe quality of the language of the place.

Even *the bone people*, which has often been treated as a triumphant break with the governing assumptions and ideological limitations of the masculine realist tradition, may be read as a complicated and subversive, but also curiously reconfirming, version of John Mulgan's 1939 classic of New Zealand humanist realism, *Man Alone*. In both novels there is a journey to the heart of the country by broken individuals who literally *fall* into the landscape and are subsequently restored, healed by notably similar figures of extreme isolation and priestly authority, and who emerge with a vision of social regeneration and a purified sense of connection to the landscape of New Zealand.[27] In other words, Hulme may reinterpret the tradition, subject it to necessary revision, but she is no more wholly 'outside' it than is Stead.

In fact, the very willed quality that surrounds the Maori cultural material in the novel, which Stead sees as a sign of spuriousness,[28] indicates the essential continuity of *the bone people* with previous Pakeha writing. The Maori spiritual beliefs we find in the novel do not need to be seen as growing directly and 'authentically' out of Hulme's experience as a Maori. They can be found in such standard works on the subject as the ethnological monographs of eminent Pakeha museum curator and recorder of Maori beliefs Elsdon Best and in the retellings of Maori myth and legend by A. W. Reed. This does not make the novel's Maoriness spurious, it merely makes it literary.

The Maoriness of *the bone people*, then, is once again and not illegitimately, a means of setting a more attractive and humane world of values against the negative ones seen as dominant in Pakeha culture. But the Maori for Hulme do not simply provide a compensating image to Pakeha society as they do for, say, Noel Hilliard in his stories of the 1950s. By dramatising the cultural dislocation in the lives of so many contemporary Maori through an unflinching naturalism, Hulme avoids being merely patronising. The novel's singular strength is its ability to inhabit while renovating the familiar house of New Zealand fiction. Its weakness is its refusal to acknowledge how much earlier New Zealand writing has shaped it.

Both Janet Frame and Stead owe as much to Sargeson as to Mansfield. It's not that their writing is 'realistic' in precisely the way Sargeson's was. It takes in all the developments in fictional practice over the last fifty years, and with that the progressive swerve away from mimesis over the last twenty. Frame's *Living in the Maniototo* (1979), in particular, is as linguistically self-conscious, as brilliantly punning, as tricky in its refusal straightforwardly to represent, as any 'metafictional' novel. Yet *Living in the Maniototo*, with its refusal to limit its fictional strategies to any single style or formal orientation, makes categories like postmodern, a term used by Wevers to describe those writers who break most radically with the assumptions of realism, seem somehow inadequate. The term accounts for a tendency in the novel's total means, but not the whole thing.

A moment in *Living in the Maniototo* when a character is 'erased' by a household cleanser makes the bizarre novels of Thomas Pynchon seem mundane by comparison:

There was a flash of light, a smell of laundry and the penetrating fumes of a powerful cleanser, then a neutral nothing-smell, not even the usual substituted forest glade or field of lavender or carnation, and all that remained of Tommy were two faded footprints on the floor.

'Things like that don't happen,' Brian said when we had arrived home. We were both shocked by the sudden plague of unreality. (p.38)

Frame here employs a species of black humour to show how advertising images permeate and condition modern life — in this country as much as in America. Yet this spillage of unreality into the world of the novel is also motivated by a desire to register the bizarre as a part of 'normal' social experience; and here it continues a line of which Sargeson remains both instigator and, Frame apart, the exemplary practitioner. There are, after all, gothic, macabre, and bizarre touches throughout Sargeson's writing, and a discernible agitation of the realist surface of the prose by a deliberately subversive homoerotic subtext.[29] Moreover, as Peter Simpson points out, Sargeson was one of the first New Zealanders to recognise in Ronald Hugh Morrieson's exuberant departures from 'realism' 'a deliberate artistic policy rather than naivety o[r] incompetence'.[30] In a novel first published in 1967 called *The Hangover*, Sargeson used the term 'brick bungalow gothic' to describe the distorted and unreal quality that invests suburbia for a boy beginning to discover the weird forms of sexuality that lie beneath its respectable appearances.[31] Realism was never, in the work of a writer as crafty as Sargeson, straightforward in its means of representation. Conversely, in the work of a writer like Frame, the anti-realist tendencies are always controlled by a complex respect for the details of social experience, a reverent attention to the actual.

At the heart of Frame's New Zealand lies a blankness and a resistance to the humanising efforts of names and familiar objects. It is a vision curiously close in spirit to that in *Man Alone*, where the novel's protagonist finds at the heart of the country an inhuman absence, resistant to *all* habitation, Maori as well as Pakeha. The antithesis of this vision is the moment in *the bone people* where the country's 'spiritual' centre is invoked. But it remains unclear whether this figuring forth of the country's magical heart in Hulme's novel is meant to be seen as a flagrantly 'fictional' solution to a cultural impasse or whether we are meant to take it as an unusual but credible variety of human experience.

As for Stead, he sees himself as so much Sargeson's true heir in his recent fiction that he feels able to indulge in occasional affectionate delinquencies. The influence of Sargeson on a generally realist writer like Owen Marshall is more obviously marked but no more fundamental. In *All Visitors Ashore* and *The Death of the Body*, Stead's prose has become more metafictional while maintaining that sense of political and social urgency that has consistently characterised his work. Stead's longstanding resistance to the 'truth-telling' propensities of 1930s English realism has always rested on a fatal attraction towards what he reproves.

The seeming contradiction between the two tendencies is a calculated strategy. The problem is that politicians have turned contemporary history into a 'comic strip' world,[32] and the novelist must reply in kind. For Stead, only by dealing directly in the magically real, can the contemporary novelist 'get nearer to reality'.[33] But 'reality' here means what both Frame and Sargeson have always understood by the term: an endless process of the transformation of the everyday by the contents of the imagination. As Frame puts it in *Living in the Maniototo*: '"Those creatures and worlds that we know only in sleep and dream and mythology — of yesterday and of today — the magical technology — are emerging as usual reality in the new dimensions of living and dying"' (p.39).

What we need is a definition of realism sufficiently generous to allow for the narrative mischiefs practised especially but not exclusively by Sargeson, Frame and Stead. Stead defends a sense of realism which seems capacious enough. He allows that 'the old realist tradition' is inadequate to all the demands placed on fiction by a contemporary writer. 'But if realism fails', he adds, '. . . it fails in surrendering the real — the truth — the actual. One goes beyond realism in order to get nearer to reality, not to dispense with it.'[34] In other words, realism must acknowledge that penetration of the ordinary by the extraordinary that Frame sees as the key feature of contemporary 'normality', yet it must not forget its reponsibilities to the common world of experience. For Stead, there is a reality prior to language and, however playful, selfconscious, or exuberant the maker of fictions chooses to be, the worlds of fiction finally pay rent to the world of fact.

The problem here is that Stead's understanding of reality does not always allow for the wholly opposed interpretations of the term adopted by those whose experience of New Zealand history has been radically different from Stead's own. This raises problems in respect of writing by Maori people in particular, where the writer explicitly sets out to oppose the dominant construction of New Zealand 'reality' by Pakeha culture. While Stead has been tolerant of writers whose sense of the real allows for playful intrusions by the imagination, he has been conspicuously antagonistic to those who depart too abruptly from the probable into surrealism, linguistic self-reflexivity, or fantasy. Stead has castigated Hulme, for instance, for departing from 'reality' into 'wishful daydream'.[35] Stead's view is that novels should not indiscriminately mix elements of historical realism and escapist fantasy writing. Magic realism, for him, has nothing in common with fantasy; it heightens reality rather than dispenses with it.

Both Hulme and Ihimaera, however, have a different understanding from Stead of the way in which the novel can include such diverse elements and a very different concept of fantasy from Stead's. For Ihimaera, 'fantasy' means not mere escape from reality or history but rather a richer engagement of the mind with experience than sober truth-telling realism allows. The terms reality and fantasy are not mutually antagonistic for Ihimaera. In *The Matriarch* the world where the gods and humans communicate is 'a fantasy as well as a real world'.[36] Fantasy is a necessary strategy in the novel for recovering *in a work of fiction* the pre-European world of the Maori.

Realism is a word that, especially in the pejorative sense in which it sometimes used these days, is becoming as unsatisfactory as romanticism has been for a very long time. When A. O. Lovejoy wrote a famous article on the discriminations of 'romanticism', he pointed to how complex and self-contradictory 'romanticism' is as a critical term; and much the same thing could be done for realism. [37]

What separates writers whose work falls under the accommodating head 'realism' is often as significant as what connects them. It is clear enough, for instance, that both Sargeson and Maurice Gee are realists. In fact, Sargeson's classic definition of the humanist realism which is often said to lie at the heart of his fictional practice describes Gee's work even more closely than it does Sargeson's own. For Sargeson, the pervading characteristic of New Zealand social life is the negative kind of puritanism that underpins Pakeha culture. He also holds that novelists must take their material as they find it; the impoverishment of human beings, the thwarting of natural inclinations that flow from puritan repression must not be avoided. According to Sargeson, therefore, 'besides representing and recreating the New Zealand scene, [the New Zealand novelist] will at the same time [offer] a criticism of it'.[38] Sargeson is not advocating preaching or propaganda. The skill of the novelist will mean that such criticism is implicit. But, for Sargeson, the novelist in New Zealand is obliged to be on the side of life against the inhibiting gods of the culture, and this has been taken as a central feature of the 'Sargeson line' in New Zealand fiction.

Maurice Gee's fiction belongs in this line of 'critical realism'. At the centre of all his work we find a body of humane attitudes pitted against the negations of Pakeha culture and the puritan legacy which runs through that culture. In *Plumb* the motif of the eels signals the potentially sinister energies that lie just below the surface of cultural repression. Here Gee looks back to a Sargeson story like 'Sale Day', where the natural desires of Victor, denied any normal means of expression, have become distorted and dangerous, manifesting themselves in ugly forms of violence. But here also the differences between the two writers emerge. The violence in Sargeson is quite unlike anything in Gee; it is at once more shocking and less real. Perhaps this difference proceeds from the different levels of negative authorial psychology that are worked into the texts. But the telling difference is generic. Sargeson's notorious use of violence is tied up with the gothic element that complicates his particular species of realism, and this is quite absent in Gee.

In Gee's fiction of the 1980s, however, a new tone and formal orientation emerge which complicate the naturalism that is so marked in his earlier fiction. It is not that he abandons realist representation and humane vision for the lexical playgrounds of postmodernism. But a radical sense of the failure of those organising principles and perspectives which had sustained both realism and humanism insinuates itself into his novels of the 1980s. The Gee of *Sole Survivor* and *Prowlers* is still a realist in the broadest sense of the term, but his novels now rest on a profound sense of emptiness behind the moral and consoling orders humans formulate in language.

Gee's is a more deliberate and achieved realism than Sargeson's. He encompasses more of 'the New Zealand experience' — social, historical, and linguistic — than does Sargeson. This does not mean that he is a better writer because he more accurately represents the

New Zealand scene. It merely makes his habitual kinds of language use and representation different from Sargeson's. These differences of procedure are related to the different senses of and attitudes towards audience between the two writers. Gee, writing since the 1960s, has been able to feel considerably more at ease with his audience than Sargeson, whose writing habits were formed in the 1930s. For Gee, a significant audience has existed which shares his anti-puritan attitudes. Sargeson, writing at an earlier time, had no such confident sense of sharing a set of values with a sizeable audience. Moreover, Sargeson wrote from the start as a homosexual who could not make explicit the homosexual values and perspectives that inform his work. Hence there is an element of antagonism in his texts towards the reader, which is much more important than that often noted toward characters or cats.[39] His strategies of reader harassment are directed in large part at allowing his 'unspeakable' preferences to find their appropriately oblique and cunning ways of inhabiting the texts.

It is the narrowness of the common acceptance of the term realism, rather than the work itself, which has for so long blinded commentators to the subversions in Sargeson's fiction. Sargeson himself, discussing the possibilities for the New Zealand novel in a 1950 radio talk, pointed out in an aside that 'there are other kinds of novels' than those loosely described as naturalistic or realistic. They are not, he added, 'the ones that New Zealand writers are likely to write — not, at any rate, at our present stage of development'.[40] In other words, there was not a sufficiently sophisticated audience in New Zealand in 1950 to support overtly non-realistic kinds of writing. But there was scope for a fiction that offered the 'accurate' representations demanded by the reader while slyly undermining them at the same time. Here Sargeson's generic complications — his 'gothic' realism — may be seen as a deliberate strategy of audience-teasing, necessary so long as the kind of readership he craved had not come into existence. And here, in this calculated playfulness with genre and with the expectations of his readers, is to be found the essential link between Sargeson and Janet Frame, his most brilliant literary heir so far. In driving a wedge too violently between our literary present and our literary past we run the risk that we shall misrepresent both.

CHAPTER 1

Janet Frame's Suburban Gothic

I have to cry out here that language is all we have for the delicacy
and truth of telling, that words are the sole heroes and heroines
of fiction.

JANET FRAME, *Living in the Maniototo* (p.92)

J ANET FRAME begins her three-part autobiography conventionally
by tracing her ancestry. It is an undistinguished line. Her father
was a railway worker. Her mother's father had been a blacksmith.
There is an 'Oxford doctor' in the distant past; a minor poet and a
publican are also mentioned. But the memory of the ancestral lineage
is unreliable beyond three generations. Even the cousins are scattered
and unrecorded. Of her grandfather and her own father, she notes
that all that remain are the homely objects they made themselves;
their presences survive not in books that tell of their important deeds
nor in family trees but in a boot-last, a pair of ribbed butter pats, a
handful of salmon spoons. 'The Ancestors' who, she had boasted as
a child, 'came over with William of Orange' were mythical. [1]

One is struck not only by the uncompromising honesty of the
record but also by the intimacy, accuracy, and *warmth* of the observation. Frame's childhood was marked by poverty, illness, and death,
but it was not all darkness. Out of a particular background —
working-class, ill-educated, struggling, and baffled as it was —
Frame gathered the strength of vision and the wealth of detailed
remembrances that provided the inexhaustible storehouse of her fiction. For that background contained its own richness, a richness
peculiar to a specific section of the working class at that time. In
Frame's case the richness came primarily by way of her mother with
her love of books and her habit of attendance upon the world. Her
father, a dour figure in the way of New Zealand males of that time and
class, is markedly less vital in her recollections.

As a young woman, Frame's mother had charred in the home of the

30

Beauchamps (Katherine Mansfield's family) in Picton. Yet the Frame children feel 'the mystery and the magic' of their mother's grasp of life when she talks not about the homes of the rich but of commonplace objects:

> She was able to imbue every insect, blade of grass, flower, the dangers and grandeurs of weather and the seasons, with a memorable importance along with a kind of uncertainty and humility that led us to ponder and try to discover the heart of everything. Mother, fond of poetry and reading, writing, and reciting it, communicated to us that same feeling about the world of the written and spoken word.[2]

Frame herself came to books not, like Mansfield, by way of the longing to escape the philistinism of the provincial bourgeoisie but by way of her Christadelphian mother's love of poetry and reading, her sense of the wonder of words as well as things. It was not only her working-class mother's 'wondrous contemplation of the ordinary world' but also her reverent attitude to language that was to prove decisive for Frame.[3]

This background needs to be seen in its wholeness and specificity. New Zealand literature has traditionally depicted fundamentalist Christianity as unrelievedly life-denying, repressive, and hostile to the natural desires of the individual. The lifelong struggle of Frank Sargeson against the wowser's God has established the theme in a single powerful image that signifies the artist's inevitable and positive withdrawal from a puritan culture. From the pre-war stories of Sargeson and John A. Lee to Noel Virtue's *The Redemption of Elsdon Bird* (1988), New Zealand fiction has shown the artist as at odds with the Calvinist God of middle-class, respectable, church-going suburbia. This line itself is part of a copious tradition of fiction, predominantly American, written against puritan culture: Melville, Twain, Stephen Crane. But in New Zealand the image of the artist has become almost indistinguishable from the theme of opposition to puritanism. The term 'critical realism' as a description of a widespread authorial attitude towards the dominant culture draws attention to the entrenchment of puritanism in New Zealand society right up till the 1970s and to the resistance offered it by so many New Zealand writers.

Yet Frame, in spite of the ubiquitous sense in her writing of the artist's separateness from the general culture and in spite of the criticism her fiction offers that society, never shows, either in her fiction or in the autobiographies, her mother's fundamentalist Christianity as anything other than humane and warm. For Sargeson, the Calvinism that thwarted and constricted his own mother's human sympathies was merely a reflection of the generally puritan cast of middle-class, Pakeha society. His rejection of his family's Protestant Christianity led inevitably to a rejection of that society. He found an alternative to that narrowness in the godless poor, the *un*respectable working class — itinerants, barmen, racecourse habitués. Frame's mother adhered to a working-class kind of Protestantism that is distinct from both the middle-class puritanism Sargeson abhorred and the working-class bohemianism he idealised. Sargeson's family served as a negative model for Sargeson the writer, who saw it as his task to criticise the life denial of the society. Frame's mother, however, served as a positive model for Frame. The sense of words and things steeped in the Christadelphian faith which Frame learned from her mother was the inspiration of her resistance as a writer to the values of the society.

In Frame's work the debt to the Christadelphians is registered chiefly in her essentially religious sense of the commonplace and in her sense of the body as the only realm of the real. In her novels language is not a means beyond the body towards spiritual apprehension. It is a means towards the discovery of the wonder and terror that lie *within* the actual. It is the end of her characters' striving after significance, not the way through to some alternative end, located in the world of the spirit. This particular sense of the body that is Christian, yet not at all dualistic, conforms with Christadelphian belief.

Frame's habitual concerns show surprising common ground with Christadelphian doctrines: mortalism, apocalypse, election, resurrection, literalism. The body is not seen dualistically by the Christadelphians as it is in orthodox Christianity. Like Milton, the Christadelphians take the promise of resurrection literally. They hold that there is no spiritual survival of death by the individual. Humans are material and in last days a great apocalypse will sweep away the present order and transform material existence. The elect will be gathered together with the righteous dead who will be raised *in the body*. As Frame's mother explained to her children, 'heaven on earth was the Christadelphian belief, not heaven in the sky. . . . [W]hen . . . you died, you died, staying in your grave until the Second Coming and the Resurrection and the Judgement Day'.[4] Like Milton also, they hold that the Bible is 'plain and perspicuous in all things necessary to salvation', going further than he in an utter rejection of allegorical interpretation.[5]

Yet the Christadelphians themselves are not the essential source of this richness Frame encountered in her childhood. Her mother's 'faith' drew on a long-buried history of working-class culture, of which Christadelphian doctrines bear the imprint, however faintly. It was the contact with this larger tradition that nourished Frame's mother and Frame herself. The tradition itself did not survive the Depression. Post-war wealth and materialism destroyed it. It was part of a protracted working-class resistance over the first half of this century to the mass culture that grew up with the wireless and the development of a consumer society and to the manufactured 'popular' culture for working people. Frame's mother belonged to the literate, book-loving, working class with its own distinctive culture, rooted in nonconformity and with links to social radicalism, though not revolutionary in the Marxist sense. At the heart of this working-class experience lies the desire not to escape the constraints of poverty by economic self-improvement — by becoming middle-class — but rather to deny to the upper classes the exclusive right to cultural significance which they maintain for themselves. Frame's mother saw no contradiction between being poor and loving poetry.

The origins of this tradition are to be found in the subversive tradition of this-worldly Christianity that influenced William Blake and D. H. Lawrence. The sense of the world as holy, as calling forth wonder, the expectation of a radical transformation of earthly life drawing on the Bible, in particular on the Book of Revelation — these are features of a distinct tradition that is 'Christian', though its Christ is human and it is not at all other-worldly. It is a tradition uncontaminated by puritanism, springing not from Methodism or Presbyterianism but from the Blakean sense that Christianity is at heart a message about transforming, not repudiating, physical existence. Ultimately, its roots are to be found in the seventeenth-century millenarian sects of the English Revolution which sought to establish the kingdom of God on earth. Its deity is not the Calvinist God of repression and retribution who prises apart spirit and matter but the Love which Walt Whitman found in the smallest joinings of material creation. 'God [is] kind . . . [God] always act[s] to love, and not to hurt, the people in the world', insists Frame's mother in the face of plentiful evidence to contrary.[6] Its characteristic heresies are those of mortalism (the denial on biblical evidence that humans possess a spirit separate from the body) and materialism (the denial of God's transcendence of material reality), heresies shared by Milton, Blake, Lawrence, and by the Christadelphians. It is opposed to religious orthodoxy and social conformity. It stresses the radical capacity of the individual to resist conventionally approved ways of seeing the world and to open what Blake called 'the doors of perception'.[7] It exhibits a particular attraction to the notion of the Apocalypse, the last days foretold in the Bible and a general renewal of the world after a time of great destruction.

This tradition rests on an openness to ultimate questions that are, after all, not the special province of philosophers but of all humans, questions which conventional religion suppresses and which a materialist culture, Marxist or bourgeois, ignores as irrelevant. It was this openness that set a young girl's head dizzy with the question: 'Why *was* the world, why *was* the world?' [8] Why should things exist rather than mere nothingness? Against the backdrop of that question Frame has never ceased to see the world. For many, this question is a sign of madness, especially when it goes with a radical questioning of the larger society's demands for conformity, institutional authority, production and consumption ('getting and spending', as Wordsworth puts it).

Yet such questions are not the sign of 'madness'; they were natural in the background Frame knew as a child in her mother's world of Christadelphian meetings,[9] poetry reciting, and constant attentiveness to being — but foreign to the adult world she emerged painfully into. It was not the entry from childhood to adulthood as such, but the expulsion from a particular family experience, one rooted in the historical experience of a class, rich and nourishing in its way, that precipitated Frame's crisis as a young woman. Patrick Evans in his study of Frame says that her 'artistic vision came early to her, fostered by the insularity of a family which turned inward from the barrenness without'.[10] This is true, provided that we acknowledge that the family's 'insularity' was not a mere vacancy, filled out by the imaginations of the Frame girls. A network of relations connected the family to cultural traditions and memories that were not peculiar or self-engendered. These traditions and memories were, however, opposed to the dominant cultural forms that emerged between the wars and which consolidated in the post-war period.

The homogeneous mass culture, ruthlessly materialistic, conformist and repressive, that emerged after World War II — the New Zealand version mimicking the international scene — provided no enclaves of resistance into which Frame could retreat. She was obliged to withdraw into the imagination, not to escape from society and its pressures, but to offer her own acts of resistance. As a confident post-war society aggressively extended existing controlling structures, such as psychiatric hospitals, to conceal those who were '[n]ot yet civilized', Frame offered to that society the threat of the artistic imagination that had been nurtured by her family background.[11]

Her early novels violently oppose the rhetoric of benevolent scientism that was used to control society and which helped to eradicate the memories of traditions of resistance that had survived into the latter half of the twentieth century. Her major novels of the late 1960s and '70s extend her critique of that society while becoming more linguistically self-conscious, more aware of themselves as artifacts. In *The Carpathians* (1988), Frame returns to the themes and scene of the novels of the 1950s, but with a new serenity and a new playfulness that qualifies the bleakness of so much of her work. In the development of her fiction over four decades we have the most complete record of the development of the novel as a form in this country and of that line of social criticism which is at the heart of the work of all our major writers from Mansfield to Gee.

*   *   *

In 1961 Michel Foucault wrote a 'History' of madness which changed the way in which the concepts madness and reason have stood in relation to one another since the Enlightenment. For Foucault, mental illness is not analogous to physical illness but is a changing, historically conditioned notion. Madness is a judgement not a fact, a judgement passed by one group of human beings on another, by one part of the human mind on another. In the words of one commentator, Foucault 'sabotages from within' the whole conceptual basis of psychiatry in the name of its victims:

The real heroes [of Foucault's book] are not the sober, white-coated scientists patiently pushing back the clouds of ignorance and painfully revealing, little by little, the true nature of madness, but rather those literary 'madmen' who, repudiating the language of reason, crossed over into the territory of 'unreason' and, in a language beyond and prior to both, testified to an experience that lay, not beyond the boundary of true humanity, but at its heart.[12]

In 1957 one of Foucault's 'literary mad[women]', Janet Frame, published her first novel, *Owls Do Cry*. Frame had spent almost a decade in New Zealand psychiatric institutions and had been considered for a leucotomy, the then fashionable treatment for chronic unhappiness. Her novel carried New Zealand fiction into a territory the society most vehemently denied and repressed, the region of the mad, who confront the reader with the simple but terrifying truth that what we find in madness is not something utterly alien to us but merely ourselves.

It is a measure of the awful fascination that attends mental illness in New Zealand that the question of her 'madness' still arises in discussion of her work and that Frame herself should continue to be at pains to separate herself personally from the dread word 'schizophrenia' which was used to imprison and punish her for the crime of not desiring what the society deemed valuable. What is significant four decades later, however, is not the accuracy of the original diagnosis (it was plainly wrong), but its continued relevance to her writing. Her work constitutes a radical criticism not only of the psychiatric concepts and the Enlightenment values which define reason and unreason but also of the cultural forms and wishes of a phase of late-capitalist consumer society in Pakeha New Zealand in the post-war period.

As for Frame's so-called 'schizophrenia', it is sufficient to recall the words of C. G. Jung, the psychologist, who, when shown the diaries of James Joyce's daughter with the view that he should treat her, compared them to the seemingly 'schizophrenic' use of language in her father's novel, *Ulysses*: 'she is falling, he is diving', he remarked.[13] Like Joyce, Frame displays a curiously double attitude towards language. There is a strong representational tendency in her work, a concern with things, and a determination to build up a solid-seeming, detailed picture of the world by way of language. She also shares Joyce's ability to capture in language the numinous quality that attaches to things in moments when they reveal their 'whatness', their essential nature, to the rapt observer. Yet there is also a Joycean tendency in her work to downgrade the referential bias of language. Words point neither out towards the lived world nor to the dark densities of meaning within the self but to their own reflections. They become self-enclosed and self-referring structures, and in this loose sense, 'schizophrenic'.

What is important in the work of both Joyce and Frame is the ubiquitous evidence of a *controlling* intelligence behind the 'schizo-phrenic' predilection for puns, linguistic tricks, errors, the taking apart of words into their constituent parts so as to wrest unexpected meanings from them. This control is present in both *Owls Do Cry* and *Faces in the Water* (1961), her earliest novels, in which she writes most directly out of the experience of 'madness' and psychiatric treatment.

Faces in the Water has been dismissed an autobiographical work, 'merely a documentary', less than a novel.[14] Yet *Faces in the Water* is not a case history or therapy or a mere documentary record, but a novel. It has the simple but elegant structure that informs all Frame's novels (the elaborate complexities of the narrative frames in the later novels are merely built on to this simple structural pattern). The novel is structured around a pattern of descent, discovery, and return (although we are perhaps meant to see the 'return' as temporary).[15] It is no less a means of controlling and organising a potentially anarchic experience, of disposing significant elements within the novel's total economy, for being simple. This pattern turns up in Homer's *Odyssey* when Ulysses goes down into the underworld. It is the informing structure of Dante's *Divine Comedy* and of Conrad's *Heart of Darkness*.

Frame reverses the emphasis in Conrad's novella. Marlowe's journey is an outward journey into an unknown continent and is centrally concerned with a stage in the West's understanding of the nature of imperialism. The journey into Africa is a metaphor for a journey into the heart of the civilised Western adventurer who discovers the darkness within and returns changed irrevocably by what he has seen. Its psychological resonances are subservient to its political and historical burden of self-knowledge.

In Frame's novel the journey seems wholly psychological. Yet Frame is not merely concerned with a private experience of madness. The novel has its own specifically political weight of meaning. The patients in the psychiatric hospital waiting for their doses of shock treatment are being punished for their refusal to abide by the rules of a society which allows only one interpretation of the real, which permits only one set of desires. When they queue at the patients' shop for the pathetic goods that are sold to them, when they scramble for the lollies issued by the Welfare Department, when they openly exhibit sexual desire at the dances put on for them — in all these ways they parody the forms of desire and consumption that rule in the society outside. Like the fallen angels in Milton's hell, the inhabitants of the madhouse continually echo the doings of the 'superior' realm whose outraged citizens have expelled them. The novel establishes a continuous parallel between madness and civilisation that allows 'madness' to speak against the voice of reason. But Istina's language is that of neither reason nor madness, although it has links to both. She knows the terror of madness yet acknowledges the prized core of humanity it contains.

Faces in the Water is a journey through madness, not madness itself. It is a map, a way through hell and back, so that we see how the journey is accomplished. For Istina, madness is a foreign land she has entered by chance and she uses the opportunity to observe the inhabitants of this strange place, to map the terrain, describe its features, and then return to the world she came from with the booty of her dark knowledge intact.

For Frame herself, madness was similarly intriguing as well as terrifying. She is impressed in *An Angel at My Table* by its strange rules and routines. She observes with interest the 'personal, geographical, even linguistic exclusiveness of this community of the insane'. The problem was her recognition that madness was both a refuge and a trap.[16] How could she visit the land of the mad, record the unique point of view it offers that is at once nightmare, treasure, and a lifelong possession, but not be lost in it? The answer was to write. Only in her fiction could Frame continue to 'construe as miracle the hieroglyphic commonplace' without being locked away for her daring.[17]

*   *   *

In *A State of Siege* (1966), Frame's major novel of the 1960s, Malfred Signal, a retired art teacher, moves to an island outside Auckland. A lone woman, Malfred is troubled by a prowler. She is terrified at night by the unknown presence who assaults her with noises, raps on her door and finally tosses a rock through her window. These attentions drive Malfred deeper and deeper into her own inner terrors, her personal 'heart of darkness'. The novel closes with Malfred dead, having been reduced to incomprehensibility by the messages hurled at her from a darkness that is both outward and inward.

Malfred has left the South Island intending to paint according to the new 'way of seeing' she has discovered. She wishes to break with the dutiful realism she has felt obliged to practise and to impose on her pupils. She wishes to paint the colours of being, unobscured by habit and convention. Seeking a new understanding of reality, she discovers instead something mocking and terrifying, a reality that is utterly inimical and destructive.

As an 'artist's novel', *A State of Siege* is predictably concerned with essentially formalist problems about art and representation that have an obvious bearing on Frame's own work. The trajectory of her work has been, like that of Malfred Signal's, away from mimesis. But these problems are not merely formalist ones in the novel. They are integrally related to the whole theme of 'New Zealandness' and of the artist's responsibilities to the country of her birth, concerns that dominate Frame's fiction.

A State of Siege, written in the middle 1960s, records a moment of deepening crisis in New Zealand's traditional means of self-represen- tation and self-understanding. The historical causes of this crisis are to be found in the anxiety about Britain's early expressions of interest in joining the European Community, a growing unease about New Zealand's involvement in the Vietnam war, increased immigration from the Pacific Islands, and the visible signs of the urbanisation of Maori people. Frame deals with these historical causes no more directly than Jane Austen in her novels deals with the Napoleonic wars or slavery, the great political issues of her day. But she registers the changes wrought by these historical issues in the minds of individuals and in the preoccupations of the culture as a whole.

In the mid 1960s the confident and homogeneous mask of post-war New Zealand was beginning to crack. It was a period in which the populace was beginning to seek a new sense of national identity in terms not governed by the old security of colonial relations. There were signs in the heightened interest in Maori myth and legend of a discomfort with the settler heritage. The widespread desire for national self-authentication that expressed itself chiefly in Pakeha identification with Maori legend is seen in *A State of Siege* to be as self- deluding and self-interested as the official rhetoric of benevolent assimilation in which, in Keith Holyoake's treacly phrase, the Maori people were 'our Maoris'.

In her retirement Malfred recalls one of her former pupils, a girl named Lettice Bradley, who had painted the story of Maui's fishing up of Aotearoa in a way that showed that she *knew* the legend. Malfred remembers being jealous of this girl who 'had been appre- hended by the soul of her own country'. [18] How could this ordinary schoolgirl, who lived in a bungalow and read Rudyard Kipling and Zane Grey, have been able not only to absorb the myths and legends of her own country but also to be absorbed by them?

In the years since Lettice Bradley had painted her version of the country's mythical genesis, Malfred has seen the envy she herself had experienced at the girl's gift 'become part of the national character' (p.123). People began 'to beat their fists' on the landscape, demanding entry, wishing to become one with their 'own' sky and sea and earth. All suddenly desire access to the treasure of a national soul contained in the Maori legends, with their 'authentic' relation to the place. Malfred's contempt for this urge to manufacture a distinct national character by appropriating the qualities of the original inhabitants is overt and scathing:

> So one by one the items of national character became the centre of the rumor and of the new probe to get at the treasure. Putting kowhai, puarangi, manuka, rata, tarapunga on postage stamps and biscuit tins (the first stage was insertion in poetry), selling Maori carvings, faked or genuine, in Lower Queen Street where the overseas ships berth — all helped, or was thought to help. (p.124)

This bogus assertion of identity reminds Malfred of children who 'disown their parents and dream themselves into the exciting newness, individuality, uncertainty, of having been "adopted"' (p.125).

A State of Siege has an unsettling power that derives from Frame's ability to straddle two different kinds of writing. The novel develops that metafictional tendency that marks Frame's later fiction, the sense of the primacy of language and the scope of invention over allegiance to fact that becomes increasingly prominent in her work from the mid 1960s. *A State of Siege* belongs to a dark species of metafiction, one closer to Samuel Beckett's fiction than to the exuberant gameplaying of fabulists like John Barth and Thomas Pynchon. At the same time the novel belongs in the line of New Zealand critical realism, though not in any provincial sense. *A State of Siege*, like the fiction of Sargeson, Duggan, and Gee, mounts a criticism of the dominant construction of reality in New Zealand. In fact, these two tendencies are inseparably linked in the novel. Frame departs from strict realism by her use of dream, distortion, and the linguistic shock of the novel's close, but she does so in part to criticise the way in which myth is used in the purposes of national self-invention. The novel's own anti-realism serves to deepen and extend its radical assault upon national 'myths'. The complexity of the novel's interweaving of different, seemingly opposed, kinds of writing raises the question of how we are to read Frame's increasingly difficult later fiction.

In the late 1980s critics like Roger Horrocks and Alex Calder, impatient with the kinds of interpretation Frame's work had received in this country, offered new readings of *A State of Siege*. Calder focuses on the novel's extraordinary ending, not so much as an 'event' as an eruption of subversive energies into the narrative and linguistic organisation of the text. Here Malfred Signal has a rock thrown through her window at night. Round the rock is wrapped a newspaper on which, as Calder puts it, 'there is a poem, a message saying: "Soltrin, carmew, desse puniform wingering brime. . ."'. For Calder, this event opens up the novel's linguistic texture to a psychoanalytic-linguistic reading. It allows the interpreter to work into 'the material side of language, its origin in the body, its connection with desire, with shouts and with screams'.[19] Calder is interested in probing the novel's unconscious by way of its nonsensical use of language. He sets out to show that the connections established by way of the novel's use of nonsense words and by the compulsive dwelling on scenes that involve violation and penetration are produced unconsciously.

The extraordinary ending of *A State of Siege* certainly does raise questions about how are we to read Frame's novels. Calder quite properly questions what he calls a 'New Zealand Reading' of her fiction, by which he means one that works within essentially realist assumptions.[20] He sketches what a 'New Zealand' kind of reading the novel looks like:

Malfred Signal used to be an art teacher. She taught her pupils to draw and shade with a stern and pedantic fidelity to representation; but she has come north to find and paint her new view, a view which comes not from her conventional training as an artist, but from 'the room two inches behind the eyes'. Malfred is in search of a way of seeing; she wants to find a reality beneath the apparent surface of things but, when reality knocks, when it wants to come inside, it is going to be other — something different, something nobody counted on.[21]

Such a reading, for Calder, does not grapple with Frame's subversions of sense, with the radicalness of her engagement with language and with the illuminating blindnesses that engagement produces. It assumes that behind the novel's delinquencies against language, meaning, and reference lies simply a more profound sense of reality than the normal one.

But in abandoning limiting realist kinds of reading we need to be careful that we do not fall into other kinds of traps. Frame's novels are larger in scope and more subversive in their characteristic procedures than either her traditional or her avant-garde readers have allowed. If the traditional New Zealand realist kind of reading of her work has tended to underestimate her linguistic subversions, the postmodernist readings she has received have downplayed the straightforward narrative pleasures her fictions offer and the deliberateness of her use of language. A Frame novel is always 'a good read' as well as being demanding and difficult. Moreover, she provides those recognitions beloved by readers, who discover correspondences in the novels to their own lives. Her early novels are realistic enough to have been used in psychiatric training courses in New Zealand, assigned by instructors who took them to be documentary records. Frame is adept at crossing the barrier between the expectations of her highbrow audience and the general reader's grateful response to familiar terrain.

Moreover, there is a significant flaw in Calder's own reading, a lapse in his attention, which signals that Frame herself is a more deliberate and *conscious* reader than he allows. Calder says that wrapped round the stone thrown through Malfred's window 'there is a poem, a message saying, "Soltrin, etc. . ."'. In fact, a piece of newspaper is wrapped around the stone and the only message it contains are two words scrawled in red crayon across the print: *Help Help* (p.244). The 'poem' Malfred reads is in fact the news itself. True, it is 'not in any language she had learned'. But this is not because the prowler has written a weird message on the newsprint and certainly not because the newspaper journalists have been allowed to write nonsense, but because Malfred herself cannot interpret the ordinary signs inscribed on the page. She turns them into hieroglyphs. She construes banality as marvel. The words, then, disclose the extent of Malfred's, not Frame's, abandonment of sense.

What happens at the close of *A State of Siege* is not the breakdown of sense altogether, as the writing degenerates into a species of glossolalia that speaks the disordered soul of the text to the initiated interpreter. The nonsense words speak *Malfred's* unconscious.[22]

Malfred, for her part, reads in the inscription the repressed memories of parts of her prior life too painful to confront directly. Immediately before reading the 'message', she spreads out the newspaper, 'thinking, as she [does] so that it reminded her of the scrap in the pocket of the old soldier home from the wars' (p.244). The old soldier figures in a dream which Malfred has. An old vagrant approaches her, picks up a discarded cigarette butt and, to Malfred's horror, puts it in his mouth. Then he stands up, 'takes a piece of torn newspaper from his pocket', approaches her, and spits his butt, globed with saliva, on to the ground beside her (p.224).

As Calder notes, the old soldier recalls Wilfred, Malfred's boyfriend from years past, who went off to the war. He is associated with death, dirtiness, and invasion of the body. All these terrors and taboos work into the 'poem' at the close of the novel. 'Soltrin' gives up soldier, 'desse' gives decease, 'puniform' puny and uniform. 'Sorrowbride' gives death and marriage in a single image. Certainly, Frame carries us here to 'the edge of the alphabet', and certainly the collapse of syntax and sense here is, as Calder puts it, 'threatening to language'. [23] But Frame departs from commonsense only to wrest other kinds of sense from its habitual ways of generating meaning. The language is at every syllable *controlled*, not spinning out into the uncontrol of true schizophrenia.

Language remains the scene of play and peformance for Frame, but she never wholly snips the strings that tie it to an audience and to a shared world. Frame's fiction moves progressively away from strictly realistic kinds of representation. Her work becomes more and more linguistically self-conscious and playful. But, for all the outbreaks of surrealism, the gothic excesses, the bizarre Lewis Carroll-like games with sense and non-sense, the novels retain their allegiance to a kind of 'truth speaking', which Sargeson would have recognised and which involves breaking through the myths and evasions that govern the social construction of reality.

To become 'emancipated' from the kind of art that 'truthfully' represents the landscape, makes the greens and blues 'lifelike', is to abandon the task of much New Zealand fiction: to uncover the 'reality' of New Zealand in the unique qualities of the place itself. It is to lose the naive sense that the artist can, in the words of Charles Brasch which Malfred quotes, '"lie with the gaunt hills like a lover"' (p.239). It is to learn to 'explore beyond the object', a phrase that may refer to the paintings of Colin McCahon (p.239). It is to stand ironically outside a culture that demands truthfulness to its own curtailed version of the real. All these are the conscious strategies the novel adopts towards the culture it draws on with a rich, exuberant irony. That they are conscious and deliberate is attested to by the sly black humour that insinuates itself into the novel when dealing with that culture. At one point Malfred even considers putting on the plate for the Art Society monthly social the head of Tom Pearce, the Auckland City councillor in the 1960s who made clear his opposition to the purchase by the Art Gallery of an abstract sculpture, 'Torso II' by Barbara Hepworth, by observing that it looked to him 'like the buttock of a dead cow washed up on the beach'.[24]

The danger with Calder's reading of Frame is that, for all its sophistication and ingenuity, it too easily becomes another version of the old theme of the *Encyclopaedia of New Zealand* entry on her work which, as Frame complains, mentions her 'tragic disordered power'.[25] We miss the force of this novel if we fail to see how ordered it is, and how consciously organised.

*   *   *

Living in the Maniototo is Frame's most distinguished work of fiction to date. Written in the late 1970s, it has none of the sense of enclosure and anxiety that marks the early works, that resentment against and fear of the society that had acted so violently against the artist's vision and difference by incarcerating her. In place of the pervasive and excoriating social satire we find in *Owls Do Cry* — the use of exaggerated cartoons of social types and mores, the hysterical denunciatory voice of the prophet-seer — we find a direct engagement with the process of fiction-making itself that is both playful and profound. The novel deals once again with the familiar romantic-modernist theme of the relation of the artist to the bourgeois world that has no place for art; yet a partial reconciliation has occurred. The artist is still by nature alienated from that world, but now acknowledges her inescapable need of its forms and habits and practices.

At the heart of the novel's concerns is the old problem of the New Zealand anxiety about 'elsewhere'. Both living in and writing about New Zealand are activities governed by the rooted prejudice among New Zealanders that their experience exists inescapably on the peripheries, at a remove from the centre, away from reality itself. The citizens of Blenheim, the New Zealand suburb where much of the novel is set, display an exaggerated consciousness of standing always in relation to somewhere else, feeling obliged to refer their own experience to that of the richer, more original, and more authentic experience elsewhere. Yet the novel itself exhibits no reluctance at having to deal with an experience thus judged to be provincial. Nor, for all its shifting between New Zealand and North America, does it discover any source of reality or originality in the places to which New Zealanders habitually compare their own country.

The novel discovers that there is, in Patrick White's phrase, a 'mystery and [a] poetry' locked within the ordinary world which only needs to be *seen* to be unlocked.[26] There is a poetry in New Zealand suburban life which is worthy of attention, of being turned into art, but not because New Zealand is a 'shining land', as Keri Hulme puts it in *the bone people*,[27] a potential Eden. New Zealand life is fit to be turned into art because it *is* the experience to hand, what is *here*, and, like human experience everywhere, is capable of eliciting moments of intense apprehension of the strangeness and terror that underlies all being. Moreover, this 'rich material culture' is found to be in its own way 'as vivid and exciting as that of a land where, say, there is a flourishing of literature or great music' (p.58). It is true that the 'renaissance' to which it lays claim lacks a soul; it is superficial. Yet 'because poetry is attendance upon the world', the suburban culture in all its vulgarity and display, with all its avoidances and repressions, solicits the attention of the artist (p.58). In *An Angel at My Table*, Frame writes that she knew she was not 'schizophrenic', although shy and absorbed in the world of the imagination, because 'I also knew that I was totally present in the "real" world'.[28]

Even the novel's protagonist, Mavis Furness Barnwell Halleton (a.k.a. Alice Thumb or Violet Pansy Proudlock), has the New Zealand obsession with 'centres' and 'peripheries'. A New Zealand writer invited to look after the home of wealthy San Franciscans, the Garretts, while they are in Italy, she explains to her hosts 'the length, breadth, and population of New Zealand and its distance from the "centre" of the world' (p.16). This recalls the old theme of distance and isolation, the New Zealand variety of the 'cultural cringe': that habit among colonial peoples of deferring to some cosmopolitan centre, of assuming that what happens locally is second hand and second rate, an imitation.

Certainly, New Zealand suburbia is characterised by imitation. The names of the streets echo the names of British lords, their country seats, and distant battles: El Alamein Road, Corrunna Crescent,

Malplaquet Place, etc. Moreover, the names are placed in absurd juxtapositions, suggesting that 'historic confusion and insinuation' that is the mark of the ersatz (p.23). The commercial architecture is modelled on that of North America, with no consideration given to the radical differences of climate or location.

Yet Mavis discovers that imitativeness is the condition of the contemporary world itself, not merely of New Zealand. The Garretts' house in Berkeley, California, is 'full of likenesses, of replicas, prints of paintings, prints of prints, genuine originals and genuine imitation originals, imitation sculptures and twin original sculptures' (p.17). In fact, Blenheim and Berkeley are mirror images of each other. Both are worlds composed of replicas that disclose the presence of no originals behind themselves. This sense of replication is so general in the novel that even the characters refer their actions, consciously or unconsciously, to prior models which themselves echo other models. Roger Prestwick, Mavis's houseguest in Berkeley, restages in absurdly diminished form the great acts of physical and spiritual exploration by venturing for a morning into the desert. He has his friends drive him to the Californian desert and leave him beside a road sign announcing: DESERT. Dressed as a mock Lawrence of Arabia and carrying a backpack, he sets off seeking 'the "real" desert, the "real" journey' (p.174). What he sees is controlled by the image of the 'real' desert he carries with him: the mirages, oases, and camels of the Hollywood movie desert. What he finds is an insignificant event to which he unconsciously attaches literary significance: his sighting of a jackrabbit becomes the 'moment in the garden' of religious discovery, a theme which runs from St Augustine's *Confessions* to T. S. Eliot's *Four Quartets*.

The world of *Living in the Maniototo* is a world of 'replicas'. Frame's New Zealand is not 'genuine' — an ideal or an essence to which the writer may appeal as Hulme does in *the bone people* — but a collection of 'simulacra' (that is, copies that have no originals). For Simon During, this ubiquity of replication signals the book's literary-historical up-to-dateness. It stands in the postmodern, rather than, like *the bone people*, in a mixture of modernist nostalgia and post-colonial gesturing.[29] *Living in the Maniototo* is here related to the postmodern condition of depthlessness, the proliferation of signs and messages which disclose no ground of meaning beyond themselves and a hectic, centreless consumerism. Frame figures forth what Jean Baudrillard calls 'the culture of the simulacrum'.[30] Yet, it is worth noting that the novel's understanding of the loss of the original owes nothing to Baudrillard and much to Plato, and that Frame's interest in the theme draws on a very ancient and honourable tradition among writers. Like Sir Philip Sidney and Percy Shelley in their 'Defenses' of poetry, Frame is using Plato against himself, borrowing his concepts and terms but rescuing a function for the poet as 'maker' whose fictions tend towards a higher kind of truth than that of the mere realist or imitator of the outward forms.

Terms such as 'original' and 'replica' in the novel have a specifically Platonic reference and source, although Frame is interested in their application not to metaphysics but to the practice of fiction. They are metaphors for creativity, not spiritual or cosmological doctrines. When Mavis observes that 'in a world of replicas the original cannot be matched in value, and the real fact is often a copy of an unreal fiction', she makes explicit the connection between fiction-making and Plato's speculations about cosmology, particularly those in *Timaeus* (pp.45-46).

For Plato, the world we inhabit, what we commonly call the 'real' world, is in fact merely a copy of an original or ideal world which lies behind its superficial appearances. The fact that we are able to group a number of discrete items into a single category indicated to Plato that the *idea* of those items corresponds to some archetypal form which exists prior to the particular thing. Thus, he held that there is an original table, an ideal form, of which all particular tables are mere copies; for the original was framed by the creative demiurge. For Plato, then, ideas are prior and superior to things. The world of outward appearances is a confusing place where humans wander about unable to recognise the truth that lies behind them. In Book VII of *The Republic* the world of appearances corresponds to the shadows on the walls of a cave. Some of the most difficult and dense passages in Frame's novel work around these Platonic ideas, which, in spite of their unmodern bias against materialism, are directly relevant to the maker of fiction.

Settling into the Garretts' house in Berkeley, which she terms 'the house of replicas', Mavis tries to concentrate on the fictional family she is writing about in her projected novel. But she finds herself unable to attend to her writing; she is 'haunted by the manifold, the replicas, and the originals' (p.117). The manifold is a term drawn from the philosopher Immanuel Kant that signifies sense impressions before they have been unified by the understanding. The replicas, in

47

Platonic terms, are the objects that make up the visible world of multiplicity, opposed to the unified world of ideas which lies behind its appearances. The originals are the archetypal forms which the replicas imitate. Mavis the writer — herself a replica and an inhabitant of the world of replicas — shapes what she discovers in the manifold into imaginary or fictive worlds (in fact, all humans, it is implied, do this merely by being sentient). In so doing, the writer discovers not the extent but the limits of her godlike powers. In the repeated shapings of experience that constitute cognition and artistic 'creation', humans come to know that they 'are not Gods' (p.118).[31]

Thus Frame qualifies the imagination in the act of asserting its constitutive power in consciousness and in the creative process. All our mental activities and the whole visible world, in this view, are consigned to the realm of imitation. But the writer is not thereby condemned, following Plato who banished the poets from his republic, as an imitator of imitations. In fact, the writer *shapes* the manifold, attends to being, pays it acts of attention, makes us see the light that surrounds objects when we attend to them reverently, and makes us aware of the nothingness against which all being is set. Because, for Frame, there are no 'originals' behind words.

Language in the novel is not merely a means of reflecting the real; it is indistinguishable from whatever reality the novel concedes it is possible for us to apprehend in a work of fiction. One cannot look through one to the other. To inhabit the world of *Living in the Maniototo* is to inhabit language, and to lose language is to enter a shadowy world of insubstantiality, ultimately to disappear, to cease to exist. Lewis Barnwell, Mavis's husband, suffers a stroke 'that burn[s] great holes in his language and scorch[es] the rest so as to make the patter unintelligible; he [has] no more sustenance or warmth from language'. Hence he is separated not only from the richness of things in the world but also from 'the wide rich tapestry of language that could cover the whole earth like a feasting-cloth or a golden blanket' (p.26). Mavis's second husband, Lance Halleton, endears himself to her in the first place because of his 'passion for the French language' (p.43). Mavis responds to the purity and vastness of this passion because she feels 'that language in its widest sense is the hawk suspended above eternity, feeding from it but not of its substance and not necessarily for its life and thus never able to be translated into it; only able by a wing movement, so to speak, a cry, a shadow, to hint

at what lies beneath it on the untouched, undescribed almost unknown plain' (p.43). This suggests that sense of the ineffable that
some critics find in Frame's fiction, the realm behind or beyond
language, towards which it continually, ineffectually gestures. But it
is Mavis who senses this plain beneath language. The novel itself
makes no attempt to figure forth what cannot be represented.

The book is rich with poetry. It echoes Yeats, Rilke, Eliot. It is
stitched together out of prior uses of language. The world the novel
represents is the world of '[a]ll beautiful words' (p.26). Words are the
'sole heroes and heroines of fiction' (p.92). The writer's code is written
down in the novel as truth to language rather than truth conveyed
through language:

a prose sentence which touches like a branding iron is good. A sentence
which keeps its feet clean from beginning to end is good. A sentence which,
travelling, looks out of portholes as far as horizons and beyond is good. A
sentence which goes to sleep is good, if the season is winter; bad, if it is early
spring. A sentence which stumbles on useless objects instead of on buried
treasure is bad, and worse if it illuminates useless objects with artifical light,
but good if it casts a unique radiance upon them. (p.50)

Language in works of fiction should seek not merely faithfully to
imitate appearances but to cast its own radiance on objects.

The novel even attends to the language of advertising. Clearly this
is a form of language that blocks attention, that offers a wholly false
promise of permanence, that is resolutely closed to being. Yet the
recurrent phrases urging people to buy household appliances are
allowed their own odd, ironic poetry. '"[W]all to wall carpet"'
inspires as much as Hopkins's '"Glory be to God for dappled things"'
in this rich material culture of the suburbs (p.52).

In *Living in the Maniototo* the visible world rests on apocalypse and
is subject to 'inevitable break[s] in the surface of things, as if a fire from
the centre of the earth or a volcano beneath its skin had at last been
forced through into an overtaking of the visible world' (p.38). The
very names of the streets tell of 'unimaginable death' (p.23). Yet these
apocalyptic 'breaks' in the visible announce not the familiar authorial
antagonism towards the citizens but an enlarged sense of the powers
of the fiction-maker to whom anything is permissible. This sense in
the book of the triumphant powers of the novelist looks forward to the
serenity of Frame's most recent novel, wherein the old anxieties and

resentments against society give way to a relaxed playfulness, a delight in narrative mischiefs. The anguished alienation of the early novels is conspicuously absent in *The Carpathians*.

*   *   *

In *The Carpathians*, Frame returns to the scene of her first two novels, *Owls Do Cry* and *Faces in the Water*. She returns, however, not to the madhouse, but to provincial suburbia, to the oppressive ordinariness of small-town New Zealand that creates and sustains the dualisms and repressions that produce the madhouse. In suburbia, to penetrate beneath the face of the normal is to invite incarceration. Here the violent dualities of the novels of the 1950s present themselves again: the artist and the philistines, the mad and the normal, the visionary and the materialistic. The 'literalness' with which this setting is depicted and the antagonism the novel directs at small-town suburbia, familiar features of Frame's novels of the fifties, led one commentator to see the novel as a sign of regression, a retreat to the 'late provincialism' of the fifties.[32] But there is a single overwhelming difference between the novel of the late 1980s and those of the fifties. In the latest novel the human faculty most under attack in the first two novels is triumphant over its old adversaries. Frame returns to celebrate the survival of that enabling condition of the imagination most threatened by the psychiatric treatments she received: memory. In *An Angel at My Table* she describes the effect of shock treatment: 'suddenly my life was thrown out of focus. I could not remember. I was terrified' (p.98). For Frame, memory makes possible imagination, culture, and fiction.

Memory in the novel is considered in its personal and cultural aspects. As a personal possession, memory is conceived of as something so powerful that at one point it takes form as a 'presence' that visits the narrator, Mattina Brecon. For Mattina, memory is felt as a living creature, a visitant from beneath the surface of the actual ('the province of Here and Now' [p.80]). Memory brings into being what is absent. As such, memory stages a reversal of that 'eras[ure]' that occurs in *Living in the Maniototo* where a character is removed from reality in an assertion of imaginative power. Both events announce the Prospero-like authority of the artist. To control language is to have the (magical) power to determine the limits of the 'real' in a work of fiction — to decide what is permissible and to break the rules.

In *The Carpathians* memory is proposed as a key to human survival. It is, in a sense Wordsworth establishes in poems like 'Tintern Abbey', the ultimate repository of human value. It stores up the significant moments of childhood vision against the ravages of socialisation. It makes possible the continuity of the self in spite of the dissolution to which subjecthood is invariably prey in Frame's fiction. It connects humans to the object world. Memory is essential to that process by which experience, language (that is to say, 'culture'), and imagination continually make up what the individual construes as 'the world'. It is 'a passionately retained deliberate focus on all creatures and their worlds to ensure their survival' (p.172). In fact, in the novel's enactment of apocalyptic breakdown, when 'reality' itself as a communally accepted, commonsense construction of the world breaks up, memory is the key to Mattina's survival. In Frame's ironic version of two biblical events, the Tower of Babel and the Apocalypse, words and concepts are demolished by the discovery of a 'Gravity Star', which exposes an anomaly in the fabric of the understood universe. Artists, of course, are accustomed to such rupturings of the 'real', albeit by way of the imagination rather than physics. Mattina is not an artist, but she has the artist's advantage of an available retreat from the constraints of probability and logic. While the inhabitants of Kowhai Street are consumed and destroyed, Mattina removes her 'real being' to Memory.

Here the novel exacts a kind of belated revenge against the world that imprisoned the young Janet Frame: the 'normal' world threatened in *Owls Do Cry* and *Faces in the Water* with apocalypse. In spite of its obsessive concern with 'Safety First', with solid surfaces, that world, for Frame, rested on destructive possibilities. The ordinary citizens in Frame's early novels are set on a meniscus over destruction that, like Hell beneath the Puritan divine's sinner, is ever waiting to consume. But in *Owls Do Cry* the threat offered to the imprisoning society was often couched in hysterical and exaggerated terms because it represented both powerlessness and resentment. Hence the markedly biblical turn of its expression. The prophetic voice here is that of the persecuted outsider possessed of an apocalyptic vision of Truth that the society deems valueless. The voice is striving not to change or reform that society, to turn it away from the false gods it recklessly whores after, but to threaten it with vengeance at the hands of a power greater than its own. It is the voice not of the true prophet (or of the New Zealand version of Jeremiah, James K. Baxter) but of the millenarian, the chiliast, the sectary, the Christadelphian on his soapbox, promising God's terrible punishment on the society that fails to heed its warnings.

Earthquake, volcano, or war are only the outward expressions of these threats. Behind all these lies the biblical apocalypse ready to carry away the many immersed in materialism, who persecute the true seers, God's chosen few (Frame's favourite images show the unmistakable influence of the Christadelphian background she mentions in her autobiography). In *The Carpathians* this apocalypse, so long threatened, is at last enacted as an extraordinary entropic breakdown of language. The old reality is swept away and a new one takes its place, in a bizarre and parodic form of a favourite Christadelphian fantasy. For the Christadelphians, the 'lovers of Christ', are ever awaiting the apocalypse foretold in the Revelation of St John, when the world will be renewed in a process of violent transformation that will see the eternal end of the unworthy and establish the chosen with Christ in a thousand-year kingdom.

Thus Frame returns to the anxious scene of the two early novels and the might-have-been, but in a sense of playful triumph. Here it is the ordinary citizens, the imprisoners of the different and the lonely, who are subjected to a sudden unhinging of their reality, made mad, and taken away to mental hospitals. Mattina, who has the elect consciousness of Frame's artist figures, is able to retreat within and escape the general destruction. She enters the transformed reality of the new 'way of seeing', prefigured in *A State of Siege* by way of memory ('and while races and worlds may die, if they are to change, to resurrect as new, they must remain within the Memory Flower' [p.151]). Like the Lord's anointed, then, the 'artist' survives the great apocalypse, with memory as the inner sign of election, and is 'resurrect[ed]'.

In cultural terms memory is more ambiguous. It is connected with the discovery of the 'Memory Flower': the discovery by New Zealand that it needs legends, the work of the imagination rather than brute fact, if it is to present to the world (especially tourists) evidence of its difference, its distinctiveness. The town has discovered the treasure that it neglected in Frame's 1950s when her own 'mad' character, Istina Mavet, carried round the signs of spiritual value — Rilke and Shakespeare — deemed valueless by the community. But in thus determining to make a soul for itself, the community displays its old utilitarian suspicion of poetry (the imagination, the spirit) as the unpredictable transformer of reality beyond the ordinary means of its apprehension. Kowhai Street is provincial, difference-hating New Zealand, with the 'Kowhai Gold' theme as a gloss to its intentions. The obsession with Maoriness has become more pronounced than in *A State of Siege*, where New Zealanders become so desperate to 'stake a claim in the identity of their country' that many falsify genealogical tables in order to claim a Maori ancestor: 'They could just as well and as happily have found that their great-great-grandfather was a boiling mud-pool or a piece of glacier or a spray of kowhai or pohutakawa blossom' (p.124). In *The Carpathians* this desperation has become more ubiquitous still, and more prominently displayed. Maori words have become fashionable, Maori legend has been put to the purposes of manufacturing a national identity. Maoriness will help develop a missing centre, a sense of belonging, of origins. It will overcome the anxiety of distance and displacement. The legend of the Memory Flower goes down well with the overseas tourists and gives them the feeling they've been somewhere (p.39).

At one point, Mattina actually stages a kind of journey to the centre or spiritual heartland of New Zealand. But instead of finding the intact memory of Maori spiritual presence as something healing and active, she finds only a nagging sense of dislocation and a boy who, left thirty years in a mental hospital because nobody noticed and, released, now apparently contentedly making baskets ('"He's a good boy"'), represents a Frameian might-have-been (p.86). Maori people figure for the inhabitants of Kowhai Street in the late 1980s as 'the people of the land', whose memory goes back before the wrench of Pakeha from 'home'. They are a 'source of memory', the means of attaining a new identity as a people. But, as in Quentin Pope's *Kowhai Gold* anthology of half a century before, they have been captured, made fashionable dress, worn in the hair, as Stead puts it.[33] Mattina's journey is a version of the journeys to the heartland in Mulgan's *Man Alone* and Hulme's *the bone people*, but one that directs the light of parody on the romantic impulse behind Pakeha attempts at home-coming. Mattina proceeds in the footsteps of James K. Baxter up the Wanganui River to a scene of romantic joining of Maori and Pakeha: the Jerusalem of Baxter's *Jerusalem Sonnets* (1970). What is uncovered is closer to Mulgan's vision in *Man Alone* of the land as inimical and unconsoling, of the Maori as also alien from it, than to Keri Hulme's vision of salvation in *the bone people*. For Hulme, the landscape is charged with spiritual presence; for Frame, it is culture that invests nature with significance.

In other words, Puamahara is New Zealand in the 1980s, but strikingly reminiscent of that of the 1950s — not because, as Evans argues, Frame has stayed within the late-provincial outlook, but because beneath the superficial changes are the same anxieties about distance, smallness, authenticity, isolation, the same fear of difference, the same proclivity for imprisoning and punishing, the same consumerism. The artist, nevertheless, has moved closer to that culture. She doesn't celebrate it, but the fierce indignation has gone from the satire. There is less of the tone of Old-Testament prophet railing against its blindness, its errors, its idolatories. There is less satiric enlarging and caricaturing in the portraits of citizens, less calling down of judgement. The artist acknowledges her own complicity, acknowledges that she feeds on ordinary reality.

Frame's habit of setting the artist radically at odds with her society undoubtedly reflects a romantic-modernist stance. Yet, like much else in her work, it also draws on those essentially religious preoccupations of her childhood. In Frame's work there is a profound sense of the spiritual bankruptcy of the many, the ordinary, coupled with a compulsion by her elect narrators to undertake journeys inwards in search of the 'true reality'. The people of Kowhai Street 'cling to their place of being' (p.16). They exist on 'a verge of darkness . . . suspended [over] . . . the spinning earth and the stars' (p.15). But they cherish and cling to the limits of their habitual ways of seeing. Confronted with the prospect of nothingness beyond or beneath or behind the familiar world, they forge links to the here and now. They refuse to 'fall into the darkness at the edge of the earth' (p.16). Those who journey beneath the surface, into the darkness, discover not separate spiritual existence but a deep anguish that is also wonder. They uncover absence, not God. Their task, then, is to remain immersed in the actual, without becoming — like the many, for whom equally there are no depths behind actuality — merely unreflective. The artist must lift up the quotidian, invest the mundane world with religious significance without resorting to the transcendent. It is the world itself that is the occasion of wonder and the mind's best fate is to know itself mortal with a religious intensity. The absence at the basis of being is both terrifying and the source of vision. For Hulme, the solution to Pakeha materialism is to turn to the gods of the Maori; for Frame, the trick is to learn to live religiously, but without the gods.

The journey inwards is necessary not because it brings enlightenment — there is no luminous centre to the self for Frame's journeyers — but because those who journey — the mad, the artistic, the lonely — are touchstones by which to measure human possibilities. They measure the world of actuality against the absence that lies beneath it, the world of speech against the silence that surrounds it (p.185). They pitch existence into the scale of death. Hence they threaten the mental structures that hold the citizens of Kowhai Street, Puamahara, together as surely as Istina Mavet did by her 'madness' in *Faces in the Water*.

*   *   *

In the second volume of her autobiography, *An Angel at my Table*, Frame describes her feelings of frustration about and love for her family as she stands on the point of her fateful decision to walk out of her teaching class on the day of her 'inspection':

I could see the pattern of their past lives slowly emerging, like a script written with invisible ink and now being made visible to me, warmed by the fire kindled simply by my growing up. I could see, too, an illumination produced by that same fire, the shadows emerging as recognized shapes of a language full of meaning for me: the language of the love and loss and joy and torture of having a place fast within a family when all my awakening longing was directed towards being uprooted, quickly, without leaving behind a cluster of nerve endings, broken threads in danger of being renewed.[34]

Like Stephen Dedalus at the close of Joyce's *Portrait of the Artist as a Young Man*, Frame here sees herself as the eager and confident fledgling, ready to fly the net of family and go off to encounter once again the nature of reality. Yet in that encounter she is almost destroyed and the nerve endings connecting her to her childhood are rejoined, not severed. They are joined not in the sense that she becomes one of those New Zealand writers who cannot escape the lure of childhood and innocence but in the sense that she finds in the culture she encountered as a child a specific means of criticising the adult world to which she was expected to adjust. The 'reality' she met as a young woman had no place or use for her; hence she sought a place in the imagination where she could observe and recall. 'Imagination' here means not an idealistic vagary but a function of those insistences on reading, seeing, and resisting that informed her family life. It is language that kept her fast, not within the living family, but within reach of the familiar shapes of family, and of the sense of wonder in words and things that she learnt from her mother.

That sense of wonder should not be seen as metaphysics or substitute religion. True, it has its source in radical traditions of Christianity, but those traditions stress not the transcendental promise of official Pauline Christianity but the terrible falling short of the world *as it is* from the vision of human possibility found in the Bible, according to the millenarian sects of the English Revolution and Blake. Yet Frame's fiction is not simply social criticism in the 'critical realist' sense that it opposes the culture's restrictions and oppressions or takes the side of life against a puritan culture's life denial. Frame's criticism is directed at the ways in which the culture creates an image of reality (and this is Blake's method also). Her fiction in the four decades since the war articulates the most thorough and consistently radical criticism that we have of the ongoing effort to create a New Zealand 'identity'. It registers the profound changes wrought on that society by all the influences from 'elsewhere' that have passed through it. Above all, it celebrates language and the power of the imagination to make out of words worlds that are terrifying and beautiful in their own right.

CHAPTER 2

C. K. Stead's Adversary Stance

Sometimes his logic was a strength; other times he seemed to get trapped inside it.

C. K. STEAD, *The Death of the Body* (p.29)

MALFRED SIGNAL in Janet Frame's *A State of Siege* is a lone woman under threat from a prowler. The prowler stalks her relentlessly. He refuses to reveal himself to her, but sends a series of threatening signs of his presence: noises, rocks, acts of vandalism. Malfred feels deeply threatened by this pursuit that withholds the pursuer. In the end the prowler breaks down the gap between them by hurling an indecipherable and threatening message out of the darkness.

Malfred is a painter. One possible interpretation of the novel's meaning is that its action represents the theme of the artist as victim of her audience. Malfred is Frame, the novelist, pursued through the text by the clumsy and aggressive reader, determined to track her down and discover her in spite of her elaborate stratagems of evasion and concealment. But turned another way, the same image of prowler and victim may be read as a sly reversal of this view of the relation between the artist and audience, between the writer and the reader of fiction. From this viewpoint, it is the prowler who stands for the author and the misapprehending victim who stands for the reader. The author tantalises the reader but will not reveal herself. The author teases and baffles the reader.

At the close of the novel, the reader, who has been waiting for the dark presence behind the novel to reveal itself, finds the author once again snatched away. Instead of the usual neat resolution of the novel of crime or terror (*A State of Siege* has affinities to both), the reader is faced by an outbreak of apparent surrealism. The message sent is less intelligible and therefore more terrifying than any so far received.

Thus the novel harasses the reader by crossing from one kind of writing into another.

Among the chief frustrations of reading a Frame novel are those that derive from the author's coy refusal to reveal herself in spite of the persistent use of 'autobiographical' material in her novels. The formula warning in *Faces in Water* that the book is a work of fiction and that 'none of the characters, including Estina [*sic*] Mavet, portrays a living person'[1] has not deterred all those readers of the 'tragic disordered power' school who recklessly conflate narrator and author. They imagine themselves listening directly to the voice of Janet Frame, speaking again and again of her long and terrible period among the mad people and about her resentments against the 'normal'. For these readers the increasing elaboration of the 'framings' of the narratives in Frame's later fiction are merely distracting attempts to distance them from the voice of the author.

C. K. Stead's novels, *All Visitors Ashore* (1984) and *The Death of the Body* (1986), contain no such warnings against confusing fact with fiction. Moreover, while Frame's shyness, her refusal to become a 'star', recalls the self-effacement of other obsessively private novelists like J. D. Salinger and Thomas Pynchon, Stead has courted publicity as persistently as Norman Mailer. When we read a Frame novel, the author's self-abnegation as a public person precedes us into the text; when we read a Stead novel, the author's self-advertising public persona goes before us.

Yet Stead's novels, like Frame's, pose considerable difficulties for the reader who forgets the fictional nature of fictions and who seeks too assiduously to locate the author's presence in the text. Frame entraps her reader by refusing to construct a public self, while threading seemingly autobiographical material through her novels. Stead traps his reader by leaving traces of his carefully constructed public persona in his novels yet at the same time distancing himself from that persona.

From the mid 1980s Stead's cultivation of a public persona as disgruntled man of letters and conservative cultural critic increasingly came between his readers and his texts. This undoubtedly led to a degree of resistance to his fiction among the significant new audience for novels that responded enthusiastically to *the bone people*. It meant, for example, that his novels of the period were less likely to be prescribed in secondary school English syllabuses than *Smith's Dream*, his 1971 anti-totalitarian novel widely studied in schools. In the middle and late eighties the class sets in use were more likely to be the stories of Patricia Grace and Witi Ihimaera. But in other respects, Stead's antithetical public stance served him well.

It drew attention to his novels at a time when 'star' qualities were beginning to be attached to a select few local novelists. Until the 1980s even a novelist as respected as Sargeson could not expect to live comfortably from his craft so long as his audience was predominately a New Zealand one. Sargeson complains about this situation in his memoirs.[2] In 1986 when Stead abandoned academia to become a full-time professional writer, retreating, Sargeson-like, to a bach (actually, a 'Lockwood' study)[3] in the garden behind his house, Keri Hulme and to a lesser extent Witi Ihimaera were in the process of becoming national figures of almost mythical proportions. This wasn't merely a matter of their receiving a greater financial reward from the local market. Hulme's novel was acclaimed overseas and noticed in a way Sargeson's work had never been. In spite of earning the respect of such English literary notables as John Lehmann, E. M. Forster, and William Plomer, Sargeson remained a provincial writer to the end, with the provincial's confined reputation.

Internationally, Hulme presented an image of the post-colonial condition that was widely successful. Without being an international novelist like Frame, she gained a metropolitan readership. Like Alice Walker's *The Color Purple, the bone people* projected a fashionable image of the 'margins'. Stead, with a modest reputation in England based largely on his 1964 critical work, *The New Poetic*, could hope neither for the major international status of Frame nor for the post-colonial *éclat* of Hulme. In the late eighties Stead strenuously culti-vated an English audience for his writing. His novels were published and reviewed, generally favourably, in England before being re-leased in New Zealand. He reviewed regularly for English literary magazines. But he needed also to cultivate the New Zealand novel-reading public.

By the late 1980s both Hulme's and Ihimaera's works were re-ceived in New Zealand as being almost beyond criticism. As a reviewer of *The Matriarch* observed, the general critical response to Ihimaera's epic was simply to say WOW STOP BUT.[4] He himself had no buts. Like Sam Hunt as kiwi bard during the 1970s, Hulme and Ihimaera represented in their persons as well as their works the fashionable idea of the New Zealand writer. Stead set out to establish himself as a novelist rather than a critic and professor at the exact moment that the novel became the vehicle of popular nationalist enthusiasm. His own fiction, however, was not the kind that attracted the adulation that greeted *the bone people*.

Stead could not meet this competition on its own ground. Too intellectual to make oracular pronouncements, too sceptical to endorse the prevailing national myths, too distant and highbrow to stand in the popular conception for the great New Zealand novelist, Stead was obliged to find other ways of generating his own publicity. This he did by exaggerating the adversarial stance which had long been his preference anyway. But instead of continuing the liberal-humanist assault on the philistine and puritan populace for its racism, repressiveness, and support of imperialist wars, he set about chastising the nation for whoring after newly fashionable, but to him equally spurious, gods, and for embracing the utopias of feminists, educational reformers, and anti-racists.

During the late 1980s Stead progressively and very publicly broke with the liberal cause he had supported until the early 1980s. He even wrote a letter to the *New Zealand Listener*, officially repudiating liberalism,[5] and stepped up the attack in subsequent reviews and in an article in the Auckland glossy magazine, *Metro*, where he received considerable attention. That is to say, he broke with liberalism *as it had become* rather than with the specific causes he had supported before liberalism had been, as he saw it, hijacked by the radicals and subsequently by politicians and others in positions of power.

This repudiation signalled the arrival of something unusual, perhaps new, in this country: an intellectual conservatism. Since the Depression years intellectuals in New Zealand have generally been identified with the liberal left. The social realist line in fiction rested on a repugnance towards the conservative and repressive attitudes embedded in settler culture. In the work of Sargeson, Baxter, Frame, and Gee the most deadening features of the national culture are consistently associated with the puritan middle class. The writer, forced outside a culture inimical to the humane values he or she holds, characteristically speaks through the little man, the marginalised figure, the unemployed, the insane. In some cases (Baxter, Roderick Finlayson, and Noel Hilliard, for instance) the writer chooses to identify with the only group he or she sees as untouched by the values of white, middle-class, puritan culture: the Maori. Stead's activities as novelist and man of letters in the 1980s have been directed at renovating this tradition: casting aside the liberal orthodoxies and the stock of characters that informed it, while retaining its critical stance towards the dominant culture and suburban values.

Stead embarked on his career as professional novelist in the middle eighties with a clear sense both of a local tradition on which he could draw and of the general movements in the novel as an international form. He also started out with a recognition of the need to address the particular problems the contemporary literary scene posed for him. He needed to adopt a calculated stance towards the contemporary reading public for fiction in New Zealand at that time. He did so in three distinct but related ways: he developed and extended the conservative aspects of his longstanding views about literary practice; he set about reformulating in the public mind the traditional image of high culture and the man of letters by writing polemical cultural criticism in popular journals; he embarked on updating and redirecting the techniques of reader-harassment in fiction that Sargeson and Frame had perfected earlier, and under different kinds of pressures, as writers who felt themselves alienated from their own society.

The antithetical public stance Stead adopted in the late 1980s did not make him a 'star' novelist. Stead's purpose, however, was not to become a 'star', but rather to stand against the assumptions and preferences which encouraged stardom among the novel-reading public. It might be argued that Stead's cultivation of a conservative persona was an attempt to win for himself a particular section of the enlarged novel-reading public that appeared in the wake of *the bone people*. By writing in *Metro* particularly, he might seem to have been trying to draw to his fiction that socially ambitious section of the middle class, liberal in matters of private morality but suspicious of Maori and feminist radicalism, which that magazine addresses (even the inclusion in *Metro* of a column by Maori radical, Syd Jackson, is a means of reminding a white audience of their true interests, not a play for Maori readers).

It is true, of course, that Stead, like any novelist, wants to win as many readers as possible to his works. It is also true that his 'anti-anti-racist'[6] and anti-feminist positions in the late 1980s coincided with and reinforced a mood of disenchantment among middle-class people with the progressive policies of the early Lange Government. But Stead did not bring into existence a new *kind* of novel-reading audience, one significantly different from that which responded enthusiastically to *the bone people*. He did not create a climate of taste to receive his own fiction; he merely reflected an existing climate. As much as drawing on a new constituency, Stead's fiction since the middle eighties has been directed at cultivating an existing one, inherited from Sargeson and Brasch but no longer tightly congregated around high culture and the literary quarterlies, and at criticising an emergent one, sprung from *the bone people*. In his essays and reviews Stead writes directly against what he sees as the follies of the liberal Pakeha middle class; in his fiction he writes against those follies less polemically but with no less animosity.

Stead's strategy of reader-harassment places him in a line of New Zealand fiction which compensates for the perceived limits of the available audience by both giving it what it wants and at the same time slyly exposing the narrowness of those wants. Katherine Mansfield bemoaned the absence in New Zealand of aestheticism, of art which took itself seriously as art. Only when New Zealand became more artificial, she believed, would it give rise to an artist who could treat its beauties as they deserved.[7] What she was complaining about was the lack of an audience in provincial, bourgeois, John Bullish New Zealand for the rich and highly crafted kind of art she wished to produce. By becoming an exile she abandoned not New Zealand itself but a reading public intolerant of her desire for a more self-conscious, more aestheticist, kind of writing.

When Sargeson decided a generation later to return to New Zealand rather than remain in England, he no more chose to identify himself with the existing New Zealand society than did Mansfield. Nor did he accept the limits a puritanical, philistine, and compulsively moralistic middle class placed upon the kind of fiction it preferred to read. He chose instead to write on two levels. His overt narrative method, while criticising the society's inhumane morality, satisfies its puritan resistance to flamboyant fiction. But his texts, like Frame's, constantly lob missiles against the reader's demand for realism and for moralising. When the narrator of 'That Summer' finds himself in prison, he cheekily asks the peeping tom warder 'for a dab of vaseline to put on [his] piles'.[8] Later he can't get to sleep because of all the creaking beds and we begin to suspect that it is the story's contemporary reader (homophobia was as entrenched among the literati as the populace in the 1940s),[9] not the narrator, whose naiveté is being exposed here.

In a sense, Sargeson's joke depends on the culture's absolute abhorrence of the concealed meaning that makes the joke possible. Because homosexuality could not be mentioned explicitly, Sargeson was unable to write directly about the subject that most interested him (if he *had* been able to do so, his stories would probably not display that curious power that derives from their indirections). But precisely for the same reason, he was able to allude indirectly to the homosexual underworld of *double entendre* and knowing jokes. What saves the story from being, in James K. Baxter's words, merely a 'bad homosexual joke' is the smallness of the audience able to share its reference.[10] The narrator is only the most obvious of the story's naifs.

By the mid 1980s the Pakeha middle class had apparently become as liberal as it had been conservative in the 1930s and '40s. Stead continues Sargeson's practice of harassing the populace for its self-righteousness, but he directs his criticism at its liberalism rather than its conservatism. For Stead, that liberalism rests on the same complacent sense of national virtue that Sargeson ruthlessly pilloried. Moreover, some of the contemporary manifestations of national virtue are directed as much against the pleasures of the flesh as were those associated with the old church-going respectability — but now in the name of radical feminism rather than in the names of Methodism or Presbyterianism.

In *The Death of the Body* Stead pokes fun not at the old theme of lower-middle-class puritanism but at the current one of feminism, which he sees as equally repressive and narrow. Moreover, by building *All Visitors Ashore* explicitly around a remembered 1950s Auckland literary scene centred on Sargeson, Stead mocks the prevailing preference for novels that break self-consciously with the 'masculine realist' line in New Zealand fiction. He affirms the Sargeson 'tradition' by altering it without repudiating it. Like Sargeson, Stead mocks the citizens for hating his particular vice. Sargeson's vice was his sexual preference, Stead's is his preference for Sargeson and the literary 'tradition' he established so single-mindedly. For both, it is the virtuousness of the citizens that is most abhorrent.

All Visitors Ashore was read as a transparent and somewhat offensive *roman à clef* when it first appeared. The accuracy and tact of its thinly disguised portraits of New Zealand literary eminences were debated in the review columns. The immodesty of Stead's own portrait of himself when younger was questioned. One reviewer described the novel as 'a piece of supremely clever naughtiness that gives us a portrait of the New Zealand artist as an awful young dick'.[11]

It is not surprising that as many of his readers have fallen into the trap of equating author with narrator as have readers of Frame. Stead actively invites his reader into the trap of identification. He mixes fictional and historical events. He tempts the reader by offering portraits of the author in various guise — as a young man and as a middle-aged professor — which both confirm and slyly deny our sense that the voice smoothly narrating the action is that of Stead himself. But having drawn us into his web, Stead eludes his pursuer, the reader, plays with him or her, remains always just beyond reach.

All Visitors Ashore is narrated by a voice that recalls the omniscient narrator of the Victorian novel. The narrator identifies himself as an older man looking back on action that is complete, carrying us into the minds of the participants and generalising a moral or political viewpoint wherever he feels the need. But the narrator is self-conscious in this omniscient role in a way his Victorian counterpart would not have allowed himself to be. At one point he even comments on the progression of the story, dismissing an alternative possible narrative method as too deliberate in its attempts at verisimilitude: 'And so the narrative, having begun concretely and dramatically, with the butter to lend authenticity, and with dialogue which did not fully explain itself and thus had the flavour of the real, would now track back and fill in what had not been explained. . . .' (p.71).

This is closer to the narrative method of Lawrence Sterne's eighteenth-century *Tristram Shandy* than to that of the nineteenth-century realist novel. The narrator draws attention to the narrative as a playful construct whose relation to actuality is oblique. Like Sterne and like contemporary metafictional novelists (metafiction is not a modern invention — it goes back to Cervantes and Sterne), Stead breaks the readers' illusions, reminding them that fictional narratives and life proceed according to different logics. But for Stead, this distance between the world of fiction and that of fact does not invalidate the novel's claim to offer a kind of truth. In an imaginary conversation which the narrator has with an absent character, his former lover, Patagonia Aorewa de Thierry Bennett (her names suggest the rich mix of cultural elements, of romance and prose, that has gone into the making of New Zealanders), he observes that the truth and the facts are not the same thing (p.52). The 'truth' of the narrative's total reconstruction of a set of events, a moment of history, proceeds from the synthesising and dramatising power of the imagination which produces it, not its correspondence to the historical record.

In this novel the record that counts is not the historical one but the literary-historical one. Not only does Stead people *All Visitors Ashore* with literary figures from the 1940s and '50s — Sargeson, Fairburn, Baxter — he also positions its version of history in relation to other fictional constructions. Some of the references to earlier New Zealand fiction are little more than knowing asides to the literate reader, as when Stead names the landlady of a boarding house Mrs Hinchinghorn. Mrs Hinchinghorn is a character in Sargeson's stories, 'A Final Cure' (1967) and 'An International Occasion' (1969). The boarding house of which Sargeson's Mrs Hinchinghorn is the landlady is very similar in period, style, and location to the one Ken Blayburn stays in in Stead's novel. Ken himself is modelled on Sargeson's longtime friend, Harry Doyle. In *All Visitors Ashore* Ken is the racecourse-loving friend of Melior Farbro, who closely portrays Frank Sargeson. The name itself draws attention to the *literary* nature of Stead's debt to Sargeson. *'Il miglior fabbro'* (the better maker) were the words which T. S. Eliot used as a dedication to *The Waste Land*, acknowledging thereby the extent of his debt to Ezra Pound, who substantially edited and revised the original manuscript of the poem. Stead thus acknowledges his own debt to Sargeson as his most significant New Zealand precursor, but he does not conceal the debts in the novel to other earlier New Zealand fiction, particularly to John Mulgan's *Man Alone*.

The debts of *All Visitors Ashore* to *Man Alone* are pervasive. Stead's novel at several points recalls the Depression riot in Queen Street which lies at the centre of Mulgan's novel. The 1951 wharf dispute, on which the action of *All Visitors Ashore* turns, is presented as a repetition of the earlier riot (behind both stand the 1981 anti-Springbok demonstrations, in one of which Stead himself was arrested). Moreover, minor actors in the historical events dramatised in Mulgan's novel turn up in Stead's. The policeman who interrupts the poetry reading is the same who the night after the Queen Street riots in 1932 had prevented a similar riot from occurring in Takapuna (p.59). The flight by sea of Cecelia Skyways/Dawn Clegg recalls that of Johnson from New Zealand in the earlier novel. Johnson also ends up in Spain.

But the debt of Stead's novel to Mulgan's is more extensive and more profound than such scattered allusions suggest. The nature of the relation between the two books becomes clearer when we compare two representative passages. The first is taken from chapter 2 of *All Visitors Ashore*:

Auckland is a harbour town, a town of two harbours, at the nether end of the world, and 1951 (properly counted) is the first year of the second half of the twentieth century. There are planes in the air, even passenger planes, but still people who travel do it by sea moving with the cargoes and like God upon the face of the waters. The ships come and go, they are our carriers and links, our assurance that our spacious and beautiful confinement though solitary is not absolute. They link us with 'Home', if there is somewhere far away we can think of as Home, or with our Catalan or Andalusian dreams. . . . There is talk of a harbour bridge and of taller buildings in Queen Street and of new methods with cargo and of huge airliners and airfreight but this is only the first year of the second half of the twentieth century — all that is to come and meanwhile Auckland still looks like a South Seas port with a predominance of wooden buildings and wooden wharf piles. At the end of the wharves — or so you will hear it said — sit men in felt hats with fishing lines dropped down into the green harbour water. These are wharfies at work and that is why the cargo moves so slowly and there are ships in the stream through which the ferries have to thread their way. The wharfies are a tight strong union who elect tough men to speak for them. These spokesmen (you will hear it said) are communists or sympathetic to communism and in Korea in this first year of the second half of the twentieth century we are fighting communism and if we fight communism in Korea and communism in the unions (so goes the prevailing logic) it is the same fight and in both America is our ally. Our Prime Minister Sidney George Holland known to the fishermen in the felt hats as the Senator for Fendalton has just come back from Washington where he has been reported as promising 'every fibre of his being' (not much fibre there, the fishermen say) in support of America and where he has said, 'Tell me what else I can do and I will do it'. Now he is going to do it and everyone knows he is going to do it, because the wharfies have cut themselves off from the Federation of Labour and they are demanding five shillings and twopence an hour (but everyone knows they would settle for four and tenpence ha'penny) and the ship-owners have offered four and sevenpence ha'penny and now the wharfies are saying they won't work overtime and that's where things stand as the wharfies gather at the Trades Hall in Hobson Street under the huge painted Vicks advertisement showing the head of a haggard old man swathed in blankets and with a handerchief up to his mouth coughing his heart out (pp.22-23).

The second passage is taken from chapter 1 of *Man Alone:*

What he saw then was the brightness of red roofs straggling down to the shore on two sides of a land-locked harbour and clustered together on one side the steel-grey cranes and advertisement-plastered buildings of the port and city. The ship moved slowly in and hung at anchor in the stream while the long business of medical inspection went on. Johnson leant on the rail, watching the shore and the small boats that went by. The deck was full of luggage and people moving and talking. Beside Johnson, a returning New Zealand soldier, still in uniform, spat carelessly into the water. The tide from the upper harbour moved swiftly down tugging at the ship. The warm mist of a day's rain that had lifted hung over them. The soldier turned and said to him:

'That's Auckland, mate — the Queen of the North.'

'The what?'

'The Queen of the North. That's what they call it — in Auckland. This is God's own, this country.'

'It looks all right.'

'It's not a bad little town — nor a bad little country neither. It looks small after London though, don't it, mate? It looks different now to me to what it did.'

The soldier had a face that was shrunken and pock-marked and un-healthy-looking; his left arm had not recovered from a shrapnel wound; he carried it stiffly in front of him. He said:

'It's three years since I seen those wharves. We was billeted in the wharf-shed two nights before we sailed. It was cold as death.'

'I didn't think it was ever cold here,' Johnson said.

'It's cold enough sometimes in winter, mate, if you're not sleeping in your bed, and we weren't sleeping in our beds.'

He coughed, lighting a cigarette.

'It's home again now for me, mate,' he said, 'and there'll be the wife and kids and all there waiting to meet us.'

He spoke without enthusiasm.[12]

In the first passage the narrator, Curl Skidmore, a professor of English in his fifties, is looking back on the Auckland of 1951. It is a set piece of description in which the historical context is established, the topography sketched, the cultural assumptions of the period briefly described, and the unfolding political events made clear. The narrator adopts the relaxed but authoritative tone of one detached from the immediate emotions of the events in their own day but undisguisedly partisan. He does not romanticise the watersiders but he is clearly on their side against the bosses and the Government of Sid Holland preparing for a showdown against the recalcitrantly leftist union. All this is straightforward enough. But there are resonances worked into the writing.

When we turn to the second passage the source of those resonances is apparent. Stead's passage knits a dense web of literary echoes to Mulgan's. Both writers use a photographic view of Auckland— Mulgan's focused from the sea, Stead's from the air — to generalise New Zealand society at a particular historical moment. Both expose the prevailing myth of New Zealand as a South Seas paradise by drawing attention to the divergences between the political and the actual climate and the paradisal stereotype (Stead picks up the theme on page 45 of the novel by revising Kipling's line, 'On thee, on thee the unswerving season smiles' to read 'On thee, on thee the unsmiling season swerves'). Both mock the paradisal view by including the obtrusive presence of advertising hoardings in the picture Auckland presents to the observer. Both concentrate on images of sickness, poverty and cold to contest the paradisal.

The image of a man coughing that occurs in both passages indicates that the later novelist is deliberately referring to the earlier one's fiction. We should, however, resist the tendency to see Stead once again as the imitator of other stronger and earlier writers, one who appropriates their forms and styles without making them recognisably his own. As a poet Stead has often been accused of being a mere pasticheur, lacking in originality.[13] It is easy to assume that the debts to *Man Alone* in *All Visitors Ashore* imply unassimilated influence. Yet they are entirely conscious, and serve a formal function in the novel. In *All Visitors Ashore* Mulgan's novel provides a constant point of reference, one that shows the power in a given culture both of repetition and of divergence. At the political level history involves repetitions that would be tragic if they were not constantly lapsing into banality. Yet the repetitions of strikes, lockouts, governmental repressions occur in the contexts of changing historical conditions that fundamentally shape culture, and these changes are governed by international shifts and developments. By 1951 the old 1930s themes of distance and isolation ('our spacious and beautiful confinement') exist in the context of a global American technology and an exported American culture. Provincial culture, in spite of its resistances and in spite of the protective walls it still hides behind, is entering 'the American Age' and being transformed in the images of American power.[14]

Mulgan would certainly have recognised the political and geographical terrain Stead traverses, although the aerial viewpoint Stead adopts would have seemed something new in New Zealand writing (it was common in 1930s English writing). Where Stead departs from Mulgan is in his prose style. His sentences are longer, more sensuous and sinuous. They are more 'feminine' in a sense Stead himself has used.[15] That is to say, instead of the short, hard, denotative sentences of *Man Alone, All Visitors Ashore* has a prose that is rich and laminated; it is more mandarin, more layered and stylistically self-conscious. Even in the idyllic scene where Mulgan describes Johnson watching his lover, Rua, swimming, Mulgan focuses the narrative entirely through the masculine view of Johnson and the prose reflects his viewpoint in its emotional understatement ('The light brown of her body was very pure and natural looking and attractive with the water glistening on her clean shoulders'). Here is a sentence from *All Visitors Ashore*: 'Unable to sleep under the blanket on the divan below Patagonia's cubist painting of lovers against a sea wall Curl Skidmore lies listening to the sound of the sea which has changed with the wind from a steady breaking of small waves interspersed with a rustling of shells to what is now a general unpatterned uninsistent agitation as of a chattering of a crowd in the dark' (p.20). This sentence is representatively rich in its balance of carefully composed phrases, precise visual images, rhythmical patternings and its mixture of aural effects. Yet such sentences co-exist with the insistent political concern of the novel, couched in taut, colloquial prose, rippling ironically with quotation and commentary.

Stead has been accused of clinging to an outdated formalism as a critic and of employing 'an aestheticising discourse' that privileges the orders of art over the political, that does not allow sufficiently for ideology.[16] Yet his effort in *All Visitors Ashore* is not directed at aestheticising history — at turning the flux of social experience into an imperishable work of art — but at finding an adequate formal and stylistic response to specific political events. If political events in New Zealand tend to repeat themselves — from the 1932 riots to the 1951 waterfront dispute to the 1981 anti-Springbok demonstrations in which Stead participated — the reason is that the country remains in the grip of dominant myths: the myth of paradise and the myth of individual self-sufficiency. By looking back in *All Visitors Ashore* so fixedly over his shoulder at Mulgan's novel, Stead recognises this repetition and the force of the myth which produces it. As in *Smith's Dream*, which explores the same national iconography, the myth of the Man Alone is exposed as blind and deceiving. Of course, that also was Mulgan's purpose in writing his 1939 novel: to lead the reader to see the inadequacy of the myth in the face of political actuality.

But Stead, respectful as his novel is towards *Man Alone*, deliberately distances his writing from Mulgan's by forging a prose that takes into account the changes in prose style that have occurred over the intervening half century and by recording the move away from provincialism within New Zealand over that period. Stead's novel takes departure as its theme, but not in the sense that it is concerned with going Home. The novel explores the process by which the New Zealand scene — cultural, economic, technological — has been progressively assimilated into a network of international relations and influences. To leave no longer involves the aching sense of uprooting; to remain behind no longer involves the consciousness of being distant and insignificant, marooned in space and time. Moreover, *All Visitors Ashore* dramatises this shift by its stylistic openness to influence. In place of Mulgan's sinewy, laconic style — objective, colloquial, unvaried — Stead puts a self-consciously rich and playful style, capable of a range of manners and perspectives, dense, intricate, self-advertising. He affirms a New Zealand 'tradition' in fiction by referring to and drawing on his precursors in a way that shows they are still present and active in his writing. But he doesn't defer to them or let their influence overwhelm him and thus foreclose his own independence as a writer.

In *The Death of the Body* Stead teases his readers in a way that recalls both Sargeson and Frame. Like Frame, he finds subtle, complex, and elegant ways of tempting the reader with hints of the author's presence while systematically withholding himself. Like Sargeson, he engages in continual sly harassments of an audience which expects a reading experience less exhilarating and inventive than the author wishes to provide. Like his precursors, Stead demands that the experience of reading his fictions will not be passive; it involves an active collaboration between reader and author. In his memoirs Sargeson described his method of drawing the reader into the text:

I learned to use my imagination to assist me in being explicit on paper, while at the same time leaving a good deal to become intelligible to the reader only upon the condition of half-way meeting: he must not expect much from me unless he uses his imagination.[17]

In *The Death of the Body* Stead's narrator, with disarming modesty, draws the reader into the story:

I introduce myself by looking out. I introduce myself only to dismiss myself as of no consequence. I'm a travelling salesman, an itinerant bard, a newsman in search of a happy ending. I'm the life-and-soul of the party-of-one. I'm the voice of the Story.[18]

In this framing technique the 'Story' itself is said to be already written. It is 'the blue folder lying on my bed under the Matisse poster' (p.7). The narrator here presents himself as a kind of automaton, a mere voice under instruction from the dictatorial, hectoring 'Story' which is determined to 'get its own way'. The narrator, then, is 'a voice without a name', a 'slave', a puppet manipulated by a will behind itself. His function is to give the reader the impression that a particular personality is speaking, that the reading experience is, after all, a confrontation with another self projected by way of language.

Yet the reader's expectations are mocked in the very moment they are met by the winning, self-effacing voice of the narrator. The narrator is, by his own admission, a convenient fiction whose function is to assuage the reader's anxieties. His voice permits the reader to listen. But it is in the process of reading itself, and by the active participation of the reader in that process, that the 'identity' of the narrator 'will be forged. Or it won't' (p.8). In the meantime, the fictional and provisional voice of the narrator serves to encourage the reader to create in his or her own mind the illusion which makes possible the novel's world: not the 'real' world that exists in space and time, nor a mere representation of that world, but an imagined world with its own laws and suspensions, its own spaciousness and detail. The novel's credibility is a function of the reader's willing creative participation in the story as well as the author's skill in enacting.

Yet how seductively 'lifelike' are the details of this imagined world! The effect of immediacy and verisimilitude is a function of the narrator's ability to convince us that the events he recounts really happened. The narrator is an author writing a novel while in Europe about a professor at Auckland University who becomes involved wittingly in a drugs scandal and unwittingly in a sexual one. Again, Stead has cunningly mixed fictional and historical events to draw his reader into the story. If part of the pleasure of reading *All Visitors Ashore* is derived from the recognition we gain from meeting 'real' literary figures loosely disguised as fictional characters, part of that we gain from *The Death of the Body* derives from the recognition that events in the novel correspond to well-publicised events at Auckland University in 1983-4. In particular, the novel dramatises the sexual politics that tore apart the English Department in which Stead himself taught until 1986.

The central character in *The Death of the Body* is Harry Butler, a professor at Auckland University. He teaches philosophy, not English, but the events he describes are very similar to those surrounding the kidnapping of the drama lecturer in the English Department, Mervyn Thompson, in late 1983. In the novel the professor is having an affair with his graduate student, Louise Lamont. A feminist clique has concocted a 'Hot-and-Cold Lecturers File' which they keep in a place called 'Womenspace'. They have targeted lecturers and professors they believe guilty of sexual harassment of female students. Information 'comes in anonymously from the victims' (p.150). They are determined to make an example of a suitable 'victimiser'. In this they are foiled.

The outcome of similar events at the English Department at Auckland University was both more tragic and more farcical. The chosen victimiser, Thompson, was kidnapped, tied to a tree, and the word RAPIST was spraypainted on his car. The event was widely publicised in the media. Thompson's plays were boycotted. His life was made a very public hell.

This event concentrated a number of crucial political, cultural, and literary issues which Stead cunningly uses as the organising centre of his novel. Thompson's crime above all was that he failed to notice that a great shift had occurred in political terminologies. As his subsequent public explanations of the kidnapping made clear, he continued long after the events of late 1983 to see himself as left-wing and progressive in general politics, liberal in private sexual matters, and sympathetic to feminism. He continually asserted his working-class origins, and pointed out that he had actively promoted feminist works in the drama course he ran. (In fact, Thompson's kidnapping was a reenactment of a similar event in a play that his drama students had produced.)[19] He did not deny that he had on occasions in the past had affairs with students. What he fiercely denied was the charge that he had 'raped' anyone.

Yet in 'advanced' feminist circles by the late 1980s the word 'rape' had a very generous definition. It meant more than the forcible act of sexual penetration. Rape was an act inseparable from power, the power held by men in society as it was presently constituted (the 'patriarchy'). Men in power who had sex with women over whom they exercised that power were rapists by definition and Thompson's notion that no rape occurred where both partners were 'willing' missed the point.

For Stead, the whole basis of the liberal culture he had defended was thus denied by feminist ideologues who saw society as expressing the naked interests of the men who controlled its economic, political, and discursive forms. To the radicals who kidnapped Thompson and to their fellow travellers (and there were many of these in the Auckland English Department with its heavy preponderance of female students and male lecturers), Thompson was not merely an aberrant male to be taught a lesson, he was a representative male in power over women to be punished *pour encourager les autres*. Here lies one of the cruxes of cultural, gender, and literary politics in the late 1980s. The problem was not that former liberals like Stead, or leftists like Thompson, had shifted their political positions significantly. They themselves had remained fundamentally unchanged; the political culture had moved under them. The liberal conscience had been made redundant by the anti-humanist ideologies of the 1980s, motivated by sectarian visions of utopia.

In *The Death of the Body* Stead deliberately calls on his New Zealand audience's knowledge of these events. But his purpose is not to record historically a minor event within academia or to titillate his readers by referring to a scandalous episode. Nor, except incidentally, is he writing a university novel, a proliferating genre in the 1980s. He is concerned with the larger underlying cultural shifts implied by the events. Here again, however, his purpose is neither historical nor polemical. He is concerned to find a narrative strategy which will confront the deep problems for the liberal subject implied by these shifts.

The problem is that the moral and philosophical issues raised by radical sexual politics in the 1980s invalidate the traditional realist and humanist resources he himself has employed in the past. His first novel, *Smith's Dream*, rests on the confidence of addressing an audience who might disagree with the political cause he dramatises but who inhabit roughly the same universe of values and assumptions. Hence his purpose is to argue a point of view, to change attitudes. He does so by transposing events in Vietnam to a New Zealand location. He exposes the threat of fascism within the New Zealand cult of the authoritarian leader and the bankruptcy of the Man Alone myth in the face of that threat ('surely he was only acting out a dream that lived in the heart of every kiwi', reflects Smith, having moved himself supposedly beyond the reach of domestic and national politics on to an island).[20] In other words, the novel assumes that reader and author share a ground of moral appeal and that fiction can have a consequence in the political sphere. Stead isn't writing mere propaganda, but his fiction is not content to 'make[] nothing happen'.[21]   As Lawrence Jones observes of the writers of the 'Provincial' period in New Zealand literature, 1935-1955, Stead's aim is the didactic one of encouraging New Zealanders 'to face up to the failure of the dream in New Zealand and work to change it'.[22]

Twenty years later the ground of that appeal had collapsed. The liberal male conscience had lost the confident central ground it once held in New Zealand left-wing politics and in the literary tradition that reflected that politics.

Stead confronts this loss by extending the playful mockery that has characterised his stance towards treasured national myths from his earliest fiction. In the 1965 story, 'A Fitting Tribute', the process by which the myth of the sporting hero as superman is produced is hilariously satirised by a boy who learns to fly with mechanical wings constructed from umbrella struts and is assumed bodily into heaven. Here the favourite national myths of the Man Alone, the do-it-yourself tradition, and the religious worship of sport are mocked by the story's wild and inventive exaggeration. In *Smith's Dream* the hero, fleeing from the fascists, actually puts his foot through the earth's crust (it is Rotorua). Thus the *Man Alone* theme of entering into the landscape is ironically invoked. In *The Death of the Body* the fascists have become lesbian feminists, but the same theme appears — the male hero harried by domesticity, seeking a ground apart from what Melior Farbro in *All Visitors Ashore* calls 'the vast bog of domesticity, the average, the norm' (p.3). The mystique of authoritarianism in the national psyche is still being exposed and the myths by which the nation constructs its ongoing identity are still being subverted and ridiculed. But a new narrative stance, a shifting of the ground from which the fiction's antithetical values proceed, has been made necessary by the antagonism towards the liberal male conscience which has traditionally held those values.

One of the ironies of 'A Fitting Tribute' is that it is narrated by a woman so that the Man Alone story is presented in a necessarily skewed fashion. *The Death of the Body* is narrated by a voice at one remove from the 'thinking head', Harry Butler, who seems obviously to stand for Stead himself. Harry is the academic male as dissociated intellect, disclosing to us the abstract processes of his thought, seeking to assert his authority over his subject, philosophy, and over the other characters. Yet the error of taking Harry for Stead is exposed when one of the other characters, Uta Haverstrom, who acts as a kind of muse to the narrator himself, is chastised for making that fundamental mistake. She mistakes the narrator for Harry, assuming that he is writing disguised autobiography. By confessing to Uta that he is 'not

Harry', the narrator limits his own power over Uta but gains power over the story itself (p.179). So long as she had conflated writer and character, Uta's emotions towards the narrator had depended on her responses to Harry's actions. When the narrator describes Harry enjoying having sex dissociated from emotion, she passionately condemns the narrator rather than Harry himself. When, still conflating Harry and the narrator, Uta at last comes to see the narrator as victim rather than unscrupulous power-wielder, he finds her within his grasp.

It lies in the narrator's power, then, to change the rules of the game that has operated between Uta and himself. Uta has figured for him thus far as desired but untouchable muse, while his own control over events has been confined to the narrative rather than the erotic sphere. Uta believes that Harry, as the victim of the feminists, has been forced to flee abroad to write the novel. The narrator realises that by changing the ending of the novel (Stead himself changed the ending of his earlier novel, *Smith's Dream*)[23] he might be able to reinforce the myth that he is in fact Harry and simultaneously arouse pity in Uta towards himself, a pity that might lead her to offer 'the consolation of [that] splendid bosom and everything that went along with it' (p.191). In the event, the narrator declines to weaken the story by confirming Uta's belief that he is writing 'concealed autobiography' (p.191). He asserts 'the power of fiction' by refusing to sacrifice his licence as an author to invent to his desire as a man to convert sexual fantasy into fact.

Harry's power is in large part the subject of the narrative. It is a power which proceeds from his head, not his body. His mistress, Louise Lamont, is initially attracted to him by his position and his authority and by her subsequent discovery that he is humane and approachable in spite of being a professor. Seeing him, after their affair, she finds him shrunken and ordinary; the desirability with which she had invested him has fled. Sexually vulnerable, a prey to doubts about the continued sharpness of his intellect, dependent on the women who surround his life — wife, mistress, secretary — Harry is less the bully than the bullied. As his given name suggests (names are giveaways in the novel), he is *harried*. His surname, Butler, also has connotations of servitude rather than autocratic power. He is even the subject of 'grammatical bullying' by the University Women's Collective, intent on removing sexist usages from language (p.131).

Moreover, Harry is uncertain about basic questions of identity. His philosophical obsession with the mind/body conundrum rests on a profound discomfort with living in the head rather than the body as a whole. His mind, which is his strength and the source of his attraction and power as a person, denies on philosophical grounds its own separateness from the body. Yet he resentfully finds himself pictured by women as merely a thinking head. It is, however, the body's pleasures not its death he seeks. He thinks of Wittgenstein, the great twentieth-century philosopher who brought a profound scepticism to bear on language, as 'a poor bodiless brilliant head—a head on a platter, thinking' (p.100). The thought occasions not awe but pity. His own power is invested in a series of authorities linked by the word, head, 'that philosophical head, head of Department, head of a household', all contained in the vulnerable object cradled by his student and lover, Claire. While Claire, who later becomes his wife, seeks to dissolve her sense of the body into a purely spiritual oneness, Harry seeks to dissolve that ceaselessly self-conscious mind, the I that thinks, into the body and its pleasures.

But if the head is so problematic a house for what it contains, where and in what consists the self, the centred ego that holds together the multitudinous expressions of a particular individuality? Harry experiences his own mind as 'a room crowded with people all claiming to be Harry Butler, and each with interests and inclinations different from all the rest'. Harry's view recalls Keats's concept of 'negative capability' and Katherine Mansfield's understanding of the self as 'multiple, shifting, non-consecutive, without essence, and perhaps unknowable' (p.51).[24] It is language that carries the fragile form of personality, 'gathering up in its repetitions their sense of themselves, like thread onto a spool' (p.46). Yet language is a treacherous instrument. It collapses under pressure. It fails to hold up the meanings and confidences placed on it. At best, it bears the signature of the self as the ineradicable mark of style. It is not words themselves, but the ways in which they are disposed, in subtle ways different for every language user, that demonstrates a core of self.

But even here words are treacherous. The narrator of the novel, certainly, has no great confidence in his ability to impose the mark of his individual style on the text he is busily constructing. It is the story, the voice out of the blue folder, that is 'commanding' (p.21). He is the commanded. Far from assuming centre stage and disposing the various elements of the story so as to demonstrate his authorial power, the penetration of every aspect of the story by his will, he is himself pre-empted by a voice behind his own, disposing him. That voice — invisible, detached, ironic, mocking — is the one who puts into the mouth of Uta Haverstrom the subversive query: 'Maybe Maestro you're the wrong person to be telling this story. Maybe it should be told by a modern woman who wouldn't make excuses for the professor' (p.82). But that concealed voice, like the creative God who has absconded from his creation leaving signs of his former presence but refusing to manifest himself, is unavailable to the reader. He invites, tantalises, but will not appear.

Literally, then, the reader is in the position of Harry himself faced by his friend Jason's mendacity: 'since Jason liked to embroider the truth, and sometimes to invent it, neither Harry nor Phil knew whether to believe him' (p.28). Harry may see himself as one who seeks to see things clearly, who respects the facts; but how are we as readers to verify where the facts end and invention begins in the novel he inhabits but the action of which he does not control?

Stead uses the Mervyn Thompson episode — or rather the reader's knowledge of that event — as a historical substratum on which to build his fiction. But he departs from the actual events, invents, embroiders, wherever it suits his purposes. He deflects the attention from the actual victim, Thompson, to an invented potential victim, Harry Butler, but he leaves the essential features of the conflict between feminist activists and academic liberals intact. The effect is to blur the distinctions between fact and fiction in a way that allows Stead both to assert his power as novelist over the facts — he can manipulate, alter, shift the emphasis where it suits his purposes — yet to retain a crisp sense of the cultural and political issues at the heart of the matter. Thus he uses a playful, even mischievous, sense of his authority over actuality as artificer to arrive at a deeper version of the 'truth' than a mere historical record would have allowed.

In fact, as Jonathan Lamb has shown, the kidnapping itself was a curiously theatrical event in which the action of a play, previously performed by Thompson's drama class, was reenacted before a national audience with Thompson recast as protagonist.[25] Stead himself has commented on this aspect of the event in an article in *Metro* and one suspects that the theatricality appeals to him as a novelist.[26] In *The Death of the Body* Stead restages a third time the drama of sexuality and power acted out in the Auckland English Department, asserting his interpretive power as a novelist over events in which he himself might well have figured as victim. The 'hit list' at Auckland University in 1983-4 extended beyond Thompson.

Few male members of a department which was accused in the student newspaper of 'a history of academic rape' could feel secure in a climate where terrorism was advocated by feminist and Maori radicals.[27]

Stead locates the historical meaning of the action not in the bare chronology of 'objective' events but within the consciousness of those who were the subjects of those events. Thus he makes the same kind of point about sexual and cultural politics that his narrator makes about politics in general in *All Visitors Ashore:*

> History is always written as if the doings of ordinary nameless faceless persons such as the young unmarried couple looking for a juice extractor were a grey and ill-defined background to the stage on which the politicians strut and strike attitudes and make decisions and laws, but of course history is not reality, it is merely fiction badly written, and in reality it is the other way about, the politicians are the grey background to ordinary lives, however their strutting and posturing and decision- and law-making may bear upon the availability of juice extractors (p.128).

History becomes 'real', for Stead, not in the history books or in Parliament or even on the streets where the strikers march. It becomes real where it impinges upon the consciousness of individuals. By dealing directly with this essential subjectivity of experience, Stead would say that the novel's deliberate fictions come closer to 'the true feel' of actual history than do the factual accounts of historians.[28]

The reviewers and readers who complained that literary Takapuna in the 1950s wasn't as Stead depicts it in *All Visitors Ashore,* or that university lecturers can't afford the Porsche Harry Butler owns in *The Death of the Body* fall into Stead's carefully prepared trap, as Reginald Berry notes in a review of the novel.[29] Their realism is literalist. They assume that events and details in a novel must be consistently predictable and 'lifelike'. They assume that conspicuously clever professors who write novels about clever professors, or former psychiatric patients who write about life in psychiatric institutions, must necessarily be writing 'disguised autobiography'. Stead's point is that by making departures from the strictly representational kind of realism the novelist arrives at a deeper understanding of reality. History, for Stead, is that continual process by which events are transformed within the minds of the individuals who experience them.

At the same time, he allows that there *is* a 'reality' out there, prior to language and independent of ideological constructions. Stead uses the terms 'real', 'truth', 'actual' without the quotation marks that signal the user accepts the conventional wisdom of structuralism and semiotics that there is no access by way of language to the real. Curiously, Stead has often been taken for an advanced, overly intellectual writer, one too intelligent to be truly creative, spontaneous, or original. He has been characterised as an 'academic' writer, where the epithet means formulaic, imitative, above all, one who writes according to some prescriptive theory. Yet Stead has never been interested in theory as such. His views on literary practice are an amalgam of modernist poetics and commonsense realism. His aestheticism has always been modified in practice by a determination to engage directly with the political issues of the day and to communicate beyond the groves of academe.

Stead's attitude towards the 'truth-telling' tendencies of realism has always been ambivalent. His poetics have inclined him progressively away from the stress on poetic language as statement towards a language-centred formalism which downgrades content. In his fiction, as in his poetry, he tends to organise the narrative events around moments of epiphanic insight, located within the consciousness of the protagonist, that hold together a disintegrating experience. These Mallarméan moments transcend history, death, disorder, ugliness by imposing on them the pure orders of the imagination. Death and disorder are able to be 'accommodated within a pattern'.[30] In *Smith's Dream* the hero, listening to music, becomes acutely conscious of the various minute particulars that make up the immediate world received by his senses, but the music dissolves all distinctions and translates him into a timeless moment.[31] In *All Visitors Ashore*, under the spell of 'Wagnermusic', Curl Skidmore and a select few 'step[] outside the boundaries of time, [and are] gathered into the heavens' (p.51).

In *The Death of the Body* the head in which such moments of imaginative unity are housed suffers various indignities. Its transcendental impulses are mocked by the inescapable facts of bodily existence. But the sense of mystery is not altogether dispelled and the word soul continues to serve as a term to express how some core of individual being which is separate from mere thought imposes its special signature, its style, on all that it produces. Thus style asserts its command over fact and the aesthetic instinct imposes unity on the raggedness of experience.

At the same time, Stead's aestheticism has always been complicated in practice by a disposition to engage directly with the political and cultural issues that interest him. Moreover, whatever he has taken from Coleridgean, modernist or postmodernist poetic theories, Stead insists that there is a real world external to and independent of individual perception and that the novelist can get 'closer' to that world by making his or her formal and linguistic means adequate to the perpetually changing nature of the real. What Stead rejects is naive realism, not realism itself. Reality for him is a joining of mental activities with external states of things, and the whole perpetually changing.

So realism, for Stead, must be flexible and inventive enough to register this process of change. He wants to capture the minute reverberations to which history gives rise in the consciousness of the individual, and this requires of the contemporary novel a greater degree of formal openness and a degree of self-consciousness, even playfulness. He wants a realism that allows for his 'delight in language, in verbal play'.[32] The naive notion of realism as the representation of experience in transparent language must give way to one which allows for that penetration of the ordinary by the absurdities of contemporary history. This balance of realistic and metafictional tendencies in Stead's fiction connects him loosely with the movement known as magic realism. In magic realist novels like Gabriel Marquez's *One Hundred Years of Solitude* (1967) and Salman Rushdie's *Midnight's Children* (1981) the departures from probability, the flagrant use of myth, legend, and fantasy, serve ultimately political and moral ends. They illustrate the outrageousness of actual history in the late twentieth century. The 'magical' powers of fiction serve a higher sense of reality than that campaigned for by the politicians and the generals.

Stead, however, does not make exuberant use of myth in his fiction, as Rushdie and Marquez do. In *Midnight's Children* Rushdie treats the various myths, memories, and cultural traditions of India as fictions. That they are not 'true' does not prevent their being pleasurable and useful. When Stead objects to the use of fantasy and myth in *the bone people* or *The Matriarch*, he shows the extent of his loyalty to the New Zealand realist tradition, which has always been sceptical of myth. Hulme and Ihimaera differ from the magic realists by forgetting at times the mythical status of myths. Stead differs from the magic realists by insisting on debunking myth rather than making exuberant use of it in his fiction.

Throughout his career Stead has stood by a view of tradition that affirms in large part that of Eliot. Stead does not, of course, share Eliot's belief that tradition cannot be separated from religion. For Eliot, culture in its most inclusive sense is the incarnation of religion; for Stead, the old gods of Europe did not make the voyage to New Zealand with the settlers and he approves of the secular temper of New Zealand society. Nor does he share Eliot's preference for orthodoxy, except insofar as the term becomes synonymous with tradition and means 'the background, "the accumulated wisdom of time" and of the civilization, against which the poet's subconsciously conceived images of "things as they are" will naturally dispose themselves'. [33] But Stead does share Eliot's view that 'tradition' for writers who share in the general inheritance of Western Europe presents a continuity that goes back to Greece and Rome, that the writer is well advised to acquaint himself or herself with that tradition, that there are objective standards in literary judgements, that the historically significant ideas and artistic productions of a culture proceed in a central flow or 'mainstream',[34] and that cultures are organised hierarchically, both internally and in terms of their relations with each other.[35]

Stead has always been a 'traditional' writer, as poet, novelist, and critic, but we need to give careful consideration to the meaning of the word traditional. He is not traditional in the sense that his writing reflects the stylistic habits of, and thereby belongs to, the past. He is traditional in the sense that he has consistently placed at the centre of his writing practice a view of the relation of the individual writer to the past which holds that the great works of the European tradition are not merely touchstones by which we may measure excellence but also the roots of our common culture as heirs of Europe. This view has put him increasingly at odds with the rhetorics of post-colonialism and postmodernism, both of which, for different reasons, eschew Eurocentrism and tend to be suspicious of high culture.

Stead's position here needs to be seen in the context of a debate in New Zealand literary circles that has gone on since the 1930s which is essentially a debate about tradition. In the 1930s Sargeson, Brasch, and Curnow insisted that the writer in this country must attend to the particular world to hand, geographical and social, as the basis of a series of adventures in search of the reality peculiar to the place. Yet all eschewed nationalism in its vulgar forms (though A. R. D. Fairburn urged New Zealanders to cease 'monkeying about with European culture').[36] They were opposed to the nationalist puffery which inflates a local reputation simply because it is local or the substitution of the outward signs of difference — indigenous flora, in particular — for the commitment to go in search of the always elusive 'realities' of the immediate world. Yet they were also opposed to the slavish adoption by writers in this country of poetic forms, styles, or fashionable theories from metropolitan centres. The writer, they held, must attend to the best that is being written and that has been written by writers working in older and more assured traditions, but writing here must be grounded in the writer's unstinting attention to the reality that is 'local and special at the point where [the writer] pick[s] up the traces'.[37]

Stead's position is a natural extension of these stresses from the 1930s. He wants the Pakeha to acknowledge their break with the source culture. There must be no hankering after the lost home. Yet he is adamant that they must acknowledge the extent of their debt to their British past. There must be no romantic identification with the landscape, no ransacking of Maori myth and legend, but rather a sober sense of the realities of the place and its people and a determined effort to find literary forms and styles appropriate to those realities. Above all, he wants them to acknowledge the extent and continuity of their debt to Europe, to what he calls 'a long and honourable tradition of Western literature — specifically literature in the English language. It is a tradition which gathers within itself a whole civilization — its spirit, its values, its historical record, its imaginative triumphs, its linguistic riches, its experiments with form'.[38] For Stead, this is the central cultural inheritance of New Zealand people. It has been 'transmuted' by New Zealanders, Maori and Pakeha, during the century and half of the country's existence. To claim that New Zealanders should accept their 'Pacific location' and turn their backs on Europe is to privilege geography over what he sees as the true location of culture which is within the minds of those who inherit it.

Stead is a nationalist, not an empire loyalist. He does not hold that the Pakeha should stress their links to the European 'home' as though the ships that brought their forebears put nothing more than an inconvenient distance between the settlers and their past. What he opposes is the liberal Pakeha desire to refashion the uneasy and guilty colonising self in a romantically conceived image of the Maori. Stead argues that culture is something people carry with them when they migrate, not something that springs out of the ground of the place to which they come. According to Stead, they can't miraculously leap into the culture of the Maori because they suddenly decide that their own culture is inappropriate to their geographical location or is politically embarrassing. Because of their British heritage, they have a particular indebtedness to the tradition of English language writers from Chaucer to the present. This lies behind and reinforces their own tradition of specifically New Zealand literature. For Stead, they can lose this heritage if they neglect it or misrepresent it or dismiss it as 'monocultural oppression', but they can't trade it for another.

Over the 1980s Stead has adopted, partly deliberately, partly as a result of his abrasive personality, an adversary stance towards the liberal culture that shaped him. This has set him apart from the intelligentsia but has moved him closer to the *Metro*-reading middle class which has adopted in the late eighties the anxieties about tradition, standards, and the state of the English language that inform the *Landfall* editorials of Brasch in the 1950s. Thus Stead's quarrel with what he sees as the mood of the country as a whole has been conducted in less splendid isolation than he sometimes suggests ('I knew at that moment how far I and my country had drifted apart').[39] In the late eighties, while the objects of Stead's annoyance have changed, the tone of the quarrel has become more intense. Yet that very intensification indicates the emotional investment that went into the relationship in the first place. At times Stead has conducted what seems like a breakup with an exasperating marriage partner, with the combatants drawing on their respective constituencies by announcing the causes of the separation in the reviewing and correspondence columns of magazines.

In a sense Stead has chosen to act as the gadfly in the current cultural climate, saying what many Pakeha are reluctant to say publicly for fear of being painted as reactionaries. There is an element of dandyism in his stance. The dandy adopts a mask, an exaggerated cast of features, which allows him or her to focus a set of attitudes in public. It is a means of complicating the way in which the voice of the author speaks to the reader by concentrating the contradictions of a given personality into a deliberately adopted posture. The force and passion of the engagement with a specific society has extended the range of available ways of discussing contemporary New Zealand literary culture.

CHAPTER 3

Keri Hulme and Negative Capability

Behind our quickness, our shallow occupation of the easier
Landscape, their unprotesting memory
Mildly hovers, surrounding us with perspective,
Offering soil for our rootless behaviour
CHARLES BRASCH, 'Forerunners'

KERI HULME's *the bone people* was published at the end of 1983. It was the literary success story of 1984, a year in which New Zealand entered a period of massive social change. In July a Labour Government was elected which promptly embarked on a programme of radical reform, the contradictions in which reflected the deep uncertainties behind the country's new self-confidence. The Government, with its anti-nuclear policy and its repudiation of sporting contact with South Africa, appealed to an optimistic, progressive, and assertively nationalistic mood. At the same time, the regulatory protections of the economy were ruthlessly demolished. Thus the Government presented to New Zealanders an image of their country as capable of isolation from the racial and technological violences of other nations and in control of its own destiny at the very moment that the unleashing of market forces was internationalising the country's economy and grossly exacerbating existing racial and social tensions.

Yet in the middle of the decade the contradictions were not apparent. It was a period, however brief, when the country was breathless with a sense of its own possibilities. New Zealand was to be remade after the long oppressive years of Muldoon in an image of self-reliance, racial justice, and inventiveness. It was to be a shining example of non-nuclear virtue. Two symbols crystallised the new mood. The Americas Cup Challenge yacht, KZ7, stood for kiwi ingenuity and local technology — small-scale but innovative and advanced—pitched against American technocratic power and Aus-

84

tralian arrogance. *The bone people* stood for literary excellence made locally out of indigenous materials alone, something utterly authentic and of this place. Here were two powerful expressions of the idea of an independent, unique New Zealand, attracting the admiration of the world for its achievements. Organic, virtuous, self-advertising — New Zealand figured in television advertisements in the mid 1980s as a truly South Pacific Eden, a mixture of brown and white faces celebrating in song a common destiny and identity. This also was the vision of New Zealand/Aotearoa contained in *the bone people*: 'a shining land', different and potentially great, a melding of various traditions around a unifying centre. That centre, the novel promised, would be supplied by the Maori cultural presence.

The novel was an unprecedented success. Its first flimsy paperback edition, published by a feminist cooperative, poorly copy-edited and cheaply printed, sold out in astonishingly short space. A myth quickly gathered around the book: that it had been rejected repeatedly by short-sighted, probably unconsciously racist publishers, unable to recognise a work of native genius when it presented itself.[1] In fact, the local publishers who had been offered the work merely requested further editing of an unwieldy, uneven and error-ridden text (on p.63 mugs of cocoa mysteriously turn into coffee then back into cocoa on p.64).[2] But the myth proved more resilient than the prosaic facts of publishing procedure and caution. At any rate, it was appropriate that myth should attach itself so swiftly to a work of which the organising principle was the manipulation and recasting of myth and legend. Five years after the extraordinary reception of the novel it is time to ask whether Hulme in writing her book, like so many New Zealanders in reading it, forgot the mythical status of myths.

*   *   *

When Henry James wrote that Nathaniel Hawthorne's *The Scarlet Letter* could 'be sent to Europe as exquisite in quality as anything that had been received, and the best of it was that the thing was absolutely American; it belonged to the soil, to the air, it came out of the very heart of New England',[3] he initiated a discussion about national literatures whose metaphors continue to haunt us. Thus *the bone people* was greeted in the *Listener* in terms that suggested that the novel's 'classic' status was a function of the generative influence of the soil and air of Aotearoa. When Joy Cowley claimed that the novel was the long-awaited 'flowering of talent which had not been transported from the northern hemisphere . . . [that it had] grow[n] — seeds, shoots, roots and all — from the breast of Papa', her words said more about what the reviewer, and an unexpectedly large reading public with her, wanted to find in *the bone people* than they said about the novel itself.

The novel's rapturous reception undoubtedly owed something to its ability to answer that recurrent question — what does it mean to be a New Zealander? — in confidently post-colonial terms. Here was a novel which granted identity to New Zealanders not in terms of their colonial origin but in terms of the native features of New Zealand: local landscape, Maori names, Maori religious beliefs, indigenous plants. The novel announced the end of the cultural cringe in New Zealand. Yet what was overlooked in all this was the extent to which the novel, far from growing organically out of the ground like some hardy native plant, had been painstakingly stitched together out of scraps and shards and flotsam and jetsam of *literature* that had been washed up on New Zealand shores from everywhere imaginable. A not too assiduous search through the novel discloses echoes of Tolkien, C. S. Lewis, Melville, Sufi poets, Virginia Woolf, Lawrence Durrell, Edward Lear, Joyce, and Yeats.[4] What is important here in terms of Hulme's overall method is the way all the influences are mixed together in the novel — the serious with the silly, the tragic with the absurd, the bombastic with the frivolous. Of course, Maori cultural material is given priority in the novel. It is the central and controlling element, but it does not crowd out the romance material or the chunks of eccentric word-spinning inspired by Joyce or Lear. Hulme's most impressive and problematic achievement in *the bone people* is to make so much disparate material — cultural traditions, linguistic registers, stylistic tendencies — cohabit in a single novel. The question is, does it also cohere?

The essential problem for the reader of the novel is that the method involves so many disconcerting shifts from naturalism to a kind of mythopoeic romance writing. Is the reader meant to respond to the sections on Maori religious beliefs or semi-magical cures for cancer with the same 'willing suspension of disbelief' with which he or she is evidently meant to respond to the realistic sections?[5] Are scenes like the pine-throwing contest and the fight between Joe and Kerewin, which have the exaggerated, almost tongue-in-cheek quality of epic duels in Westerns or martial-arts films, meant to be taken as probable and realistic or as tall tales? Certainly, the fishing trip that Joe, Kerewin, and Simon make contains elements of the outrageous tale such as we find in Australian novelists like Joseph Furphy and Peter Carey (even Zane Grey in *Tales of the Angler's Eldorado* never manages a catch as prodigious as Kerewin's). More troubling are the supernatural elements in the novel, especially in the crucial 'Kaumatua and the Broken Man' section (Chapter 10). Here Joe meets an old man who has been waiting quite alone all his adult life for a predicted visitor who will take over the care of the little god he guards. The promised visitor is Joe, which suggests a divine scheme operating behind the randomness of events to fulfil its own obscure purposes.

The problem is that the relation between the supernatural and naturalistic elements in the novel is confusing and lacking in clear demarcating signposts. In Coleridge's *Rime of the Ancient Mariner* the realistic details encourage us to believe in the unbelievable for the space of the narrative. But we are not meant to grant the reality of phantoms and spirit ships except as symbols of some abstract metaphysical scheme. In *the bone people* the supernatural is not consistently treated as fictive. The world of Maori spiritual presences, of gods and visits by the ghosts of ancient Maori people, into which Joe stumbles in Chapter 10 is depicted as real — not 'real' in the sense that the pub scenes and squalid domestic scenes are, but not merely fanciful either.

By and large the novel's reviewers were not inclined to explore such problems. What was clear was that *the bone people*, by announcing so vigorously that something distinctively New Zealand could be made out of different elements united by a prodigious authorial will, offered a *cultural* vision that suited the moment. The specifically *literary* matters of form and style were touched on only in the most generalised fashion, as though all the conflicting elements of style, the difficulties of organisation, the floridness of the prose were signs of Hulme's necessary and beneficent leap into a new way of writing, one that corresponded to a distinctively Maori and feminine vision of harmony, healing, and spirituality.

The matter of style in the novel is crucial in terms both of Hulme's sense of the literary context she is contesting and of the cultural programme she wishes to advance. The *literary* style of *the bone people*, in its richness, its self-consciousness, its mixture of mandarin and colloquial tendencies, and the eclectic range of its diction, is set against the restraint of 'traditional' New Zealand fiction. This is what Lydia Wevers means when she says that the tradition the novel belongs in is 'outside' the masculine-realist line in local fiction. It is true that that tradition, derived from Sargeson, male and Pakeha in its outlook, shows the residual force of the puritan influence it opposes in the habitual stylistic lack of display of Sargeson heirs like A. P. Gaskell and Maurice Gee. Realism and puritanism here are joined together. Of course, this view of the Sargeson line ignores the subversive tendencies in the master's own style, especially notable in the later stories, tendencies which become manifest in the work of Stead, Frame, and to some extent Owen Marshall. But, for Hulme, fiction writing in the mid 1980s is an activity to be carried out in conscious opposition to the prevailing forms and features of that New Zealand literary inheritance which Wevers identifies with the Pakeha male.

One of Hulme's chief means of opposing this 'realist' tradition is her use of a style compounded of conflicting elements. Both in terms of the novel's overall organisation and at the level of its individual sentences, *the bone people* mixes naturalism and romance. This blending of antagonistic tendencies permeates the novel and is crucial to the vision of literary, social, and personal wholeness it contains. We need to look closely at the novel's use of different linguistic registers.

In Chapter 1 Kerewin Holmes overhears Joe Gillayley, as yet unknown to her, sounding off in a bar. His language is 'a rambling drunken anecdote' in a language, English, whose dominance of his own thought is a sign of his cultural loss, the profound limits of his being as a Maori in a Pakeha-ordered reality. Listening to his litany of fucks, Kerewin reflects:

Why this speech filled with bitterness and contempt? You hate English, man? I can understand that but why not do your conversing in Maori and spare us this contamination? No swear words in that tongue . . . there he goes again. Ah hell, the fucking word has its place, but all the time? . . . aue (p.10).[6]

What depresses Kerewin here is not the word 'fuck' — it is a vivid, colloquial, concrete Anglo-Saxonism that appeals to her herself — but the *narrowness* of Joe's linguistic world, the poverty of its expressiveness in telling of any more than his imprisonment inside his helpless anger. Her own language spills from a hectic word hoard of Anglo-Saxonisms, Latinate words, the specialised terminologies of medicine, pharmacoepias, floral taxonomies, craft-derived terms, especially nautical and carpentering expressions, New Zealandisms, especially sporting idioms and 1950s slang ('Struth'), Maori words, literary borrowings, and poeticisms. On the facing page, she slyly picks up a line from John Masefield's schoolboy favourite, 'Sea-Fever' ('I must go down to the seas again'), with 'my soul . . . go down to the pools' before a passage of submarine description, the particularity and vividness of which recall D. H. Lawrence:

A small bunch of scarlet and gold anenomes [sic] furl and unfurl their arms, graceful petals, slow and lethal . . . tickle tickle, and they turn into uninteresting lumps of brownish jelly . . . haven't made sea-anenome [sic] soup for a while, whaddaboutit? Not today, Josephine . . . at the bottom, in a bank of brown bulbous weed, a hermit crab is rustling a shell. Poking at it, sure its empty? Ditheringly unsure . . . but now, nervously hunched over his soft slug of a belly, he extricates himself from his old hutch and speeds deftly into the new. . . . (p.11)

The interjections, expostulations and musings supplied by Kerewin root this description securely in the mind of its observer. The concreteness of the passage indicates Kerewin's quick sense of things in themselves as her mind catches at a given moment of perception. But the linguistic range from the Old-French-derived 'furl' to the Greek-derived marine-botanical term 'anemone' to the Middle-English 'ditheringly' and the Latinism 'extricates' reveal Hulme indulging her taste for wordy gameplay, investing her character with her own playful, pleasurable ranging across the possibilities of the English language. Immediately below this passage she ironically includes a homonym for Joe's favourite expletive in a mock-pompous scientific phrase: '[t]he sole midlittoral fuccoid'.

Part of Hulme's linguistic endeavour in *the bone people* is directed at finding a dialect that is vigorous and colloquial rather than literary or borrowed. Hence the novel's conspicuous display of the expressions of fishing, building, making, drinking, and inventive cursing. But she is also motivated by a literary magpie's sheer love of 'bits of language', whatever their origin (p.219). She makes up words, or joins together existing ones, Lewis Carroll-fashion, as in 'tremble and sniz' (p.204). She uses *Lord of the Rings* mediaevalisms like 'wraithness' (p.273). She uses a mediaeval Scottish word like 'hirpling' (p.246). She self-consciously employs a ridiculously elaborate Latinism like 'neonmarinepiscator' (p.221).

There is an element in this of mere word-spinning. Hulme cannot resist wordsplicing, puns, lexical jokes, neologisms. Yet oddly, this tendency towards wordplay in its various forms does not make the novel linguistically self-conscious as Janet Frame's novels are. The subject of Hulme's novel is not, as it is in Frame's novels, language itself, but social regeneration and her understanding of language is essentially realistic. Words in Frame's novels do not reliably provide a way through to the world; they are not consistently mirrors of the real. Words in *the bone people* name things and represent a solid external world.

In fact, *the bone people* is a very traditional novel in terms of the understanding of language, representation, and character on which it rests. In these respects it owes more to the nineteenth-century novel of character than to modernism, in spite of its passages of Virginia-Woolf-like 'poetic' prose, its use of stream-of-consciousness, and the *Waste Land* symbols of towers, bones, and deserts scattered through the novel.[7] As in a Dickens novel, we are encouraged to identify emotionally with characters whose eccentricities contribute to their human credibility, to the lifelike sense of depth and complexity they convey. Hulme's fictional world has the extensiveness and detail of realism. The language of the novel, for all its word-spinning tendencies, serves ultimately to require us to make moral discriminations about the actions and intentions of the characters as though they were actual humans, not fictional constructs.

Moreover, in spite of its habit of continually veering towards the numinous and the mythical, the novel is loaded down with a weight of horrifically naturalistic domestic detail. At the novel's heart is the harrowing dramatisation of a specific social evil, child abuse. We are made to identify emotionally with the victim of an evil, and our identification is so total that we forget that what we are reading is a representation of life, not life itself: this ability to make us identify is the source of the novel's disturbing but undeniable power.

Take, for instance, the scene in which Joe beats Simon almost to death. This stands at the heart of the novel's naturalism. It is the antithesis of those moments of mythic assertion of visionary wholeness and healing which the novel offers. The scene of the beating is conveyed to us in the some of the tightest and most compelling prose in the novel:

> When Joe comes back into the kitchen, he is carrying his belt by the leather end. The buckle glints as it swings just above the floor.
> His stomach convulses, knotting with fear.
> He swallows violently to keep the vomit down.

Joe is surrounded by pulses and flares of dull red light.
He says in a low anguished voice.
'You have ruined me.'
He says,
'You have just ruined everything, you shit.'
He doesn't say anything more, except when he has turned the chair against
the table.
He says, 'Get over.'
He does. He lays his arms in front of him, left hand stiff, and his head on
his arms.
He sets his teeth, and waits.

* * *

The world is full of dazzlement, jewel beams, fires of crystal splendour.
I am on fire.
He is aching, he is breaking apart with pain.
The agony is everywhere, hands, body, legs, head.
He is shaking so badly he cannot stand.
The hard wood keeps griding [sic] past him.
He keeps trying to stand.
Joe's voice is thin and distant.
'When did you get this?'
'When did Bill Drew give you this?'
'How long have you kept this?'
He is pulled up and held onto the door frame.
The wood gnaws his body.
He pushes forward with all his strength against the hand that pins him
down.
He is thudded back into all the teeth of the wood.
'When did you do this?'
'When did this happen?'
Sliding the sliver out of the wrapping, his hand trembling uselessly. He
fists forward. It seems a foolish, feeble blow.
But I need to stop the wood coming through.
Joe screams.
The first punch hit his head.
His head slammed back into the door frame.
The punches keep coming.
Again.
Again.
And again.
The lights and fires are going out.
He weeps for them.
The blood pours from everywhere.
He can feel it spilling from his mouth, his ears, his eyes, and his nose.
The drone of flies gets louder.
The world goes away.
The night has come. (pp.319-20)

91

Hulme writes here with uncharacteristic economy. The details are exactly observed. The perspective of the whole piece is skilfully focused through the eyes of the child who is the subject of the attack so that we feel its full horror as the action crowds upon his consciousness in a chaotic sequence of colours and sensations, the significance of which remains at a distance from him. There is no overwriting. The clarity and control of the prose allows us no escape from the terror of what it records. Precisely because the narrator avoids intruding emotion and because the boy himself is too numbed and disconnected from the event's meaning to experience it emotionally — it is direct sensation for him — the reader's emotions are the more fully engaged.

This passage of uncomplicated naturalism is certainly the strongest moment in the book. It dramatises, makes 'real', a widespread social evil. It does not simplify, preach, or propagandise. It registers the humanity of the man who beats the child as well as that of the child who suffers. When Joe says to Simon, 'you have ruined everything, you shit', we recall Kerewin's first encounter with him as a drunken Maori male, hiding the brokenness of his own culture under swear words in the very language that signals his loss. When Simon sees the lights and pulses that fade into darkness at the end of the passage, we recall the child's apparent gift for discerning 'auras', but here they register not the novelist's eccentric reading interests but the child's terrified apprehension of what is about to happen to him and his ineradicable love for Joe.

The violence in *the bone people* is so shocking because it is described *realistically*. It remains with us, troubling and unshakeable, as the often-remarked-on violence in Sargeson's stories does not. The violences in Sargeson are *literary* ones. They partake of the gothic. They occur in surrealistic suspensions of normal social codes as in 'A Great Day' (1937), where the little bloke Fred kills his muscular fishing mate Ken, or as the calculatedly outrageous turn at the end of 'Sale Day' (1939), where the sexually repressed Victor throws the randy tom cat in the fire. But Hulme's novel, for all its continual departures from the actual into the mythical and the magical, deals with the preoccupying core of violence at its centre in a realistic manner.

The novel's compulsive playfulness with language, then, amounts to a kind of decoration. It does not thwart the referential tendency of the novel. In fact, far from showing a disposition to disconnect words from their referents, *the bone people* is continually seeking to reconnect words to things, both by its realism and by a bias in the choice of diction which shows Hulme's desire to establish an organic link between language and lived realities. Hulme retains throughout the novel the sense of a known world of particular things, lovingly invoked by names which have a beauty in themselves as sounds. Behind this lies the novel's pervasive hankering for the lost pre-industrial world in which the names of trades and tools of trades seemed to have a closer connection to actual things than they have in the 'fallen' post-industrial world. Maori names have this kind of significance in the novel, particularly the names of weapons, stones, trees, and woods used in the making of furniture or the tower. The names of precious stones and of the stars also have the numinous quality of spiritualised things.

The personal language of signs used by Simon, the mute boy, is a form of language in which there is no gap between thing and sign; hence its special place in the novel's linguistic order. Simon's 'language' is pure because it is so close to the things of which it speaks. It is, as Joe puts it, 'mainly derivation', that is to say, its origins in objects or ordinary things are uncontaminated by the abstraction of being turned into written characters which need to be reinterpreted (p.49). Behind this notion of linguistic purity lies a venerable romantic theme. Simon prefers things to names because he does not want to separate his subjecthood from the object world: 'Names aren't much. The things are' (p.134). He even builds versions of that romantic cliché, the aeolian harp (p.107).

Hulme's 'modernism' has a romantic base. It belongs in what Paul Fussell describes as a lyrical complaint against industrial civilisation:

One large intellectual and emotional atmosphere enfolds writers as different as Yeats, Eliot, Hemingway, and Lawrence, and from this distance what the four are doing seems to look more and more like the same thing. They are mounting a rhetorical critique of industrialism; they are prosecuting a perhaps more richly dramatized and lyricized continuation of the complaints of Ruskin, Arnold, and Morris.[8]

Like all those eminent Victorians and moderns Fussell cites, Hulme belongs in a line of resistance to a world in which the old 'natural' bonds between humans, and between humans and things, have been replaced by the 'artificial' bonds of money and machinery. Hulme's romantic modernism is expressed in her desire to avoid abstraction by returning to a time when human life was still connected to the simple elements of daily existence. Kerewin's world in the tower she builds is atavistic; it is not urban, alienated, mechanistic. It has none of the anonymity, the miscellaneity, the disorder of modern urban life. And the speech she prefers (or rather the several dialects she affects) is not the demotic language of utility and commerce which is spoken in large cities. Joyce and Eliot made works of formal beauty out of that urbanised language, and Wedde continues the same modernist endeavour in *Symmes Hole*. Hulme is fighting a rearguard action against the modern world and its debased dialects.

Hulme's achievement in *the bone people* should not be underestimated. In a period when prose fiction in this country tended either to a played-out version of Sargesonian realism (see the short stories in *Landfall* during the late 1970s and early '80s) or to an impenetrable postmodernism (see the fiction in *Parallax* or Michael Morrissey's *The New Fiction* [1985]), she managed to forge a prose style that has range, density, and vigour, yet which is not, allowing for some lapses, onanistic, self-regarding, or excessively conscious of itself as performance. Her writing is flexible and capable of employing a range of stylistic manners. She never allows her prose to become journalistic in the manner of much realist women's fiction — Sue McCauley, Joan Rosier-Jones, or Heather Marshall, for instance.

Lawrence Jones has placed Hulme's fiction in the line of feminine writing that derives in this country from Katherine Mansfield.[9] It is true enough that Hulme's novel foregrounds material that falls outside the usual range of realist writing by men in New Zealand. Where critical realism opposes the puritanical cast of Pakeha culture from a consistently secular and sceptical stance, Hulme displays a promiscuous attraction to religions in general, provided they are not Christian. Where much realism in this country has been concerned with the observation of outward manners and behaviours at the expense of inward states of mind, she is interested in such observation only sporadically. But several prominent features of her writing are closer to 'masculine' traditions, both local and international, than to feminine ones.

Certainly, she has none of Mansfield's fluency with symbolism, none of the rich ambiguity in Mansfield's stories as to motivation. Mansfield is concerned to register emotional nuance, not to trace motivation naturalistically. In the Mansfield story 'Bliss' the symbolism concentrates a great complexity of desire in Bertha whose true object of passion is perhaps the other woman in the story. But all this complexity and obliquity is left delicately unresolved in the story. It is focused through the symbol of the moon, tenuously drawn out, while the key to Bertha's emotion is left as a hint, a suggestion, a raised eyebrow. Hulme tells us explicitly and at some length about Joe's background and his motivations. We know why he acts as he does because we know about his race, milieu, and environment in straight-forwardly naturalistic terms. She indicates the details and mechanics of the deterministic production of mental qualities by social conditions — by his menial work, his cultural dislocation, his sufferings as a child, his drunkenness. Even where Hulme focuses this material through Kerewin's consciousness, casting it in the form of questions drifting through her troubled sense of Joe's relations with Simon, the bias of the writing is naturalistic. Here is a key passage that locates the sources of Joe's problems — in a way that is quite foreign to Mansfield or Frame:

What would it feel like, to want to be priest, to want to be teacher, to want to be husband and father of a family, and be thwarted in them all? How would it feel to have that macabre kind of childhood, blighted by insanity, beset with illness? And those veiled hints he dropped of violence done to him . . . no wonder he's sparse on knowledge of how to deal with children. (p.242)

Nor does Hulme's prose have anything significant in common with the 'feminine' line of modernism, the long sentences and the concentration on sensibility we find in Dorothy Richardson and Virginia Woolf. Where she does use long sentences, they are long by the accumulation of independent clauses, not because they have the meandering clausal complexity of Woolf's sentences. Like Woolf, she is a psychological realist (part of the time anyway), but there is nothing refined or upper-class about the sensibilities she chooses to open up to the reader's explorations. In many ways, Kerewin with her determination to assert a practical, no-nonsense, muscular outdoorsiness has more in common with the preferred types of the Edwardian novelists and poets than with Woolf's female characters. Hulme's public persona recalls the 'huntin' and shootin'' poets of the early 1900s who were put off aestheticism by the scandal of Oscar Wilde and affected a loud heartiness. The 'cult of beer and Sussex, of walking and simplicity which ended with Masefield, Brooke and Squire'[10] has been turned into the cult of Okarito and Scotch, mead, pipes, bush-craft, and whitebait fishing.

Like that of the Edwardians also, Hulme's writing is charged with a pastoral patriotism. As the Edwardian poets eagerly looked back to an England before the rise of commerce and industry, finding in the countryside unspoiled reminders of the old order of organic connection and national virtue, Hulme discovers in pre-European Aotearoa what the kaumatua calls 'this country's soul' (p.380). The kaumatua, a direct link to the old Maori world, reveals to Joe 'the heart of the country' (p.380). This is the spiritual significance contained in the little god he protects. This vision of a purified New Zealand/ Aotearoa is offered as a substitute for Christianity, which is associated with the Pakeha conquest and with the alien gods of commerce and rationality. (Oddly, in spite of Kerewin's expressions of Nietzschean scorn for Christian values [p.343, for instance], the novel offers us a complete version of the Holy Family with Simon as Christlike victim, Joseph as the celibate human father, and Kerewin as the virgin mother.) The memory of a Maori reality in New Zealand's prehistory provides the central spool around which the various strands of cultural inheritance wind themselves. The country, in the old days, the kaumatua tells Joe, was 'different and special'. 'Something very great', he continues, 'had allied itself with some of us'. Aotearoa was 'the shining land' (p.374).

The irony here is that Hulme has projected backwards into prehistory the familiar settler myth of New Zealand as a possible Eden. Eden, of course, is always located in the past, although promised in the future. Culturally or individually, it constitutes the dream of one's own childhood. The pre-European Maori are not romanticised in the novel. Joe considers the tradition, taught in schools and preserved in standard texts, that the ancient Maori was 'a noble fighter': 'God, what lies we get taught. Exemplify the honourable incidents, and conceal the children who get the chop, the women and old men stampeded over cliffs, the bloody endless feuding' (p.346). He acknowledges the gallantry and 'the wit in the face of inevitable death', but he admits also the cruelty and the horrors (p.346). Nevertheless, the spiritual side of the ancient Maori world, which is expressed most cogently by the kaumatua, includes the organic and pastoral values of childhood. This is the world of romance, which is why the ancient Maori metaphysical order is dramatised in the novel by way of magic and myth. There is, of course, no *realistic* way of presenting that world, just as there is no *historical* way back to the pre-European Maori and their way of life. Contemporary Maori people like Joe and his friends and relatives are treated realistically in the novel. They suffer all the ills and exhibit all the frustrations of people at the bottom of the social heap in any society. But the attempt to represent the spiritual world of the old people necessarily means the abandonment of realism, even though Hulme has tried to grant a kind of 'reality' to that world.

This pristine Maori presence, a spiritual reality that traces its origins to the pre-contact Maori order, is what saves New Zealand from being merely another former British colony being formed in the image of American consumer capitalism. Australia is tellingly described as a 'dead-hearted' country by Kerewin who has just vanquished two stereotypical Australian Returned Servicemen's League racists in a pub exchange (p.305). New Zealand, on the other hand, has 'a dream marae at its core' (p.271). Here Maori spirituality becomes the enabling condition of a form of romantic nationalism, centred on race, culture, and land. In other words, the novel's vision of the past is influenced by a species of spiritualised nationalism.

At this point the novel's desire for authentic belonging coincides with the wish to purge New Zealand of the corrupting layers of European influence — to eradicate the colonial heritage — and to purify the nation by placing specifically Maori values at its centre. *The bone people* does not, of course, deny that the Pakeha have a place in New Zealand, but it does call on Pakeha to accept the priority of Maori culture and Maori values. It calls for a reversal of the hegemony of cultures that colonisation established and perpetuated. The novel deliberately points a way beyond the colonial legacy and envisages a new wholeness for all those cultures that have been fractured by colonisation.

When the kaumatua describes to Joe the spiritual plenitude of the old people's world, he uses a phrase that invokes a famous line in one of the first literary dramatisations of imperialism, Shakespeare's *The Tempest*: 'All the land is filled with mysteries, and this place fairly sings with them' (p.378). There is an echo here of Caliban's speech to Stephano, 'the isle is full of noises,/Sounds and sweet airs, that give delight, and hurt not'.[11] Thus Caliban, the conquered 'savage', attempts to instruct his conqueror in the value and completeness of the world from which he has been displaced. Shakespeare's play defends the imperial ethos and grants a benign magic to Europeans. Hulme's novel attacks imperialist attitudes and reconstitutes the power of primitive magic. It may also be significant that Kerewin first encounters Simon through footprints left in the sand, thus recalling Robinson Crusoe's first encounter with Friday in another great defence of imperialism, Defoe's *Robinson Crusoe*. Again, the meaning of the event in the prior text is reversed: here the sea-borne European arrives as a lost innocent and is seen from the perspective of the existing inhabitant.

Hulme's effort in *the bone people* to envisage a way past the legacy of colonialism is one of the sources of the novel's power and of its appeal. The problem here is that, for Maori and Pakeha alike, the pre-European world can only be recovered in terms of the intervening century and a half of European presence. The Maori concept of that world has inevitably been affected by Christianity. The view that Maori people are more spiritual than Pakeha overlooks the extent to which Maori religious beliefs were influenced by the teachings of the missionaries in the early nineteenth century. Ironically perhaps, Maori culture has kept alive a Christian tradition of opposition to materialism and of love for one's neighbours that has partly disappeared from the dominant Pakeha culture.

At any rate, the Pakeha presence in New Zealand, however contaminated by its association with colonialism, cannot be removed to reveal the pristine outlines of the original culture. After 150 years of cohabitation, after having been so long and so intimately, albeit unwillingly, intertwined, the two cultural presences cannot be neatly separated. The version of that pre-contact order glimpsed in *the bone people* has inevitably been touched by European influence, particularly by the romantic stereotypes of 'noble savage' culture that were worked into the governing assumptions of the British founders of the colony in the middle of the nineteenth century.

With this in mind we can approach the most contentious aspect of the novel, its treatment of Maori religious belief, which has implications for its vision of New Zealand's redemptive future, its picture of New Zealand society, and for its design as a whole. C. K. Stead in an article on *the bone people* has complained about the novel's habit from time to time of 'tak[ing] a dive from reality into wishful daydream'. Stead objects to the Maori spirituality in the novel which he sees as spurious and willed. His objection is worth quoting in full:

> Worse, however, is the sequence in which Joe comes close to death and then is rescued by an old Maori man who has waited his whole lifetime under semi-divine instruction to perform just this rescue, so he can pass onto the

man he saves proprietorial rights over a piece of land and the talisman in which its spirit is preserved. There would be no point in recounting in detail the physical and mystical experiences which make up this section of the novel. It should be enough to say that I found it, read either as Maori lore or as fiction, almost totally spurious.[12]

Stead here refers to the crucial chapter, 'The Kaumatua and the Broken Man'. Despite Stead's cautionary remarks, I want now to look closely at this chapter both in terms of its Maori spiritual elements and in the light of Stead's question about whether it is permissible in a novel to depart from 'reality' and, if so, whether there are proper limits to such departures.

In the first place it is worth noting that the Maori religious and spiritual ideas in this chapter are not at all esoteric. They are not the kind of cultural belief that is passed from generation to generation exclusively within the group. Much of the material can be found in Elsdon Best's 1932 Dominion Museum Monograph No. 2, *Spiritual and Mental Concepts of the Maori*, which was reissued in 1954 and 1973. On page 360 Joe dreams that his dead wife visits him in the form of a moth. In Best's monograph we find that 'certain moths are viewed as being *he wairua no te kehua* (souls of ghosts)'.[13] A fuller explanation of the same belief is found in Best's *Maori Religion and Mythology* (1982), where we learn that spirits after death pass through ten stages of existence in the underworld and some then reappear as moths, which is why moths are called *wairua tangata* (human souls). Moreover, this is the final stage of existence in the underworld, which corresponds to what the kaumatua tells Joe about the dream and his wife's spiritual condition.[14] The kaumatua's teachings on Maori religious lore in Chapter 10 of *the bone people* bear closely on the concept of mauri, which Best deals with extensively. As Best points out, '[d]eep-sea voyagers apparently carried a *mauri* of their vessel with them'.[15] The material mauri was regarded, in Best's words, as 'an abiding place of the gods'.[16] This is what the kaumatua tells Joe.

There is no clear indication that Hulme has used Best as a source. The point is that the sources of the religious material in the novel could be found in a number of basic texts, most of them of the kind that Joe himself characterises as 'useful books his grandmother gave him' (p.346). Hulme has mentioned in an interview reading the Maori legends in English at school in 'A. W. Reed's retellings'.[17] There is nothing unusual about her having turned to such sources for information. Inevitably, what we come to know about cultures other than our own (and Hulme is Maori more 'by heart, spirit, and inclination', in Kerewin's words, than by 'blood, flesh and inheritance') is influenced by what we read (p.64). It would be surprising if Hulme had not been influenced at some point by such sources, just as it would be surprising if no traces of earlier Pakeha literature were to be found in her work. The Maori spiritual material in *the bone people* is not pure and unmediated, a direct link back to the source. It bears the imprint of the Pakeha reception and interpretation of that material.

The important point is that Hulme has *dramatised* readily available material and made it serve the particular purposes of the novel. Hence the kaumatua receives his instruction in Maori religious lore from his grandmother, although a woman would not have had access to such material in traditional Maori society. Moreover, Hulme enlarges the concept of mauri from one that applied to canoes, rivers, and tribal areas to one that embraces the whole country. As the pre-European Maori had no concept of New Zealand/Aotearoa as a unified entity (although they did see the North Island as a geographic entity, te ika a Maui), it is highly improbable that they would have held that there was a special god for the whole country. Gods were brought from Hawaiki and distributed round the specific areas. But it is unlikely that there was a mauri for Aotearoa. Who would have guarded it? Where would it have been placed? The notion involves a transcending of tribal affiliations that was not possible till the arrival of the colonists made Maori aware of their unity as well as their differences as a people.

In Chapter 10 Joe, recently released from prison, goes alone into a stretch of rough bush with the object of suicide. The suicide attempt itself is reminiscent of Gloucester's similar attempt in *King Lear*. Joe stands above a cliff, soliloquises, jumps, and survives. And like Gloucester, he now begins a process of learning true wisdom. His mentor is an aged kaumatua who has waited a lifetime for just this moment. Before he passes out, Joe reflects on the waste he has made of his own life and his relationships. He sees himself as 'a wilderness of alien gorse and stone' (p.352). It is the kaumatua who will lead him back behind the 'foreign images' to a buried core of wholeness and healing associated with both childhood and the pre-European Maori world.

Slowly the kaumatua reconnects Joe to his true past, his Maoriness. He works through the images of his dreams attaching them to authentically Maori spiritual and folk lore. He purges him of the bitterness and of the legacy of imposed ('alien') images. He prepares Joe to receive as truth rather than mere fancy the reason he has waited so long:

'I guard a stone that was brought out on one of the great canoes. I guard the canoe itself. I guard the little god that came with the canoe. The god broods over the mauriora, for that is what the stone is home to, but the mauri is distinct and great beyond the little god . . . the canoe rots under them both . . . aie, he is a little god, no-one worships him any longer. But he hasn't died yet. He has his hunger and his memories and his care to keep him tenuously alive. If you decide to go, he will be all there is left as a watcher, as a guardian.' (p.373)

Joe's response to this is initially sceptical. He considers the kaumatua mad and reflects that the museums are full of canoes and little gods. Yet at the same time his Maori unconscious (the archetypes and figurings of the unconscious are racially determined for Hulme) responds to the old man's words. An 'unseen current', a deeper and darker intuitional level of his being, answers the specifically Maori address of the kaumatua. The layers of Pakeha false consciousness, the imposed colonial heritage of alien cultural conceptions, are in the process of being turned aside by authentic knowing.

At this moment the old man 'mumble[s]' the core of his truth, and discloses the astonishing 'message' of the novel itself: 'it is the heart of the country. The heart of this land' (p.373). This theme, thus quietly insinuated into the reader's initially sceptical mind, is taken up, developed over the rest of the chapter as Joe swings between doubt and acceptance towards the affirming high note on which the chapter ends. What the kaumatua tells Joe needs to be thus prepared for and made persuasive because it is the myth the novel seeks to substantiate, the wish it seeks to make dramatically true, the cultural vision it seeks to promulgate:

'I was taught that it was the old people's belief that this country, and our people, are different and special. That something very great had allied itself with some of us, had given itself to us. But we changed. We ceased to nurture the land. We fought among ourselves. We were overcome by those white people in their hordes. We were broken and diminished. We forgot what we could have been, that Aotearoa was the shining land. Maybe it will be again . . . be that as it will, that that [sic] thing which allied itself to us, is still here. I take care of it, because it sleeps now. It retired into itself when the world changed. It can be taken and destroyed while it sleeps, I was told . . . and then this land would become empty of all the shiningness, all the peace, all the glory. Forever. The canoe . . . it has power, because of where it came from, and who built it, but it is just a canoe. One of the great voyaging ships of our people . . . but a ship, by itself is not that important. And there are many little gods in the world yet, some mean, others omnipotently benign, some restless, others sleeping . . . but I am afraid for the mauri! Aue! How can I make you understand? How? How? How?' (p.374)

The final appeal is directed as much at the reader as at Joe. Our own layers of rationality, scepticism, doubt need to be swept aside so that we may, like Joe, believe without understanding, affirm without questioning. Yet what we are asked to affirm is, in the last analysis, a form of mystical nationalism. The little god spiritualises New Zealand by reaching down beneath the Pakeha presence to an intact core of Maoriness. Thus it makes possible the unembarrassed use of the old language of sub-imperial patriotism: 'shiningness', 'glory', 'forever'. This renovated nationalism allows the Pakeha reader to feel at home in New Zealand by expelling from consciousness all those qualities associated with rationality that prevent the anguished post-colonial subject from fully empathising with the people his or her ancestors displaced and the land they made their own.

Thus the journey of the little god to Aotearoa that is recalled in the novel offers to the Pakeha an object of worship that might replace the Protestant God in whom they had long since lost interest. The gods of the old world made the journey to New Zealand with the missionaries and settlers, but their presence here was always ghostly and they faded over time, leaving only their injunctions and maledictions behind them in laws concerning liquor and homosexuality. In the 1980s, however, the descendants of the settlers discovered in large numbers a terrible absence where the religious sense had once resided. So they turned to the gods of the Maori. Frame notes the turning towards Maori legend and spirituality in the middle sixties in *A State of Siege* and finds it unconvincing. Two decades later Hulme gives the Pakeha what they wanted: gods who have made the passage and been established in the country over centuries, fit deities for an anti-nuclear ethos.

Here, tellingly, the desire to discover indigenous legends that Frame exposes in *The Carpathians* is met. In place of the old canoes of the Egyptians Joe remembers seeing as a boy is something 'much more exciting': 'one of the fartravelled saltsea ships, that knifed across great Kiwa centuries ago' (p.376). So Joe encounters the canoe in a moment of religious intensity that is at once personal and cultural. He touches the water that contains it and is electrified and illuminated in the same instant. Thus translated into the world of spirit, he is able to receive the kaumatua's recollections of visitations from the old people in the appropriately reverential mood. Significantly, here in the midst of the novel's most flagrant departure from any recognisable reality, the writing becomes less floridly romantic and more realistic and detailed. The kaumatua recalls one of the old people throwing a piece of cooked kumara at him. The world of ordinary experience has penetrated that of romance and hence, we are to assume, made it 'real' (p.378).

In all this the novel follows with curious echoes the story of Christ's passion. Joe's agony in the garden gives way to his passion and transfiguration. After the great event has ended, an earthquake shakes the land and signals the passing of the old order and the dawning of the new one. Joe sets forth into the world that does not know of its own transfiguration, bearing the cornerstone of the new spiritual dispensation. In spite of the anti-Christian remarks scattered through the novel, Christian, often specifically Catholic, imagery is pervasive in *the bone people*. When Kerewin first sees Simon, the boy is 'standing stiff and straight like some weird saint in a stained gold window' (p.14). When the kaumatua dies, Joe softly echoes Christ's words from the Cross, 'it is ended' (p.383).

The essence of Stead's charge against *the bone people* is that Hulme's departures from reality are in the direction of cultural wish fulfilment rather than historical responsibility. The elements that complicate its realism do not enrich it but constitute mere fantasy, in the *Lord of the Rings* sense, and this is inappropriate in the novel as a form. For Stead, Hulme offers in her novel a way of forgetting, an avoidance of the complex actualities of history. And he specifically identifies the Maori religious elements in the novel with such reprehensible escapism.

There is, however, another sense of the word fantasy, another understanding of its place in the novel. For Hulme, fantasy is a part of the novel's total means, one element among all those it may reasonably include. Her novel is a national epic, with the inclusiveness and the didactic, celebratory purpose that goes with the genre. Hulme may point out the society's flaws and violences. But she is motivated by a profound desire to teach the society how it might heal itself and become whole. She focuses on those features peculiar to the place and its people. She wants to connect the nation to its past, to point to a possible future, to revivify legendary material. Unlike Salman Rushdie, whose *Midnight's Children* is also a national epic, her purpose is not fundamentally satiric but constitutive. Rushdie sees chiefly the lies and shoddiness of national life, the enormous falling short of the actuality from the rhetoric of beginnings. He sets the follies of the present against the legends of the past (the novel's debts to Hindu mythology are extensive and elaborate), but finds no point of value in the past from which to stand aloof and judge the corruptions of the present. Hulme sees the evils of the present, but envisages a wholeness and healing in the past which she offers as a positive and possible model for the future.

But the only way of dramatising that possible future in the terms she sets is by way of myth. Hulme's 'mythic method' is one that attempts to make the reader accept the mythical material that informs and shapes the novel, to take it as true. That is not to say that she means us throw away commonsense altogether and enter the world of faery — or not quite. She does want, however, to bring about a deep change in the reader by which he or she will be led to respond to the spiritual content of the novel in that condition of selfless empathy which Keats describes as 'negative capability', without, that is, any 'irritable reaching back towards fact'.[18] In Eliot's *The Waste Land* myth serves to provide a continuous parallel between the past and the present so that the fallenness and shoddiness of contemporary history — its 'immense panorama of futility and anarchy' — are able to be worked into the formal order of art.[19] In Hulme's novel myth serves as a means of erasing the corrupt ways of seeing and responding to the spiritual realities of the past that are inseparable from Pakeha consciousness. Thus, reshaped in Maori terms, the Pakeha and modern Maori themselves are pointed towards a reformulated, purged, and spiritualised version of their being as New Zealanders. The novel's deliberate blending of past and present and of various cultural elements is intended as a metaphor for and an encouragement of national regeneration.

Like that of Robin Hyde, whose *Nor the Years Condemn* (1938) has similarly been accused of 'varying unpredictably between the pedestrian and the fantastic', Hulme's realism is harnessed to a 'utopian politics'.[20] The introduction to the 1986 New Women's Press edition of Hyde's novel concludes in terms that echo the contemporary reviews of *the bone people*:

The images that give the book its odd fluidity and elusiveness, its difficulty and especial power, speak of a desire to heal the conflicts that batter the human spirit — conflicts between male and female, Pakeha and Maori, people and land. But the book evokes this healing only in the dream languages of fiction. Divided within itself, divided between its different modes of speech, the text enacts the conflicts whose resolution it can only gesture towards.[21]

That this passage so accurately characterises Hulme's novel as well as Hyde's bespeaks the cultural mood that made the novel's reception so favourable. *The bone people* addresses a deep-rooted and wide-spread desire to find some way beyond the shoddy impasses at which history and race relations become stalled. In these terms realism and fantasy are both essential elements in the novel's overall design. They are a means of envisaging a wholeness otherwise unthinkable. Against the centrifugal tendencies of history, Hulme asserts a centre. Against the degradation of values, Hulme asserts a core of meaning. New Zealand in *the bone people* signifies an idealised essence by reference to which the actual New Zealand is a continual disappointment. Thus *the bone people* oddly recaptures the sense we find in colonial writing of 'home' as a distant ideal by substituting the buried spiritual presence of Maori New Zealand for the lost Pakeha one of England.

The mixture of elements in the novel — of styles and sources — is crucial to an understanding both of the novel's formal organisation and of its determination to offer a redeemed version of New Zealand as a post-colonial country. What is significant is that Hulme evidently feels easy about acknowledging the extent of the novel's debts to her wide reading (see the eclectic mix of books ranging from Westerns to scientific works and mystical treatises in the bach at Moerangi [p.189]), yet has denied the influence on her work of previous writing by Pakeha New Zealanders.[22] This denial involves a curious and significant act of repression. It is as though a truly 'New Zealand' literature can only be established by the melding of all those elements that contributed to the making of the New Zealand cultural picture — Maori, Celtic, even the acceptable English influence represented by Tolkien and Lewis — but not that body of work chiefly by white New Zealanders, usually male, directed at establishing New Zealand literature as a separate but related part of the general European inheritance. Hulme is prepared to acknowledge the literariness of her novel, but determined to censor out those literary debts which do not suit her cultural purpose, which is no less than the formulation out of conflicting elements of a distinctive and original cultural whole. In other words, she seeks to establish a 'tradition' of writing in this country which bypasses the existing tradition on ideological grounds. Hulme makes clear the novel's view of the proper relation between imported and indigenous elements when Kerewin coments on the exotic forests:

'TEA TIME,' says Kerewin, and turns the car off the main road.
'Bloody pines,' snarling to herself.
'Huh?'
'Look at it.'
Cutover bush going past in a blur. Where it isn't cutover, it's pines. They start a chain back from the verge and march on and on in gloomy parade.
'This place used to have one of the finest stands of kahikatea in the country.'
'And they cut it down to make room for those?'
'They did,' she says sourly. 'Pines grow faster. When they grow. The poor old kahikatea takes two or three hundred years to get to its best, and that's not fast enough for the moneyminded.'
She pulls up hard. 'I hate pines,' she says unnecessarily.
Joe grins. 'I gathered. They've got their uses though.'
'O there's room in the land for them, I grant you, but why do they have to cut down good bush just to plant sickening pinus? Look at that lot, dripping with needle blight, dammit . . . this land isn't suitable for immigrants from Monterey or bloody wherever. Bring the kete, eh.' (p.163)

In other words, foreign influences are permissible provided that they remain subservient to the indigenous features of the place. The final phrase with its glaring signpost of the Maori word 'kete' and its closing Maori idiom, the lifted 'eh', makes clear the connection between the silvicultural and the larger cultural and linguistic contexts.

Yet Hulme's novel cannot escape the influence of earlier New Zealand literature. The very effort of resistance to that influence is a sign of its continued force, even if in a negative fashion. Moreover, the presence which lies behind that effort of repression shows itself in the way in which recurrent themes of New Zealand literature are worked into the novel in new and subversive shapes. In a sense *the bone people* is a prodigious act of revisionary reading in which the content of the New Zealand literary inheritance is recovered and reconstituted in the terms of a powerful reinterpretation of what the description of New Zealand actually means.

Certainly, there is a strong indebtedness to the Man Alone theme which runs from John A. Lee and Mulgan down through Barry Crump and turns up, in parody, in Stead's short story of the middle 1960s, 'A Fitting Tribute' and in his novel, *Smith's Dream*.[23] In a sense *the bone people* rewrites Mulgan's novel with a part-Maori woman substituted for an English male as the protagonist and with the concerns of the eighties — feminism, Maori culture, the indigenous — substituted for those of the thirties — economics, socialism, internationalism. Kerewin Holmes has the familiar features of a New Zealand literary type: the outback, laconic, do-it-yourself bloke with his tall tales and adventures. Part of her concealed and presumably shameful paternal lineage is Barry Crump. One can understand Hulme's desire to conceal such origins. Yet, it is the novel's ability to offer what seems like a new view of New Zealand's possibilities and its past, all the while curiously reconfirming the familiar themes of New Zealand literature, that accounts, in large measure, for its success in this country.

The novel is, after all, extraordinarily powerful. This is accountable partly by its subject, partly by the force with which Hulme evokes it, the unflinching directness of its naturalism. Stead has said that there is 'something black and negative' about this power, something 'deeply ingrained in [the novel's] imaginative fabric'.[24] What this implies is that some deep-rooted imbalance or unhealthiness in the author's psyche spills into the novel, makes it troubling and compulsive at the same time. This view too confidently locates the book's power in the personality of the author, albeit at one remove, and it does not explain the novel's cumulative effect on the reader. Yet it is not enough to say that the novel's power is a function of the ideas it contains.

It is true that these ideas stand outside the rationalist and sceptical values on which Stead's criticism is based. His scepticism can accommodate Frame's religion of absence but not Hulme's predilection for weird religions. Yet what is most troubling about the novel is not explicable in terms either of its commitment to Sufism, mandalas or magical oncology. Nor can it be explained in terms of the peculiarities of Hulme's psychological makeup. The source of that power is to be found in a vision of the human capacity for evil that is almost Manichaean in its intensity and scope.

Hulme is committed to the view that the the human soul has depths in which darkness seems to predominate over light. *The bone people* finds something dark and negative that will not fritter away when the light of reason has been cast on it. At the heart of the novel is a sense

107

of the capacity of humans for unimaginable destruction of what they love as well as what they hate and this is inseparable from their sense of beauty. Most disturbingly, it is their capacity to love not only what they injure but also what injures them that redeems them. This is a significantly different viewpoint from other studies of the capacity of human beings for evil. Ultimately, the exploration of evil in works like *Macbeth* or Malcolm Lowry's *Under the Volcano* (1947) asserts human value. Lowry's consul in *Under the Volcano* has marked similarities to Kerewin. He too wills an evil out of his own troubled soul. He loves but destroys the objects of that love. He is doomed, large-souled, immensely self-destructive, almost at times magnificent. He represents the form of tragedy acted out in a world that has grown too small for tragedy. We respond to his complexity and to the largeness of the scale on which he has been conceived. But the evil that he wills is simply that: evil that is political as well as personal. It is the Western world stumbling into war; it is the rise of fascism. In *Macbeth* we are taken into the mind of a murderer and we discover ourselves. Macbeth's intellectual being asserts the value of the mind, in spite of what it is responsible for. But when Macbeth kills Macduff's wife and children we are intended to see that as evil pure and simple. We are not invited to conclude that because Macbeth has a prodigious soul he should be allowed to continue as king in spite of his crimes.

This is precisely what *the bone people* implies: because Joe's love of Simon is shown ultimately to be more sustaining of his humanity than the abstract Pakeha justice which would remove him from such dangerous care, we are meant to agree that Joe should be allowed to keep the boy. At this point the novel's relation to the social evil it dramatises comes dangerously close to complicity. Dickens's novels led to legislation against child abuse and other social evils because Victorian readers were moved to sympathy for the victims he portrayed. *The bone people* encourages identification with the victimiser as well as the victim.

The second source of the novel's power is attributable to its cultural resonance, specifically to its ability to tap the deep unconscious wishes and blindnesses of culture — to enact them, in fact. Hulme's book is one of those that are interesting because of, not in spite of, the ideological confusions they disclose. This is because its uncertainties reflect a profound and unresolved self-doubt in the culture out of which Hulme writes. Take the novel's treatment of the cultural themes of love, sexuality, and family. Stead has observed that what gives the novel its imaginative strength is 'that it creates a sexual union where no sex occurs, creates parental love where there are no physical parents, creates the stress and fusion of a family where there is no actual family'.[25]

This is true enough, but one would like to add that that the imaginative act that resulted in the novel corresponds to a widespread desire to imagine new forms of the family, of sexuality and of parenthood, where the legitimising myths that have so long given those institutions force have come under immense stress. Hulme seeks to *reenvisage* these bonds and the very force of the desire to remake them in a more acceptable form produces the air of strain in the novel and its telling absences. The absent centre of the novel is the curious reticence about the family histories of Kerewin and Simon. Why are we not given an adequate account of the sources of Kerewin's alienation? Perhaps because they are Pakeha. In Kerewin's journey away from a past and a family which are hidden from us, we see a flattering mirror image of Hulme's journey, and that of many Pakeha, away from the Pakeha past regarded with embarrassment and charged with guilt.

To seek to discover the fullness and meaning of Maori culture is a commendable wish, one that Pakeha culture as a whole could well embrace. But to do so at the cost of the knowledge of one's own past is self-defeating. It serves the interests of neither Pakeha nor Maori. Hulme's favourite image in *the bone people* of interwoven threads is a useful one. It implies that cultural traditions can be allowed their discrete integrity, yet worked together into new patterns. It is also noteworthy that she seeks to include a variety of traditions, including European ones, in that reworking. The problem is her determination to leave out so much of Pakeha culture. Michael Neill has talked about the novel's 'astonishing political innocence'.[26] He means the sanguine view it offers of the country's future prospects. Equally problematic is its view of the country's past.

CHAPTER 4

Witi Ihimaera and the Politics of Epic

All truth is fiction really, for the teller tells it as he sees it, and it
might be different from some other teller. This is why histories
often vary, depending on whether you are the conqueror or not.
                                    WITI IHIMAERA, *The Matriarch* (p.403)

INTERVIEWED in the *New Zealand Herald* shortly after the publication
of his first novel, *The Frigate Bird* (1989), Rarotongan-born poet
Alistair Campbell said that he felt that 'the most exciting developments
in writing . . . in this country' are to be found in the work of
Polynesians. 'In a 100 years' time, it will be writers like Albert Wendt
and other Polynesian writers who will be remembered', he continued,
singling out Wendt, Keri Hulme, and Patricia Grace as writers who
have 'something new to write about'. While he granted that there are
some fine Pakeha novelists and short story writers, Campbell argued
that these writers 'are mostly going over ground that's largely
exhausted'.[1]

According to Campbell, while their stories and novels may be well
done and finely expressed, Pakeha writers have no rich ground of
spiritual or family life to draw on, as Polynesian and Maori writers do.
This viewpoint holds that a significant shift needs to take place in
New Zealand's cultural outlook. Writers should turn away from
Europe and its colonising legacy and look towards the Pacific and the
cultures indigenous to the region. Campbell's viewpoint is more
broadly Polynesian than that of the Maori writers he cites. Like
Wendt, he situates New Zealand writing generally within a pan-
Polynesian concept. For Maori, the organising and energising centre
of the general decolonising effort in this country is naturally the Maori
presence and Maori culture *within* New Zealand. Maori writers and
artists intent on shifting the cultural emphasis in New Zealand away
from Europe see themselves as participating in a 'Maori Renaissance'.

110

In the words of Witi Ihimaera, delivering one of the 1981 Turnbull Winter Lectures, 'We still have a long way to go. We still need to force a reconsideration of New Zealand's monocultural perception of itself.'[2]

Ihimaera is one of the most forceful writers to have emerged in the cultural movement termed the Maori Renaissance. Ihimaera's fiction constitutes a powerful critique of the colonising culture, a passionate defense of the indigenous one, and a prodigious attempt to forge a way of writing that embodies a specifically Maori sense of life.

Ihimaera began to publish stories in the early 1970s in the *Listener*, in *Te Ao Hou*, the journal of the Maori Affairs Department, in *Landfall*, and in *Islands*. His first collection of stories, *Pounamu Pounamu*, was published in 1972. Set in the rural world that Ihimaera knew as a child, his stories evoke nostalgically but with remarkable vigour and conviction a way of life that was by the seventies part of the past for many, perhaps most, Maori people. In this world the Maori language was still 'intact and localised enough for preservation and transmission of the culture itself'.[3] With the massive shift of Maori to the cities during the fifties and sixties, the continuity of traditional Maori life and custom was inevitably ruptured. The next collection of stories records this process of loss. The stories in *The New Net Goes Fishing* (1977) deal with urbanised Maori life, with the 'fault line [that] had suddenly developed in our history — on one side was a people with some cultural assurance, on the other was a generation removed from its roots'.

Yet, according to Ihimaera, in spite of the pervasive presence of an alien and dominant culture, in spite of 'the massive discontinuity in Maori life' occasioned by the shift to the cities, a core of Maori value remained intact.[4] For Ihimaera, the memory of a Maori world, linked to the past by a network of traditions, is both a continuing point of value and a means of organising the formal properties of his fiction. His use of narrative voice, his choice of formal conventions, his stance towards the reader — all these are governed by his sense that the old Maori world view was a complete and satisfying explanation of life. But an important shift in the way that memory figures in the fiction occurs between the stories in *The New Net Goes Fishing* and his next published work, the novel, *The Matriarch* (1986).

In the early stories Ihimaera describes the idyllic village of Waituhi as resolutely pastoral and beneficent. Ihimaera himself describes his early stories as 'tender, unabashedly lyrical evocations of a world that once was' and has characterised them as out of touch with the hard political realities of contemporary Maori life, lacking a necessary anger and engagement.[5] But the world evoked in these stories is not meant to be seen simply as that of childhood or innocence, the world from which all humans pass into the loss and betrayal of adult experience. It is presented as an actual world, faithfully and accurately recorded, one which occupies a threshold between the traditional Maori way of life and the encroaching world of the Pakeha. Waituhi is depicted as a reality that remains under threat from the dominant mode but which has not yet been squeezed out of existence. Because the old order remains a continuing presence there, the village offers a vantage point from which the ongoing brutalities offered to the Maori as a people can be observed and measured. As Janet Frame retreated into the literary imagination in order to describe and judge a violently unsympathetic experience, so Ihimaera in his early stories and in the novels *Tangi* (1973) and *Whanau* (1974) retreats into the world recalled from his own childhood and invests it with a nostalgic and romantic aura.

In *The Matriarch*, however, the sentimentality and naive realism of the early stories give place to a more complex sense of the way in which historical experience can be represented in a work of fiction. The world of childhood has become the self-conscious world of pastoral convention — a literary means of holding together a disintegrating experience. The pre-European order of Maori life is included in the book, but not in a way that suggests an unbroken line of contact has been maintained. Instead it is presented as a kind of fantasy, but fantasy in a very particular sense. Here fantasy is regarded not as a mere departure from reality, an escape into daydream or wish fulfilment, but as an imaginative means of giving expression to interpretations of experience other than the dominant one. In this shift there is both loss and gain for Ihimaera's fiction.

In all Ihimaera's fiction, including *The Matriarch*, his major work to date, this matter of organising perspective, of the place from which the narrative voice proceeds, is a cultural as much as a literary problem for the author. To see what this means in practice, let us compare three passages of prose which deal with Maori life and which set out to demonstrate how Maori culture differs from Pakeha culture. The first is taken from a story by Roderick Finlayson, 'The Totara Tree', first published in 1940. The second passage comes from 'A Game of Cards', included in Ihimaera's first collection of stories,

Pounamu Pounamu. The third passage is taken from *The Matriarch.*
Finlayson's story dramatises a conflict between a small rural Maori
community and the Pakeha authorities who are putting a power line
through their land. An old woman, Taranga, has climbed into a
sacred totara tree to save it from being felled.

> 'It's the wires,' Panapa explained loftily. 'The tree's right in the way of the
> new power wires they're taking up the valley. Ten thousand volts, ehoa!
> That's power, I tell you! A touch of that to her tail would soon make Taranga
> spring out of her tree, ehoa,' Panapa added with impish delight and a sly dig
> in the ribs for old Uncle Tuna. The old man simply spat his contempt and
> stumped away.[6]

Finlayson's depiction of Maori people is not wholly uninformed.
He sets their actions and emotions in terms of the cultural attitudes
and practices that make up the traditional Maori world. The story
turns on the particular attachment of an old woman to a tree that has
a special Maori significance for her. It is her birth tree, where her
umbilical cord was buried, a sign of her connection to a particular
place and people.

Bill Pearson has noted that 'Finlayson's Maori characters are
simple in conception' and that Finlayson 'is best when he is sympa-
thetically observing; when he enters his [Maori] characters' minds,
the triteness of their thoughts is not convincing.'[7] The Maori world
depicted in the passage above is naive and Finlayson's tone is patronising. It is opposed to the Pakeha world in terms of a set of typological
attitudes. Pakeha culture in the story stands for force, size, dominance of nature, mechanisation, commerce, practicality, and utilitari-
anism. The Maori stand for simplicity, native cunning, connection to
nature, and attractive superstition. The Maori see their traditional
ways as under threat from Pakeha modernity, but they remain
unperturbed in their essential being. Finlayson thus projects on to his
Maori subjects a simplicity that compensates for a state the Pakeha
themselves have lost.

At times, indeed, the Maori in 'The Totara Tree' are not so much
romanticised peasants as comic figures who display the exaggerated
mannerisms of clowns. The epithets which describe them generate
comic effects by attributing to them an endearing effort at self-
aggrandisement ('Panapa explained *loftily*') or exaggerate and dehu-
manise their expressions ('with *impish* delight'). The elaborate attempts to represent Maori speech habits only accentuate this diminu-

tion of the subjects of the story. The use of 'ehoa' as a Maori colloquialism is a stereotyping mannerism, like the expressions of comic
negroes in sentimentalising Hollywood films of the same period. The
word 'stumped' to describe the way the old man walks is less a
realistic detail than a convenient sign of his simplicity.

When we compare Finlayson's passage to one from Ihimaera's 'A
Game of Cards', we see immediately the immense difference that
proceeds naturally from the evocation of Maori life *from within*:

Nanny Miro . . . among all my nannies, she was the one I loved most.
Everybody used to say I was her favourite mokopuna, and that she loved me
more than her own children who'd grown up and had kids of their own.

She lived down the road from us, right next to the meeting house in the big
old homestead which everybody in the village called 'The Museum' because
it housed the prized possessions of the whanau, the village family. Because
she was rich and had a lot of land, we all used to wonder why Nanny Miro
didn't buy a newer, more modern house. But Nanny didn't want to move.
She liked her own house just as it was.

— Anyway, she used to say, what with all my haddit kids and their haddit
kids and all this haddit whanau being broke all the time and coming to ask
me for some money, how can I afford to buy a new house?[8]

The use of language here is very different from that in Finlayson's
story. Ihimaera is writing out of his intimate sense of what it is to be
Maori, not from within the categories and perspectives of white
liberalism, and this is reflected in the immediacy and vivid accuracy
of his use of Maori-English speech. In Finlayson's story the Maori are
presented in terms of their opposition to all the negative qualities of
Pakeha culture. They are unconcerned with money, resistant to
technology, innately spiritual. In Ihimaera's story the Maori people
are concerned with money and appearances. They are not technological innocents. Significantly, cars are very important in Ihimaera's
fiction. The matriarch's Lagonda, for example, signifies beauty and
nostalgia rather than mere consumerism.

But all this functions within a particularised set of cultural norms.
Money is not something alien; it has been assimilated into a coherent
and organised set of values which do not coincide with those of the
ruling culture. It serves to bind the family together. To dispense
money to relatives is to gain prestige, to maintain authority within the
whanau, and this is more important than buying a new house or
painting an existing one. The point is that display is important in
Maori culture, but while display within your own group is appropri-

ate, conspicuous display of possessions in order to impress outsiders is abhorrent.

The trouble with Finlayson's treatment of Maori people is not that he grossly misrepresents them or that he is unsympathetic to their culture. It is rather that he is not really interested in illuminating Maori values; he writes from a Pakeha perspective with Pakeha concerns. Finlayson is continuing that long-drawn-out quarrel with industrial civilisation that comes from *within* European culture itself and which goes back chiefly to the romantic period. Gypsies, Greeks, Polynesians, Mexican villagers, children, and the mentally deranged have all at various times served as representative figures of the organic and spiritual values of the pre-industrial order, destroyed by the rise of commerce and the triumph of the commercial middle classes.[9] In New Zealand many writers have considered 'Pakeha' and 'Puritan' as virtually synonymous and have felt antagonistic to a 'Pakeha' culture that they deem grossly materialistic and destructive, especially of those values most cherished in pre-modern societies. Hence Maori serve as convenient projections of ancient and desirable values deemed to have vanished from Pakeha culture.

What Finlayson offers as an alternative to Pakeha reality is not a peculiarly Maori vision of alternative values. The conviction that before the triumph of commerce and machinery humans were bonded to the land, to their own cultural past, and to the gods is a view of the past that most societies call on, not just Maori. The sense of the land as a 'living geography text and history book in one' (p.103), the sense of spiritual connection to the land — these are not exclusive to Maori. They indicate the widespread belief that life was fuller, more rounded and complete, before the triumph of industrial civilisation.

The appropriate literary form of such desires is pastoral, and they are evoked with especial poignancy by the narrator of *The Matriarch* in a passage where he adopts briefly the idyllic voice of pastoral:

Waituhi. It was the close kinship the whanau shared with one another so that we never lived apart from each other. It was the place of the heart. This place of old wooden shacks and scrub-covered foothills. This place where the Waipaoa was wild in the winter and strangely menacing in the summer. This place of the painted meeting house, Rongopai, with its eaves sloping to an apex like an arrowhead thrusting at the sky. This place of people growing older, where flax and flowers grow untamed in the plots where houses once had been. This place of the village graveyard where the tribal dead slept in the final resting of the body. This place, this Waituhi, was family. The whanau was my home. The love and affection they held for each other were the ridgepoles of my heart. The sharing and enjoying of each other were the rafters. And within these walls and roof, my heart was shared with my whanau, so closely intertwined that I never ever wanted to leave Waituhi. Taku manawa a ratou manawa. My heart was their heart. (p.107)

The desire for connection between family, place, values, and meanings can be found in D. H. Lawrence, F. R. Leavis and in many of the writers of the 1920s and '30s, both English and New Zealand. A. R. D. Fairburn shared many of these nostalgic, organicist hankerings.[10] That desire is expressed by Ihimaera more sentimentally than by Lawrence, but there is surprisingly little difference in the stances taken towards the past. Lawrence is mourning a traditional rural way of life that had almost vanished in England by 1918, but of which he himself had some first-hand experience at Haggs Farm, where he loved the Miriam of *Sons and Lovers*. Ihimaera is mourning his own childhood and the traditional rural Maori world that persisted in New Zealand until the 1960s. For all the obvious differences between the English and the Maori pre-industrial ways of life, they represent to both Lawrence and Ihimaera the same myth of the past as whole and satisfying in contrast to modernity.

Ihimaera, however, is not concerned in his early stories merely to mount a rhetorical critique of Pakeha culture using the Maori as convenient repositories of all the values it excludes. He is concerned rather to dramatise and particularise a world whose value is not only that it is in opposition to the existing order but also that it has rituals, preferences, ways of seeing and acting which are meaningful in their own right, which exist in their own discrete terms. In other words, for Ihimaera, Maori culture does not exist merely *in relation to* the dominant culture. Its value is not merely negative and adversarial, but is also that it presents to those who live within it an order of positive and interlocking meanings that are self-sufficient. Where he does develop a rhetorical critique — and he does so very powerfully in *The Matriarch* — that critique is directed not at an abstraction like commercialism or industrial civilisation but at the specific historical impact of European people on the Maori people in New Zealand since colonisation. He does not repudiate European culture as such, although he expresses a fierce indignation against the Pakeha, the local version of that general cultural inheritance.

For Ihimaera, 'the Maori Renaissance' fundamentally involves the giving of dramatic expression to Maori life *from within*, without showing any need to cut off the sources of knowledge that are available to modern Maori as much as to modern Pakeha. Ihimaera's later work is steeped in European sources, and this gives an enriching density to the cultural sense conveyed, but in no way diminishes the essential core of Maoriness that governs the design and outlook of the fiction. A passage from *The Matriarch*, a far more ambitious and complex work than Ihimaera's early stories, will illustrate the distance travelled since Finlayson's story of 1940.

All the homes are like the matriarch's, strung along the road and getting dustier and older by the year. There is a concentration of houses around three areas: Pakowai, where the church is; Rongopai, where the painted meeting house rests; and Takitimu Hall, just below the village graveyard where the dead sleep. Oh, once, there was such magic here, in those long greenstone years of my youth. Takitimu Hall used to be ablaze with lights on Saturday nights when a dance was held, or a wedding, or a haka night. And all Waituhi would be there, attracted to the celebration of life itself. And from the hill further up from Takitimu Hall, as Te Ariki and I were cutting back the scrub from the graveyard, my heart would catch fire with love for Waituhi. You could see all of the village from that hill. The road curving away and the houses of the whanau. And the seasons seemed kinder in those days long ago. In winter, the mist cascaded down the hills or sleets of rain covered Waituhi with a gray haze. In summer, it seemed that the land extended its boundaries as the hills receded into the sky. Spring brought green fields and crops of maize, and the orchards grew ripe with fruit. Autumn was the season of falling leaves. But no matter what season, it seemed to me that in those years of the greenstone, Waituhi remained unchanged. Sometimes when the sun was going down, the hills would be set alight with a coronet of fire. At such times I would look at the streets of Waituhi and be calm because it would last forever. (p.106)

This is pastoral, of course. What is important is that it is deliberately and self-consciously pastoral. Ihimaera represents here the world of childhood, of tribal tradition, and of seasonal flux. It is a world in which human lives are surrounded and nourished by larger cycles of meaning and recurrence. It is a world of family and continuity, a world which is essentially unchanging. But this world has its meaning in terms of the novel's use of conflicting voices: the pastoral voice which is restorative and the prophetic voice which tells of the brokenness of the people and expresses their anger against their oppressors. At one point, describing the Matawhero 'Retaliation',

Ihimaera's narrator, Tamatea, sets the two conventions, pastoral and prophetic, side by side:

> Oh, Major Reginald Newton Biggs, I wish to give you a lyrical and rhapsodic interlude, something to balance the cruel reality of death, the smashing of your head to pulp during the dawn of the tenth of November. Let me conjure a family picnic, yes, by the banks of the Waipaoa River. . . . And you dive into the river, and the nurse laughs and pulls her dress away from the cascading splash. And your sweet son reaches up to catch the splashes as they fall. (pp.144-5)

This idyll, with its calculated allusion to the pastoral scene of the Waipaoa River and the childhood of the narrator, prepares the ground for the brutal realism by which the violence of the massacre itself is conveyed: 'He heard chopping sounds cutting off the lives of his children. Then he felt a sharp warmth as his throat was slit' (p.163). Ihimaera moves the narrative from the pastoral scene to the massacre scene by strategically undermining the reader's natural repugnance against violence towards women and children. The narrator attacks the reader's resistance by linking Te Kooti's violences to accepted ones. He recalls the Old Testament accounts of war acts carried out against oppressors: 'And as Pharoah had done unto the prophet, so did the prophet do unto Pharoah. And just as God had done unto the Egyptians when they would not let His people go, by sending death to the first born of the Egyptians during the time of Moses, so did the prophet do so to the Pakeha because they would not let the Maori nation go' (p.152). Finally, the narrative voice backs off from the described events to scorn the 'tender sensibilities' of the Pakeha reader, offended by the violence detailed by the prose.[11] He connects the 'massacre' to other religious wars and speaks directly to the reluctant reader: 'And do I hear you protest at the detailed descriptions of death?. . . Again, your protests fall on deaf ears' (p.170).

The publication of *The Matriarch* followed a decade in which Ihimaera had deliberately stopped writing. In 1975 he had felt that his fiction was inadequate to the political urgencies of the day. He felt dissatisfied with the nostalgic, pastoral form of his early writing. *The Matriarch* is more politically engaged, more angry and antagonistic than the early stories. At its heart no longer lies the loving evocation of a pre-industrial world of bucolic Maori simplicity, enclosed within tradition, in harmony with the earth. That vision must co-exist with a sharper one of Maori as 'bottom-barrel' citizens of a world they have no part in, workers and poor people, tramping through the morning streets (p.66). The latter, realist vision is present in the early fiction as well, of course, but there its force is blunted by a pervasive sentimentality.

But *The Matriarch* does not simply substitute for the pastoral vision of the early fiction a social realist one of violence, material deprivation, cultural alienation, and family breakdown. Tamatea in *The Matriarch* is more sophisticated than the narrator of the early stories. He is also angrier. Ihimaera employs a greater range of narrative voices than in the early fiction. He also offers a wider range of conflicting stylistic tendencies. There are recollections of childhood combined with affirmations of family. There is also the voice of the prophet, railing against the injustices the Maori people have suffered. The narrator addresses his Pakeha readers directly, condemning them and holding them responsible for those evils: 'For most assuredly *you*, Pakeha, began taking the land from us as you were signing your worthless Treaty. *You*, Pakeha, began taking away our culture' (pp.73-74). There is also the mythic voice speaking of the religious and cosmological concepts of the Maori ('Then from Te Kore and Te Po arose the first gods, the primal parents, Rangi awatea and Papatuanuku . . .'[p.2]).

The novel is not simply more political than the early fiction. It is altogether larger in scope and more complex in its organisation. Behind the novel's formal organisation lies Ihimaera's need to show how the wholeness, connection, and meaning he finds at the heart of traditional Maori life were subsumed under the brokenness, alienation, and loss that have permeated and shaped Maori life since colonisation, and especially since the drift to the cities.

The Matriarch is a historical novel which attempts to record the whole response to colonisation, political, military, and psychological, of the Maori people during 150 years of Pakeha occupation. It is also an epic because, although the novel concentrates on only that part of the Maori people whose traditions and heroes form part of Ihimaera's own background, that experience is meant to be representative of the *whole* Maori experience. It tells, in Kipling's phrase, 'the tale of the tribe' and by extension the tale of the race. Moreover, in spite Ihimaera's belief that Maori culture is fragmented, he is fundamentally concerned about capturing a sense of life as something whole and integrated. There is a tension between his message and the medium by which his message is conveyed. *The Matriarch* is a novel, a modern literary form which reflects the lack of integration of post-industrial civilisation, in which meaning is never inherent in existence but must always be sought for. But it is also an epic in the sense that it attempts to dramatise the memory of a time before the worlds of subject and object became separate.

For Ihimaera, the tragedy of the colonisation of the Maori is deepened by his sense that in places like Waituhi it was possible still to remember a time before the worlds of inner and outer, of self and nature, had flown apart. In the story, 'The Greenstone Patu', included in *The New Net Goes Fishing*, the narrator observes that some of his young urbanised Maori friends had returned to their villages to find 'the culture submerged beneath the thick European patina'.[12] When Tamatea, the narrator of the novel, cries, *'where has the mana of the land, and the tapu of the land gone? Have the gods departed entirely from us and left the world only to man?'*, the lament draws attention to lost presences, traces of which are still discernible (p.105). The grandeur of the little village of Waituhi has gone. Its poverty and dilapidation are the visible signs of defeat. Yet there is another, invisible, Waituhi: the Waituhi of the family, the whanau, the ridgepole connecting past and present. This Waituhi is absent from the lives and even from the broken dreams of most of the present inhabitants. But it is operative for those, like the matriarch, in whom eternity still lives and moves because they possess the imaginative and spiritual capacity to envisage it.[13] It is in terms of this living fiction that we are meant to read passages like this:

All of a sudden, the veil between day and night lifted, and the matriarch and the child were in some otherworld where gods and men commune. Where timelessness begins and there is no separation of past and present. A world energised with glowing forces and creatures of light fading in and out of the hills, the plains and the physical landscape of Waituhi. The child saw into the essence of things. He saw the gleaming sap ascending the trees, and the sap and the dark red blood coursing his transparent body were one and the same. He saw the geological structures of the earth, and the diamond sparkling structure of the mountains were one and the same as the gleaming cellular structure of his body. He saw the movement of light and wind and cloud, and they were one and the same as his own life force.

Then he looked up into the heavens and saw that worlds beyond this earth, and the worlds spinning into darkness, and the creation of new suns and new nebulae, were the same as the worlds in his blood. He looked into the faces of the gods and was not blinded. He was in the universe and the universe was in him. (pp.108-9)

In the context of a realistic historical novel, this would be merely purple prose — overblown, charged with romantic primitivism ('some otherworld where gods and men commune') and biblical pastiche ('He was in the universe and the universe was in him'), continually gesturing towards the ineffable ('He looked into the faces of the gods and was not blinded').

Indeed, it *is* overblown and represents the most consistently troubling aspect of Ihimaera's prose. The tendency is already present in the early fiction but it does not there overwhelm the realist and humanist tendencies that characterise Ihimaera's most compelling work. The strength of these stories is their exact registration of Maori English ('When Mum had her wild up, Dad always did as she said')[14] and in their engaging and vivid portraits. In 'The Greenstone Patu', for example, a sacred weapon makes its own choice between two families competing for its possession:

> The sun glowed upon a wedge-shaped object swimming towards us. Swiftly it approached, twisting and gliding through water shafted with sunlight. As it came, it cried out its name. Its calls grew louder, ringing in our ears.
> Suddenly they were accompanied by sharp cracking sounds snapping loudly through the room. The sounds came from a cabinet panelled with glass like silver mirrors. As we watched, the panels began to buckle and snap and splinter into sharp broken shards. Imprisoned behind the glass was the patu pounamu.[15]

Here the animism that invests the object with magical properties is focused through the rural families squabbling over heirlooms and observed by the affectionate but detached narrator, Tama, who stands between the two worlds and is able to interpret one to the other. In Ihimaera's 1987 novel, *The Whale Rider*, the writing has been entirely taken over by inflated word-spinning that dresses up Maori mythological beliefs as fantasy. In the following passage a child is riding a whale and communing with the creature:

> The sea was a giant liquid sky and the whales were descending, plummeting downwards like ancient dreams. On either side of the koroua and his kuia entourage were warrior whales, te hokowhitu a Tu, swift and sturdy, always alert, a phalanx of fierceness.[16]

The prose here is strained and self-conscious, for all its effort to sound flowing and attuned to natural rhythms. The images are imprecise and uncontrolled. Why is the sea like a 'giant liquid sky'? The repetitions increase the air of meaninglessness. What does 'descending' add to 'plummeting downwards'? What is the function of the closing alliteration, 'a phalanx of fierceness'? The writing is overloaded, mannered, striving after effects.

It is a pity that reviewers and critics have failed to direct close critical scrutiny at Ihimaera's style since the heady days of his early success. No doubt, they were reluctant to seem to quibble over minor flaws in what was clearly a significant new voice, and above all a significant new *Maori* voice. As the publisher of *Pounamu Pounamu* and *Tangi* noted with satisfaction on the dust jacket of *Pounamu Pounamu*, it was 'the first collection of short stories by a Maori author to be published'. Yet, had the enthusiasm which has greeted Ihimaera's fiction been tempered by a close critical attention to the flaws as well as the strengths of the writing, the overblown habits of the prose might have been curbed before they produced *The Whale Rider*. The rise of the novelist as 'star' in the middle eighties, with Hulme and Ihimaera as revered figures, helped book sales, but it did little for the state of the novel as an art form in New Zealand.

In *The Matriarch* the tendency towards rhapsodic evocations of the spirit world is counterbalanced by the novel's political anger and by its realism. The word-spinning mysticism in *The Matriarch* is merely one among several styles and voices adopted in the novel. Its function is to give form to a vanished but remembered way of life. In part, Ihimaera is attempting to convey in prose the force of oral culture. Consequently, he stresses genealogy and spiritualises nature. He tries to capture in print oral conventions: repetition, onomatopaeia, formulaic expressions. Ihimaera himself has suggested that a useful comparison might be made between Maori oral forms and Anglo-Saxon imagery and symbolism.[17]

In *The Matriarch* the narrator likens the oral tellings of the journey of the great kahikatea tree that became the ridgepole of Rongopai to the Old English poem *The Dream of the Rood* (p.185). This suggests how we are to read the account. We are expected to enter into the world view of another culture — heroic, tribal, organically connected to the cosmos and to nature. This requires of us as readers not so much that willing suspension of disbelief by which we enter into supernatural tales as a capacity to look behind the prose correlatives of oral cultural forms to the world view that sustained them. The reader is not meant to respond to this material as mere escapism, as fantasy in the *Chronicles of Narnia* sense. What Ihimaera offers is closer to Tolkien's *Lord of the Rings*, in which old forms are consciously mimicked and reproduced, although Tolkien is much more skilled linguistically than Ihimaera. Ihimaera offers a representation in a modern novel of what the myths of an oral culture might look like.

The result is not entirely successful. It is difficult to read the passage dealing with the voyage of the canoe Takitimu without thinking more of the film epics of Steven Spielberg than of the ancient oral genealogies and mythological accounts of the Polynesian voyagers. Certainly, any resemblances between Ihimaera's oral narrative and mediaeval heroic tales like *The Dream of the Rood* or *The Seafarer* are merely superficial. Attended by gods, serpents, fabled monsters, spirit creatures composed of light, earthquakes, and other marvels, the casket of the gods is brought from Hawaiki (p.260ff.). At the climax of the account a greenstone adze carried by a huge wave splits open the wall of a gorge and the holy ark is borne into a greenstone altar (p.277). Ihimaera's purpose here, like Hulme's in *the bone people*, is to dramatise the bringing of the Polynesian gods to Aotearoa and thus spiritualise the land in terms of a time scale that dwarfs the colonising efforts of the Pakeha. But the special effects, mystical flourishes, and inflated rhetoric of the writing produce unconscious self-parody.

In *The Whale Rider* such fantasy has subsumed all the other elements in Ihimaera's fictional repertoire. In *The Matriarch* the contrary elements are still working inside a single frame. The problem arises where the spiritual fantasy seems to be presented as oracular messages from a higher reality, something like what George Plumb in Maurice Gee's Plumb trilogy calls 'cosmic consciousness'. When the matriarch passes on to Tamatea the knowledge that was taught in the traditional Maori schools of learning that were 'destroyed by the Pakeha', it is hard not to feel an approving authorial presence behind the teachings. The portentousness of the prose collapses the distance between narrator and author:

Her voice struck the reverberating drum of the land, and the sound boomed out, loud and long, and it seemed to open a crystal gate, lifting the portcullis between ourselves and the past, and *we were in some otherworld*. A world where gods and men commune. Where timelessness begins and there is no separation of past and present. A world energised with glowing forces and creatures of light fading in and out of the landscape. (p.293)

Later the narrator states that well after the establishment of Pakeha domination in Aotearoa (as late as the 1890s) 'the world of the Maori, of communion between gods and man, the fabulous with the real, still manifested itself in apparitions of immense power' and goes on to relate an incident in which the officers on board a ship reported sighting a taniwha (p.340).

Yet a distance *is* maintained by the author from the marvels and myths of which he avails himself, although his stance towards the Maori religious material is never merely ironic. Later a similar sighting is explained in purely naturalistic terms: 'The reality is that a surge in the river had swept under the foundations of the meeting house and carried with it wirenetting which made arrow patterns in the currents' (p.389). A psychologist suggests other possible ways of interpreting the manifestations of Maori spirituality when he tells Tamatea 'you're telling me a story, a fantasy, and you have used your intelligence to make it so believable that you believe in it yourself' (p.409). When the narrator characterises the sighting of the taniwha as a reminder of the past 'ripping through the fabric of the real world and bringing with it the remnants of fantastic dreams', we are reminded of the moment in Frame's *Living in the Maniototo* when the fantastic erupts into the actual world, tearing up the fabric of the normal (p.341).

Ihimaera is not a metafictional novelist like Frame, but neither is he a naively propagandistic one who seeks to convert his readers to the religious viewpoint of the pre-European Maori. The spiritual elements in *The Matriarch* are a deliberate strategy he employs as a novelist rather than religious propaganda. Ihimaera treats those religious beliefs as 'fantasy', by which he means not mere escape from reality or history but a different understanding of experience than Pakeha rationality allows for. The terms 'reality' and 'fantasy' are not mutually exclusive for Ihimaera. The world where gods and humans communicate is 'a fantasy as well as a real world' (p.192). Fantasy plays an important role in Ihimaera's fictional method. The pre-contact world of the Maori can only be recovered *in a work of fiction* as 'fantasy'. The source of the matriarch's 'magic' is her ability to make tangible that vanished world.

By this use of fantasy, Ihimaera means to open up a way of seeing the world that is alien to Pakeha rationalism. He offers us a fictional version of the Maori world view and bolsters it with a series of comparisons to the world views of the ancient Hebrews, the Anglo-

Saxon tribes, and the Italian nationalists of the Risorgimento. The novel continually establishes links between Maori culture and other peoples with perceived similarities. The link to the ancient Hebrews is one sanctified by the Maori love of the Old Testament and identification with the Jews as a tribal people exiled from their land. The Hauhau prophet Te Ua Haumene preached that the Maori people were 'one of the lost tribes of Israel, living in "New Canaan"' (p.79). The links to the Italian culture of the Renaissance and to the nationalist political movement of the Risorgimento are more complicated. Essentially, they provide a way of getting outside the Pakeha way of seeing Maori. They diminish the New Zealand Pakeha by referring to other Europeans who were as rooted and traditional as the Maori were and who were, like the Maori, subject to fierce oppression. They allow Maori cultural expressions to be rescued from the denigration they have suffered by Pakeha indifference and condescension. The meeting house at Rongopai may look drab and desolate on the outside, but *'open the door and walk in, and you are in the Sistine Chapel of the Maori nation'* (p.133). Its builder, Moanaroa Pere, is a Maori Leonardo da Vinci (p.184). Similarly, Maori religious belief is compared to the 'philosophical speculations of the earliest Greek philosophers — Empedocles, Anaxamander and others' (p.252).[18]

The link to Italy also provides a frame for the elements of cultural fantasy surrounding the voyage of the Takitimu canoe from Hawaiki. Venice, like Hawaiki nui, is a city attended by gods, where reality and fantasy, the supernatural and the real, collide (p.431). It is a city out of the Apocalypse, covered in 'gold and azure' (p.430). It is a world where myth has a role in the details of everyday life. This interpenetration of the real and the fantastic connects the Maori people's ancestral home with the actual home of the modern Venetians and neatly bypasses the Pakeha, quotidian British burghers recreating English lower-middle-class suburbia in the Antipodes.

The matriarch's Maoriness is so secure that it can include the richness of Verdi's colourful romantic nationalism. The Maori nationalism she expresses is identified with that of the Risorgimento as found in Verdi's operas. 'With her voice at the pitch of its passion, ah, that is the matriarch indeed, commanding and at her most imperious. *A costoro schiava non sono . . . della mia patria degna saro. I am not a slave . . . I will be worthy of my native land'* (p.13).

When Ihimaera describes the matriarch entering by magical means into the ancient Maori metaphysical world, he does so with a mixture of operatic effect, fantasy writing, and pastoral convention. The last, in particular, is very strong: 'She felt the elements coming alive, the long silent dynamo of creation beginning to hum. The earth, breathing. The sky taking the form of a giant tattooed god. The forces of life, animate and inanimate, stirring in the wind and flooding through a widening cleft of light' (p.108). There are passages in Lawrence not far removed from this. For Lawrence, Christianity and industrialisation had destroyed the old pagan sense of life as a vital connected whole. In *Apocalypse* (1931) he describes how Christianity broke the ancient contact with the cosmos: 'The sun, the moon, the planets, instead of being the communers, the comminglers, the life-givers, the splendid ones, the awful ones, had already fallen into a sort of deadness'.[19]

Lawrence is concerned with the way in which the language of Bible, particularly of the Book of Revelations, insinuates itself into the consciousness of those exposed to it, however determined they may be to resist it. Ihimaera is not resistant. The frequent references to precious stones, crystals, angelic figures, apocalyptic events suggest the presence of the biblical Apocalypse behind *The Matriarch*. As in *the bone people*, Christianity is ambivalently present in Ihimaera's novel. At times it is explicitly rejected ('the fatal ascendancy of Christianity'), yet the language of the Bible is worked into the fabric of the writing (p.272). Like the meeting house at Rongopai with its mixture of realistic and surreal paintings, of Maori and Christian symbols, worked into its decorations, *The Matriarch* is a mélange of conflicting elements and styles. Although this mixing is clearly intended by Ihimaera to reflect the variety of traditions that have gone into the making of modern Maori culture, the effect in the novel itself is to contribute to its sense of structural incoherence.

Similarly, the overwriting in the novel is to some extent at least deliberate. In *The Matriarch* the heightened quality of the prose when dealing with Maori spiritual lore is contextualised by the opera references worked through the novel. Opera allows the excess of colour and emotion that Ihimaera wants. Indeed, Ihimaera justifies his own overwriting by comparing his novel to opera, the most excessive of art forms. The matriarch herself is like an operatic diva able to summon stage effects to her assistance. When she sings at night a song to the people and the land, the moonlight 'etch[ing] her profile with beauty' is a stage moon; the words she sings are Verdi's: '*O patria mia mai piu, mai piu te rivedro*' (p.121). As a journalist friend of Tamatea's puts it, describing one of her 'scenes' to Tamatea, she specialises in 'brilliant coup[s] de théâtre' (p.92). At one point she pulls her veil down and light falls as if she were on stage. We even hear the kettle drums rumbling thunder offstage as the lights fade:

> The veil slowly descending. As it did so, the clouds began to join across where once had been a brief space of sunlit sky.
> 'So be it,' the matriarch said.
> With a ponderous rumbling, like iron gates closing, the sun began to go out.
>
>   * * * *
>
> *La luce langue, il faro spegnesi ch'eterno scorre per gli ampli cieli. Notte desiata, provvida veli la man colpevole che ferira. Light thickens, and the beacon that eternally courses the far-flung heavens is spent . . .*
> The prelude to the Te Kooti retaliation—that too was like the sun going out. (p.78)

This imaginative force which links the Maori metaphysical world to Italian opera is why the matriarch and not Tamatea is the novel's central focus. In the early stories Tama Mahana, the modern Maori, is more sophisticated and more central than the traditional Maori characters who figure in the stories. He interprets them to us, without condescension but as one not wholly belonging to the world of marvels, spirits, and magic to which they owe allegiance. The matriarch, however, is much fuller as a character and more commanding intellectually than Tamatea. In her the old world survives into the modern, not as superstition or nostalgia but as power and resilience.

The ground on which she chooses to assert herself as a Maori is uncontaminated by that sense of self-hatred which haunts the attempts of colonised peoples to define and assert themselves. It is true that the matriarch knows from the time she enters adulthood that, as a colonised person, she is a 'slave'. But, because her *imagination* has retained a connection to the spiritual world, because she spans the worlds of opera and actuality, her possession of her Maoriness is unassailable. Neither Te Kooti nor Wi Pere, lineal ancestors of the matriarch, who represent respectively violent public resistance to and private rejection of Pakeha hegemony and who dramatise those separate Maori responses to colonisation, holds as securely as the matriarch does the keys to that world where the shadow of the Pakeha has not fallen. The matriarch allows Ihimaera to present a perspective that is outside Pakeha-ordered reality. With her rich imaginative connection to the old Maori world, she provides a means of speaking for Maori that is untouched by the denigrating bias of the colonisers' way of seeing. The matriarch, inviolate and pure, is one of the immortals; she is in touch with the gods.

There is a metaphysical side to all this, but it is not necessary to accept that spirit world in the novel as 'real'. The metaphysics in the novel are a means of representing the old intact Maori world. What is gestured at is a complete cultural order, one quite distinct from present-day reality. Thus, inside the meeting house dedicated to Te Kooti at Rongopai the visitor gradually becomes separated from the ordinary world: 'You were in another world, the interior of Rongopai, in itself complete and self-sustaining, its own world without end, its own time-lock' (p.190). This is very close to the language Ihimaera uses in his Turnbull lecture to describe rural Maori before the drift to the cities: 'Culturally, they were a rich and vital entity, self-sustaining and secure'.[20]

This world is able to blend elements of Christianity (stressing Old Testament rather than New) with traditional Maori belief, old ways with new ideas. The paintings inside reveal in their wild colours 'the subconscious of the Maori, the persona, in highly romantic and yet realistic terms' (p.191). Thus Rongopai is 'a fantasy as well as a real world' (p.192). It stands at the centre of the novel's meanings and method of procedure. The architecture and decoration at Rongopai, by their method of borrowing from a number of sources and mixing together seemingly antagonistic elements, correspond to that of the book itself.

As Alex Calder observed in *Landfall*, welcoming and praising Ihimaera's novel, *The Matriarch* 'borrows from everywhere to make something new from the ruins of the old'.[21] Calder here identifies a practice that is at the heart of Ihimaera's method of composition in *The Matriarch*. Ihimaera draws material from a variety of existing sources — Sir Peter Buck's *The Coming of the Maori* (1949), J. H. Mitchell's *Takitimu* (1944), J. B. Mackay's *Historical Poverty Bay*, and others — and works it into his novel. As is well known, not all these sources are adequately acknowledged. In particular, Ihimaera has taken passages from Keith Sorrenson's entry on Maori land tenure in *An Encyclopaedia of New Zealand* (1966), edited by A. H. McLintock.[22] This aspect of Ihimaera's writing practice needs to be examined closely, not simply because the charge of plagiarism that has been levelled at the novel is a serious one but also because Ihimaera's 'borrowings' involve complex issues of authorship, ownership, and the novelist's responsibilities to historical fact.

The problem of 'plagiarism' is a very complex one, but the bare facts of *The Matriarch*'s debts to Sorrenson's work seem straightforward enough. Essentially, Ihimaera has lifted a substantial passage from *An Encyclopaedia of New Zealand* without acknowledgement and has then worked it over, interpolating his own (or rather his narrator's) comments into the 'borrowed' passage. In the technical legal sense this would seem to constitute an infringement of copyright. The work from which Ihimaera borrows is still in copyright. Ihimaera takes over not just the ideas in Sorrenson's piece but also the wording.

In the first place it needs to be said that Ihimaera should have acknowledged Sorrenson at the outset, as he acknowledged several other sources of *The Matriarch*. (Recent editions of the novel do acknowledge Sorrenson.) Moreover, he should have made clear that his use of such sources involved more than simply consultation. This is particularly the case in a work like *The Matriarch* that includes so much historical material. Ihimaera makes copious use of fantasy in his novel, but *The Matriarch* is, among other things, a historical novel which claims to offer an accurate account of New Zealand history since colonisation and which rhetorically condemns traditional colonialist interpretations of that history. By drawing on Sorrenson, Ihimaera is borrowing the prestige of the historian for his fiction, claiming a truth for its central account of the past. Historians naturally disapprove of flagrant departures from demonstrable facts. By including historical material in his novel, Ihimaera is grounding the book's account of the past upon what is purporting to be his own historical research and is relying upon the historian's reputation as a reliable and accurate recorder of what actually happened.

However, *The Matriarch* is a literary rather than a strictly historical work. Ihimaera uses historical sources because he is dealing with historical events, but he includes them within a fictional frame. The novel *as a novel* stands or falls on the total picture it offers of dramatised characters enacting historical events. Te Kooti, as we meet him in the novel, is conveyed to us largely by way of the matriarch's account of his character and of the events in which he figured so prominently. Here the novelist's effort is directed at giving substance to a historical villain, placing him in the context of the culture and the specific historical wrongs which shaped his personality.

Moreover, Ihimaera does not simply take over Sorrenson's account. He works over the passage he borrows, inserting new sentences and deleting others. This process is deliberate, even calculated. Ihimaera does not simply add passages of his own or rephrase his source, as one might expect of someone trying to disguise a debt. Rather, he writes *against* Sorrenson's account and *against* the historical kind of writing Sorrenson uses. When one separates Ihimaera's interpolated sentences from Sorrenson's passage, they make up a thread of commentary and protest on the context in which they have been placed. Sorrenson's writing, although it expresses an opinion about the events it records, is exact, restrained, balanced, objective, unemotive, factual. Ihimaera's is angry, at times hysterical, subjective, partisan. No effort has been made to fit the two seamlessly together. Instead, the distance between them has been exaggerated.

Thus Ihimaera inserts between Sorrenson's bare statements of fact about confiscated land mocking lines about the slave handler's whip and adopts the stereotypical white Southern voice crying, 'Get back, niggahs, back into line' to make his point (p.239). Then he makes a telling change to Sorrenson's sentence about the amount of land returned. Sorrenson writes about '"friendly" or "loyalist" Maoris'.[23] Ihimaera drops the quotation marks and the distancing epithet 'friendly'. The effect of this is to distort Sorrenson's meaning so that his words appear to defend the biased term, 'friendly Maoris'. In the next interpolated passage Ihimaera adopts the Old Testament prophetic tone that runs through the novel: 'They were like a plague of locusts in the land of Egypt'. At the end of this paragraph Ihimaera seemingly interrupts the method he has established so far—taking a sentence from Sorrenson then adding one of his own—by deleting a passage. This deleted passage deals with tribes who surrendered and co-operated with the Government, 'only to sell most of their land recklessly within a few years'. It is difficult to avoid concluding that this passage was deleted because its content is so dangerous for Ihimaera's rhetorical stance. It indicates that not all the land lost by Maori was taken by force or perfidy but that quantities of it were sold, foolishly perhaps, but willingly and legally.

Ihimaera's additions to and subtractions from Sorrenson's text all serve to vilify the Pakeha. They adopt a rhetoric of grievance and condemnation. When Sorrenson writes that the land legislation 'was part of a wider policy designed to fulfil the promise of the Treaty of Waitangi to grant Maoris the rights and privileges of Europeans', Ihimaera adds to the front of the sentence: 'Oh, it could make you weep, but the Pakeha foisted this one on the Maori by claiming that. . .'. Here Ihimaera's distortions of history have nothing in common with those of magic realists like Rushdie or Marquez who distort in order more truthfully to represent history. Ihimaera misrepresents history in order to make his partisan case more convincing.

The way in which Ihimaera has worked over Sorrenson's text is a deliberate process that does not conceal his indebtedness to Sorrenson. Sorrenson's writing is not merged into Ihimaera's. In fact, the rhetorical distance between borrowed and interpolated material is increased. By changing the historical source, Ihimaera sharpens the antagonism between historian and narrator-rhetorician. But by not reporting Sorrenson accurately and by distorting his analysis to serve his own purposes, Ihimaera stacks the argument in his own favour. The way in which Ihimaera has drawn on Mitchell's *Takitimu* (mentioned as a source in the 'Acknowledgements' to *The Matriarch*) further reveals the process of the novel's composition.

Mitchell prefaces his account of the building and voyage of the canoe by abjuring the 'mythical' side of the traditional oral stories surrounding the Takitimu:

It is true that in the reciting of the story certain claims are made that can only be held as mythical. Being fond of boasting of their superiority, by comparison and by the adding of supernatural powers, the Maori has embellished all tradition. But, holding such romancing to be the mere garments to the story, let us consider the main body of the facts.[24]

Here Mitchell is carefully separating himself from oral tradition and from the fantastic stories of Maori myth and religion. He adopts the objective, understated approach of the ethnographer or historian — the scientist — as against the boasting and embellishments of the traditional Maori storyteller who cannot distinguish fact from fancy. Ihimaera's method is to reinsert the romancing into the account. But he relies very heavily on Mitchell for the story itself.

Mitchell writes: 'None but selected chiefs were fit to be carried by *Takitimu*, these men and the sacred relics of the past. No common man, nor women, nor children, nor cooked foods were carried by this sacred vessel on its voyage across the great Southern ocean.' Immediately below, he cites Sir Peter Buck's *The Coming of the Maori*: 'Tamatea-ariki-nui (Tamatea the high priest) gave forth the order: "Let a giant canoe be made and be called Takitimu. We will journey far across the seas to this Southern land of which they tell."'[25] Ihimaera splices these two passages together: 'It was Tamatea ariki nui who gave the order to his iwi, "Let a giant waka be made and be called *Takitimu*. We will journey far across the seas to this southern land of which they tell. Let it be made sacred, carrying none but selected chiefs and the sacred relics of the past. Let no common man nor woman, nor children, nor cooked foods be carried by this sacred vessel across Te Moana nui a Kiwa"' (p.253).

It is worth noting that the extent of the debt here is not indicated by the 'acknowledgement' at the front of Ihimaera's novel. Sir Peter Buck is not mentioned at all, while of Mitchell's book Ihimaera merely notes that *Takitimu* 'was consulted on tribal and genealogical aspects'. But what is significant is the way in which the material has been assimilated into *The Matriarch*. Ihimaera uses the sources as a narrative substratum on which he imposes layers of embellishment, romantic colourings, mythical flights of fancy. The ancient Maori supernatural world is reconstituted in the novel as a kind of breathless high prose — excited, extravagant, almost camp:

> The cargo of the gods. The more mundane minds have imagined them as being mere carvings of wood and stone, relics representing the children of Ranginui, the Sky Father, and Papatuanuku, the Earth Mother. I like to visualise the gods as being creatures of light and of darkness, gods of the Maori pantheon, covering all that life itself was dependent upon. Here they are, within the crystalline altar, ready to be carried from Hawaiki to Aotearoa, gifts for the new land to bring vivacity, and a new glorious season to the people lacking in godliness. Tawhirimatea, god of the elements, like a swirling cloud of wind, thunder and lightning shimmering in the altar. The glowing crystal of sparkling greens of all hues. . . . (p.260)

Crystals, creatures of light, rainbows—Ihimaera's mythic vision is a mixture of *The Wizard of Oz*, New Age rhetoric, and the Book of Revelations imposed upon the standard accounts of Maori religious beliefs found in Mitchell, Buck, and Best. Similarly, his epic history consists in the imposition of a prophetic voice constructed from the language of the Old Testament upon the standard historical accounts found in *An Encyclopaedia of New Zealand* and elsewhere.

There is nothing intrinsically reprehensible about Ihimaera's method of composition, provided that the sources are respected and acknowledged. Stevan Eldred-Grigg's *The Siren Celia* (1989) is stitched together out of direct and extended borrowings from George Chamier's *A South-Sea Siren*. But Eldred-Grigg acknowledges not only his source but also the way in which he has used it in the book. Thus the attention of the reader is concentrated on the interesting dislocations that arise when a text is rewritten in a different time. Ihimaera's own 1989 collection of stories, *Dear Miss Mansfield: A Tribute to Kathleen Mansfield Beauchamp*, announces its own status as a deliberate rewriting of some of Mansfield's stories from a Maori perspective. Had Ihimaera acknowledged and treated his sources adequately in *The Matriarch*, the focus of attention might have been directed at its proper object: the way in which historical and ethnological sources are *employed* in the book and to what effect.

The use of borrowed material in *The Matriarch* suggests that the book is written in terms of an understanding of authorship and ownership that is at odds with the view that a literary text is a piece of property owned by the individual who wrote it. *The Matriarch* does not place the author as an authoritative ego at the centre of its attention. The main narrative voice is a generalised one, speaking for a whole community rather than for Ihimaera or a mask he chooses to assume. The novel borrows from a variety of sources as well as from Sorrenson. In some cases Ihimaera has borrowed quotations and facts, as when he follows the account of the 1975 Maori Land March in Michael King's biography of Whina Cooper.[26] In other cases, sections from the works of various authors have been spliced into the writing of *The Matriarch* and worked over. The novel's sense of writing as a process is at odds with one which assumes that a single coherent personality is responsible for a whole text, owns it individually, and stamps every syllable with the mark of its ownership.

There is good literary precedent for this. Wedde shares the same sense of language as communally owned and downplays creativity and to some extent originality. As his mock writer of the introduction to *Symmes Hole* puts it, after listing the novel's collisions of fact and invention, 'Not only was Melville the first Pacific novelist, he was also one of the first to do what postmodern writing now finds familiar: recycle material, make use of existing texts, regard the act of writing as redistribution rather than creation'.[27] One of the ironies here is that Dr. Keehua Roa, dutifully acknowledged as copyright holder for the introduction on the verso of the title page, is himself a 'fictional' character — Wedde in academic disguise.

Even a writer who clings as tenaciously to the notions of authorship and authority as Stead, relies in his 'Clodian Songbook' on the Penguin translations of the Roman poet, Catullus.[28] There is no question that Stead has plagiarised Catullus, or the Penguin translator, by doing this. Stead expects his reader to be aware of the debt, which is quite explicit and well signalled, and to take pleasure in the skilful way in which the contemporary poet sets the work of the ancient poet in a local context. In poem number 7 in the sequence his persona, Catullus, writes, 'Tell her/Catullus loves her/as the lone lawn daisy/loves/the Masport mower'.[29] Here the force and effectivess of the lines rest on the relocation of the original in a contemporary suburban setting.

Some distinctions need to be made here. At the heart of the matter lies the author's understanding of audience. When T. S. Eliot translated Mallarmé's *'donner un sens plus pur aux mots de la tribu'* as 'to purify the dialect of the tribe' and included the line in *Four Quartets*, he was paying homage, not stealing a good line. He expected his readers to be familiar with the sources on which he draws. He was also asserting the classical principle that the essence of good writing is not the originality of the thought but the fineness of its expression. It may be that a novelist finds some obscure work in a foreign language, translates it, and passes it off as his or her own work. This constitutes true plagiarism, but is undoubtedly rare. More commonly, a novel will show evidence of influence, traces of style that reveal the force of some previous writer on this particular novelist. The writer may be quite unconscious of such influence.

This kind of influence is universal and not at all reprehensible. Writing comes not from the ground or the air or our uncontaminated minds but from other writing. We object when the influence shows itself in a novel as, in the words of Malcolm Lowry, 'maldigested and baleful'.[30] But we applaud when the influence has been assimilated, made part of the new work. Since Joyce, readers have become accustomed to novelists who deliberately foreground their debts to other writers. Pastiche has become a feature of contemporary writing, while 'intertextuality' has become a feature of contemporary reading. As Keri Hulme has usefully put the matter in relation to *the bone people*: 'there's nods to many writers . . . as well as outright quotation (particularly Sufi Jalal al Rumi) because I'm buggered in this day and age *how anyone can be a virgin writer*. We've all read far too much to be untouched by the wealth of the world's creations.'[31]

Another reason that novelists may 'steal' from other writers is to expose the 'bourgeois' concept of property that lies behind the concern with originality, the horror of plagiarism. The Scottish poet,

Hugh MacDiarmid, worked very substantial sections of other writers' work into his poetry because he was a Marxist and despised the notion of intellectual property rights. He actually characterised his own mode of composition as 'the new plagiarism'.[32]

The question of intellectual property is a complex one. Publishers, of course, have an interest in extending intellectual property rights further and further, as do authors. This continues a process which goes back to the Renaissance when the notion of the author itself was formulated around the rise of publishing houses, the definition of property rights, and the emergence of the concept of the playwright as the individual with authority over a written playscript, a concept which had no precedent in mediaeval theatre. In the seventeenth century the notion of authorship was still unstable. Ben Jonson's poems are frequently translations of classical originals. But this was considered perfectly proper in his own time. Jonson took pride in demonstrating how much of classics he knew and he assumed an audience with a similar education. Quotation marks and permissions were superfluous here.

Stead seems to do same in 'The Clodian Songbook'. What is similar is Stead's expectation that his reader will be alert to what he is about. Because Stead considers the classical heritage of European literature a vital legacy, he expects his reader to be prepared to see how he has adapted Catullus. But in spite of his classicism, Stead holds an essentially romantic view of the author as a unique individual, expressing his or her individuality in a style that reflects the authentic self. He values 'originality' and thereby assumes that authors own the works they make.[33]

The question, then, is what function do the borrowings serve in Ihimaera's novel? Do they constitute acts of tribute to respected writers, playful pastiche, sly assaults on the concept of intellectual property rights, or are they outright plagiarism? The most simple explanation would seem to be that borrowing from sources occupied an important role in the process of Ihimaera's writing of *The Matriarch* and that he has insufficiently acknowledged those debts, perhaps inadvertently. After all, why would Ihimaera steal from a source as widely known as *An Encyclopaedia of New Zealand*, which stands on the bookshelves of thousands of New Zealand homes, and whose contributors might reasonably be expected to read the novel and recognise their own writing? Certainly, it seems unlikely that Ihimaera would invite litigation and compromise both his own reputation and that of his publisher in order to challenge property rights. Neverthe-less, there is at least an unconscious irony in the fact that the material he has appropriated from Sorrenson deals with a much more signifi-cant act of appropriation: the taking of Maori land after the Land Wars of the mid nineteenth century.

The Matriarch, as Calder observes, 'borrows from everywhere', but it sets out to make a new kind of whole from all that it draws on. The novel speaks to us as an epic, an epic which is concerned not only with restoring the past but also with piecing together a future out of the hopes of the past. The question is, what sort of epic is it possible to write in the late 1980s in New Zealand? What relation should the book's enactment of the past have to actual history? And whose history should the epic detail? As Maurice Shadbolt in *Strangers and Journeys* (1956) set out to write an epic for Pakeha, Ihimaera thirty years later has written one for Maori. Clearly, it *is* possible to write a national epic from the viewpoint of a part of the whole that constitutes the nation. But the problems raised by the effort are massive. To construct a possible future such a book must actively refigure the past. To what extent, then, is it permissible to reinvent the past in the process? The effort the epic as a form directs at reinterpreting history and at constructing possible futures is deeply political by its nature. Ihimaera's epic novel addresses the politics of New Zealand in the late 1980s; its strengths and weaknesses are inseparable from its relation to that political climate. They are also inseparable from the different cultural understandings of history that became so marked as the country approached the sesquicentennial celebrations of Pakeha domination.

Stead, reviewing the novel in the *London Review of Books*, saw it as a failed novel, historically misleading and insufficiently realised.[34] Stead objects most strongly to the novel's distortions of history. There is no contesting that Ihimaera has misrepresented history, in Stead's definition of the term. Ihimaera rewrites the past (or rather an eminent historian's analysis of the past) in order to suit the politics of the present. In this sense the novel must be judged a failure. But Stead's view fails to do justice to the novel's ambitions and to the particular pressures — cultural and historical — which influenced its manner of construction. Ihimaera's understanding of history is so radically different from Sorrenson's or Stead's that to accuse him of misrepresenting history is, from one perspective, simply to miss the point. The question is, *whose* history is being misrepresented? To

Ihimaera, the 'objective' history of patiently gathered 'facts' and impartially written accounts is no less fictive than the mythical universe of the pre-European Maori he conjures up in his novel. His whole novel, with its angry rhetoric and accusations, is pitched against that history, offering in its place a history of the subject and victim rather than one of the observer. Within *The Matriarch* these opposed constructions of history collide.

The Matriarch is built out of conflicting elements: realism and fantasy, social prophecy and myth, violence and spirituality, history and epic. At the heart of Ihimaera's effort in the novel lies the desire to construct a fictional edifice in which the various imported elements and styles — opera, the Bible, and so on — are included in a context that is distinctively Maori. If the result is flawed, the scope and difficulty of the attempt deserve to be acknowledged.

*   *   *

Alistair Campbell's novel, mentioned in the preamble to this chapter, is one of the first three titles in a new series published by Heinemann Reed, the Pacific Writers Series. The other two are John Cranna's *Visitors* and Nick Hyde's *Earthly Delights*. In conception the series deserves high praise. It reflects the diverse energies of current New Zealand writing that includes work by Pakeha, Maori, and Polynesians. It signals a welcome broadening of the sources of fiction in a society increasingly aware of its internal differences rather than its homogeneity. At the same time the early novels in the series are steeped in a sense of contact with the larger world rather than the old consciousness of distance and isolation. In a sense, all are travel books. The series also indicates a necessary attention among New Zealand writers to New Zealand's Pacific location. It is one among the various series of fiction brought out by Heinemann to represent the distinct regions of the English-speaking world, notably Africa and the Caribbean.

It is true that Maori and Polynesian writers are playing a very large energising role in New Zealand writing in the 1980s, as Campbell has stressed. But it is not true, as the series itself attests, that the fiction being produced by Pakeha is merely going over 'exhausted ground'. What we are seeing is the emergence of relatively distinct traditions within the national picture. There has been a forceful Maori presence in that scene, in which Ihimaera's fiction over more than two decades has been crucial. But we are not witnessing the rise of a purely Polynesian cultural outlook on the ashes of the Pakeha one. As Ihimaera's (and Campbell's) own work demonstrates, the influence of Pakeha writing is inescapable.

What we are seeing is the emergence of a new context for Maori writing, and Maori culture generally. Ihimaera in the early 1980s protested at the 'invisibility' of Maori writing.[35] He meant the way in which it exists within a context that demeans it by not seeing it as alive, vital, part of the present. In *The Matriarch* Tamatea remarks on the museum in Poverty Bay which was notable for its Maori artefacts, but which installed them 'in a European-looking building, like memorials to a people who no longer existed!' (p.67). Ihimaera's own fiction, particularly *The Matriarch* despite all its flaws and floridness, constitutes an impressive attempt to make a structure in which the European features (chiefly Italian) still have a place, but in which the work as a whole reflects the Maori cultural presence which he places at the centre of New Zealand life.

Ihimaera has stated that his endeavour as a writer has been 'to convey an emotional landscape for the Maori people'.[36] Because Ihimaera organises his fictions from within this emotional landscape, the relation of his work to the novel form is necessarily ambivalent. The novel is essentially an *ironic* form, opposed to the epic, which is celebrative and constitutive. The novel as a form characteristically enacts the quest for meaning the ancient epic takes as a given. The great Marxist critic, Georg Lukacs, described the novel as the epic of the broken modern world.[37] The world of the novel is alienated, broken off from any sense of meaning as something inherent in experience. The novel typically records in a detached and ironic manner the fatal split between self and other that is inseparable from modernity.

This ironic sense is precisely what Ihimaera struggles against. His preferred form is that of the epic because it stands for wholeness not brokenness. The epic, for Ihimaera, stands pre-eminently for that connection between the gods and humans, between nature and culture, between self and other, spirit and matter, which figures forth the world that is essentially Maori, the world of a heroic people who have persisted into an unheroic and antagonistic world.

CHAPTER 5

Ian Wedde's Relocations

You never arrive. You never leave. There's no centre.
IAN WEDDE, *Dick Seddon's Great Dive*[1]

IAN WEDDE's childhood was a series of uprootings and dislocations. He was born in New Zealand in 1946. His early childhood was spent in Blenheim. At seven, he went with his family to Bangladesh and thence by stages to England, where he was sent to boarding school. He returned to New Zealand when he was fifteen. By 1967 he was publishing poems in *Landfall*. In 1970 he was back in London, living in Brixton, where 'the air was thick with herb smoke, and we were beginning to move differently'.[2] In the late sixties Wedde went to Jordan, where he became sympathetic to the Palestinian cause. Significantly, he did not head for the popular counter-cultural destination of the day, San Francisco, or take the hippy trail to India. Although his writing was formed by and has remained closely identified with the general cultural upheaval of the late 1960s, Wedde has maintained an ironic detachment from the styles, fashions, and factions of that period. This has been a consistent mark of his stance towards the counter-cultural positions he is often associated with: seemingly immersed, he remains separate. Similarly the stance he adopts towards his reader is deceptive: the voice speaking to us seems intimate and relaxed, but the author's presence behind it remains inscrutable.

In the mid sixties Wedde attended Auckland University where he sharpened his interest in modern American poetry. As Bill Manhire has pointed out, the effect of this was not to turn young New Zealand poets like Wedde 'into American clones'. Rather, it made 'diversity and possibility available' and freed New Zealand poetry from the longstanding dominance of English literary culture.[3] It was part of the general opening up of New Zealand culture to new influences, the liberation of previously repressed energies, that characterised the late 1960s and early '70s. Ezra Pound, William Carlos Williams, Denise Levertov, and Robert Creeley were important influences on Wedde's poetry at this time. He was also reading American postmodern novelists such as Thomas Pynchon and William Gaddis. Wedde's fiction and poetry both derive from similar sources. He is one of those writers whose lines, phrases, sentences can be tracked through the writing in its various forms and various stages. His fiction echoes with lines from his poetry and vice versa. In his earliest novel, *Dick Seddon's Great Dive* (1976), the distinction between prose and poetry breaks down altogether at times.

What is important in both Wedde's poetry and his prose is the *range* of language sources on which he draws. His writing is rich in debts to the authors who have influenced him: Dante, Melville, Charles Olson, Ezra Pound, Thomas Pynchon, A. R. Ammons. Phrases and themes from their writing appear throughout his own writing, drifting from poem to poem and working into the fiction. The theme of the earthly paradise, for example, which he picks up chiefly from Dante's *Paradiso* and from Pound's *Cantos* ('Paradise now indestructible in the mind'), runs from *Earthly: Sonnets to Carlos* (1975), through *Dick Seddon*, to the story 'Paradise' in *The Shirt Factory* (1981), to 'Dark Wood' in *Castaly* (1980), and on to *Symmes Hole* (1986) and *Survival Arts* (1988) as a single leitmotif.

But Wedde's linguistic sources are by no means exclusively literary. On the contrary, his writing is steeped in the colloquial. Wedde is keenly attentive to the energies of ordinary language, of used speech. In *Symmes Hole* the languages of 1980s street-kids and early-nineteenth-century whalers form a fugue. In his linguistic preferences, as in his political ones, Wedde is instinctively on the side of the colloquial, the informal, the marginal, and the subversive. He is against the official, the canonical, the approved. He favours the language and the politics of the street over that of the salon. The energies of his early writing spring from his opposition to the well-made poem fashionable in England in the post-war period — tight, claustrophobic, repressive. By comparison American poetry was irresistible to Wedde and his generation. It was easy, vernacular, endlessly open, and assimilative. Here, along with Bill Manhire and others, he found a way of using language that was informal, without politeness, flexible, street-wise. In prose too, he shows a conspicuous attraction towards the energetic and the vernacular rather than towards the restrained and the mandarin. Jack Kerouac was an important influence.

In Jordan, Wedde was also influenced by Islamic poetry because of its closeness to used language, to speech:

In Jordan I encountered for the first time two languages: an official *lingua franca*, classical, oratorical; then the local language. You'd find people sitting round the coffee shops reciting new vernacular poems by Darwish, Samir al Quasim, or Muin Besesieu . . . and that was their first 'publication'.

Wedde was impressed here by what seemed to him 'a totally different attitude towards language' from that which he was used to.[4] This new attitude rested on the notion that, especially in non-Western societies, people possess a store of common codes, of formulas. A popular poet can refer to these codes naturally and effortlessly. This allows the poetry to circulate among a readership that is broad and popular, but attuned to a common store of meanings and gestures. Thus the need for an elite clergy is eradicated. Such practice avoids the tendency of literary avant gardes in Western countries to base themselves in the universities and produce obscure, modernist texts which need to be decoded, 'taken away into an obscure, definitely not popular area'.[5]

From the very beginnings of his literary career, then, Wedde was formulating an understanding of tradition opposed to Stead's high modernist sense of tradition as something clerical and canonical. Wedde has also consistently opposed Stead's idea of writing as property. For Stead, style is a sign of the individual ownership of writing. For Wedde, the individual ego is less central and authoritative and he sees language and tradition as ideally communally owned. In Jordan he found a sense of style as representative of the community, not simply of individual poets producing particular pieces of writing. Later he was to find the same sense of community in Maori writing.

As a New Zealand writer, one who has chosen to make use of the characteristic forms of English as they have evolved in this country, Wedde has kept this democratic sense of writing. He distrusts literary culture, particularly elite culture, because 'most people, whether they read the so-called higher forms of literature or not, are actively participating in the same material and history'.[6] Pop songs and advertising, for Wedde, are rich in significance. They contain signs which cue the reader into a communal body of knowledge and experience just as sophisticated verbal forms like Allen Curnow's poems do.

One of the things Wedde is interested in doing as a writer is to draw on popular-cultural forms, to catch 'the mysterious and potent latencies' which he says exist even in street signs. He says that the more we look at the evidence around us, the less the traditional distinctions between high and low forms of culture seem to matter. This seems to place him in the camp of the postmodernists, for whom the old hierarchies of high and low have been made redundant by the triumph of mass culture. According to the postmodernists, artists can no longer pretend to transcend the cultures they belong to, positioning themselves above the masses. The romantic notion that the individual self is the ultimate repository of value, the modernist anguish over the collapse of metaphysical meaning, the realist conviction that the artist's job is accurately to represent the world in paint or language — all these are outmoded 'bourgeois' assumptions, according to the postmodernists. They reject high culture's preoccupations with depth and meaning and look approvingly to the superficial forms of popular culture, advertising, and consumer schlock.

But Wedde's stance towards popular culture differs from that of the postmodernists. As Wystan Curnow points out, Wedde's dislike of the 'high seriousness' of early modernism opens him up to popular culture. But he remains committed to 'the myths of depth and the self'.[7] Moreover, his attitude is sentimental and nostalgic in a way generally foreign to postmodernism. Wedde abhors the mass popular culture of the fast food industry. *Symmes Hole* is full of diatribes against McDonalds hamburger franchises. He yearns for older popular forms untouched by McDonalds and Coca Cola imperialism. His researcher in *Symmes Hole* becomes lyrical in defense of milk bars and fish and chip shops. For Wedde, the older traditional forms of popular culture rooted in working-class life enjoyed a subversive relation to the dominant culture, while contemporary ones, especially McDonalds, reinforce and represent the most aggressive and inhuman aspects of that culture.

This determination to stand against official culture, to champion the subversive and the marginal against the powerful and the oppressive, stands at the heart of Wedde's concern as a writer. It accounts for the messianic tone that creeps into his writing at times. It accounts for his uneasy relationship to the more doctrinaire advocates of postmodernism like Wystan Curnow, who has described Wedde as a 'laid back' modernist.[8] It motivates his effort to write counter-histories and to bring to the surface buried aspects of official history. It also informs his anti-colonialism and his linguistic nationalism.

*   *   *

Wedde's first novel was called *Dick Seddon's Great Dive*. It was published in 1976 as a complete number of the literary journal, *Islands*. In a sense *Dick Seddon* is a 'head novel'. It gives the appearance of having being written by someone with a copious supply of drugs to hand, its changes in pace and tone (there *is* 'tonal variation' in the novel, in spite of David Dowling's doubts)[9] attributable to the different effects of particular drugs. The narrative speeds up at times as though amphetamines are the motivating force. It slows down as though for opiates, and becomes disjointed and surreal for hallucinogens. *Dick Seddon* consists of random journeyings, interspersed with passages of stream of consciousness. The various elements of the novel seem unrelated, without any coherent design. But an attentive reading of the novel shows considerable discipline at work both in its individual sentences and in its overall organisation.

Here is a representative passage. The central character, Chink, is conducting two policemen through his flat after having been robbed. He takes a bottle of amyl nitrite and mescaline into the bathroom to dispose of it:

Ah shit. . . . The mescaline caps floated on the surface of the water when he threw them into the lavatory. He shook the amyls into his palm . . . 'Fuck it!'. . . cracking caps under his nose, snorting hard . . . the reek of cheesy football socks. He heard the D's come into the main room of the flat. He threw the remaining caps into the dunny and pulled the chain. The objects swirled and disappeared. He opened the window and flapped his arms, then washed under the hot tap, scalding his hands. He dried them and fumbled at the catch of the door. His fingers were shaking. He felt terrific. He put his hands on his knees, bent, and breathed deeply. Blood strutted finely through his body. He opened the door and went into the room where the police were.
'Sorry', he said. 'I must have got a bit excited.' (p.134)

What is significant here is the degree of deliberate organisation in the writing, in spite of its seeming to be recklessly uncontrolled. The prose moves deftly from the mind of the protagonist to the swiftly unfolding action. The sentences are crisp and economical. Yet Wedde can shift tone suddenly and lightly. Here the sentences are short, denotative, Hemingwayesque, as they move with Chink's hard, masculine energy; elsewhere they wind and circle with Faulknerian indirection through Kate's scattered, neurotic thought-stream: 'And the music isn't an accompaniment to his death, but has gone forever, though when I imagine it it's close to the pitch of "killing the fish"' (p.199).

Even in the paragraph above, Wedde executes neat little swerves whenever he needs to vary the pitch of the writing. The image of 'cheesy football socks' is characteristic, with its concentration on smells and bodily excretions. A few sentences further on the prose leaps with an excited little charge as the drug takes effect: 'Blood strutted finely through his body'. Then the whole frantic scene is brilliantly undercut as Chink goes into the adjoining room and plays the part of the outraged citizen to the detectives.

The presence of control is richly evident at the level of Wedde's individual sentences. It is also evident in the shape of the book as a whole, although *Dick Seddon* seems formless. The events it recounts are random and pointless. The characters are involved in endless, frantic movement at the end of which there are no arrivals. The novel is a picaresque for the seventies; Chink is the picaro on amphetamines. James Bertram has described the novel as 'romantic (or erotic) picaresque'.[10] Yet Wedde has attended carefully to its design. Its shape is not predetermined by some design imposed by authorial will on the raw mass of events that comprise the novel; rather, it arises out of the inconclusive attempts of a particular consciousness to discover meaning and shape in a set of ambiguous events which are already in the past. The action of *Dick Seddon* is framed by a retrospection. Kate, Chink's former lover, recalls her time with him before his death by suicide. This means that the novel's action is already concluded, but that the meaning of that action remains unsettled and incomplete. Kate searches restlessly and inconclusively back through her time with Chink and her own breakdown, seeking to come to terms with her loss.

Towards the end of the novel Kate moves towards a tentative epiphany, a moment of insight which might control and confer meaning on the material of the novel itself. She cannot imagine his death separately from the images of landscape and of music that are tied to it in her memory. The landscape, she discovers, is not merely a setting for his death: 'his death creates it, as he moves towards that moment when death will complete its creation of him' (p.199). This lovely Faulknerian sentence conveys Kate's recognition that the object world through which we move takes its life and significance from the mind that perceives it and which, however briefly, dwells in it. The more intense the mind's *apprehension* of a particular landscape, the more 'real' it becomes to the perceiving subject. The 'shape' of Chink's death, then, is governed not by whether he accidentally drowned or committed suicide, but by the shape of his life leading up to that moment of completion. The meaning is thus not closed and finalised by the event. It exists in the continuing echoes to which Chink's death gives rise in Kate's mind. Here is to be found the tentative kind of ordering the novel allows. In the course of Kate's retrospection '[a]n order has emerged . . . and it's happened in spite of my struggle to work to a design' (p.200).

While Kate is seeking the emotional significance and shape within human relations, Chink is seeking other kinds of meaning in the past. Chink's concern is largely with history. Kate recognises this instinctively quite early:

Yet I suppose I had some kind of intuition early on of what his wandering up and down the country meant, and saw that those barely perceived migrations of mind and spirit which were the real, the massive correlative of the main trunk road — saw that those almost invisible migrations were substituting for something. (p.161)

Chink's wanderings are a correlative for that uncelebrated symbol of the making of the country: the main trunk road—except that the road constitutes a sign of unity in contrast to his restless and inconclusive journeyings. It holds the country together and enables orderly travel and business, all the controlling mechanisms of society, to be conducted. Chink is concerned with other buried and ignored kinds of nation-making: the records and language of the whalers and sealers. He is interested in the gaps between the official versions of history and history itself. He reads the inscription on the Maori Wars memorial in Auckland, 'Through War They Won the Peace We Know', as the use of a public monument to disguise reality. The edifice functions as a sign which announces the power of the dominant culture to determine the way in which history shall be interpreted. Chink opposes this bullying display to the 'little wooden hutch' in which Te Wherowhero was buried (p.164). To read the meaning of both buildings, one needs to look behind outward appearances to the cultural practices and attitudes that determine them.

The matter of control of the prose is essential, as it bears upon Wedde's distance from the experience he evokes. In a sense he is writing from within an area of New Zealand social life that has not previously been expressed in its own terms, as Ihimaera's early stories evoke Maori life. James K. Baxter had written before Wedde on the world of urban drug-takers, of hippies and students. Sargeson had written before Baxter of the demi-monde of artists and sexual eccentrics. Robin Hyde and John A. Lee had written of the world of pimps and petty thieves. But, however sympathetic these writers had been towards the marginal kinds of social experience they had portrayed, none had been able to write of them naturally and exclusively in their own languages: that is, as lived rather than as observed worlds.

Lee and Hyde elicit moral sympathy from their middle-class readers for the poor they describe. Sargeson is full of knowing winks and nods to those of his readers 'in the know', but he still writes from a distance about the sexual eccentrics he loves. Baxter dons his prophetic robes, railing against the hard-headed populace who fail to see Christ in the figure of the hitch-hiker, the down-and-out, the dope smoker.

Wedde writes wholly without this tone of negative moralising. The world of students and lovers and drug-takers is not presented to the reader as a morally superior alternative to mainstream suburban society. Wedde is interested in the buried repetitions of culture and history that surround and shape all social life: mainstream or counter-cultural. He is concerned with the ways in which we take meanings from the explicit forms and interpretations of official history and with the ways in which other possible meanings elude us. The buried meanings are already there. The trick is to see them.

In 1981 Victoria University Press and Price Milburn jointly published a collection of Wedde's short stories, *The Shirt Factory and Other Stories*. The novel, *Dick Seddon's Great Dive*, was also included. At the time the collection was important because it indicated an *achieved* shift in fictional method, a new sense of possibility and openness in the way fiction could be written in this country and the kinds of experience it could include without strain. The stories in *The Shirt Factory* were not the first which took the post-sixties youth culture as their terrain or which adopted the disjointed street talk of contemporary

American fiction, but their publication in book form showed that postmodern fiction was becoming less marginal. Moreover, Wedde was writing about contemporary cultural phenomena — rock music, fast food franchises, drugs — through voices that were at once involved and removed. The familiarity of Wedde's narrators with the worlds evoked in the stories goes with a sly, ironic distance in authorial stance towards the material.

In 'The Gringos' a middle-aged rock-and-roller from the fifties finds his preferred period style already historically redundant, faintly amusing to his own fourteen-year-old son. As in Sam Shepard's play, *The Tooth of Crime* (1972), the rock and rollers' obsession with authenticity is counterposed with the slick, commercial forms of popular music that emerged in the seventies. The nostalgia of the Gringos' music depends on a belief in tradition, authenticity, selfhood, depth. The seventies world in which the Gringos find themselves has no use for their music or the values it embodied. The new world is one of surfaces and rapid shifts of fashion. They themselves are marooned in their working-class lives and the nostalgia that prevents them from seeing their own situation historically.

A decade after their publication, the stories in *The Shirt Factory* are important as a quarry from which Wedde systematically took material for his subsequent fiction. 'Snake' is a kind of preliminary sketch for *Symmes Hole*, complete with passages from the 'pirated transcript of James Heberley's journal' and a monologue against 'McDonalds Fast Foods in Courtenay Place'.[11]

In one other respect *The Shirt Factory* is of interest. The brief preface by Wedde looks forward to the increasingly arch and impenetrable introductions and prefaces he will attach to his books throughout the eighties:

(You think of fiction as a kind of rhythm beneath the endless obsolescence of fact; a swell beneath the surface chop; oxygen you can't see in the blood whose warmth you can sense under the skin you touch.) (p.7).

This is a representatively opaque sentence. For all Wedde's concern with counter-traditions, his antagonism to literary and social elites, his interest in popular culture, his stylistic manner has been consistently 'high'. Wedde's statements against highbrow culture have tended to be ultramontane in tone. Ironically, Stead, the advocate of cultural elitism, has become more and more accessible to the general reader in his critical prose throughout the eighties. Wedde, the anti-elitist, has remained recalcitrantly knotty and difficult.

Symmes Hole uncovers the buried and alternative meanings of New Zealand history that obsess Chink in *Dick Seddon*. The narrative of *Symmes Hole* is structured around two interlocking stories. The first of these is focused through a 'researcher' who is searching through historical records for submerged versions of New Zealand's past. This story is set in Wellington in the early 1980s. The second story tells the adventures of James Heberley, a nineteenth-century whaler, beachcomber, and unofficial 'settler' in early New Zealand.

The method Wedde employs in *Symmes Hole* is borrowed from Herman Meville's in *Moby Dick*. Dick Seddon's 'dive' in the earlier novel has been deepened in its significance. In that novel Chink repeats the picnic feat of the New Zealand prime minister by diving beneath the surface of things. But he dives to his own death. In *Symmes Hole* the researcher finds himself repeating Melville's 'dive' into the depths of history and consciousness. Melville's idea in writing *Moby Dick*, according to Wedde, was that underneath the movements of official history 'is another shape altogether'.[12] *Symmes Hole* goes down beneath official versions of the nation and its history to a realm where history, politics, sexuality, and metaphysics disclose their dark and concealed aspects. What he finds there is an elaborate historical plot, a dark concatenation of economic and military interests, that lies behind the nation's interpretations of its own past and its destiny.

The researcher in *Symmes Hole* thinks of Melville as one driven 'to construct and plant the slow time bomb that will fumigate the quarantine hulk of his nation's consciousness' (p.161). Wedde's novel attempts to do the same for New Zealand. But Wedde is not as radical in his criticism of the nation's 'consciousness' as was Melville. In the person of Captain Ahab in *Moby Dick* Melville expresses the rhetorical excess, the romantic imaginative daring, and the fierce idealism that went with the confident, expansive mood of America at mid century. Ahab also expresses the Yankee will to reduce nature to commodities. He concentrates the most destructive forces in the America of the 1850s. The ship he captains journeys towards a general catastrophe associated with the grave faults Melville discovers in the national character, for all its confidence.[13] In Worser Heberley, Wedde rediscovers the nation's beginnings and embodies them in a subversive figure. Heberley, like Ahab, concentrates traits that Wedde finds at the heart of the national identity, but traits that are more positive and less exaggerated than those of the monomaniacal whaler. Although he is touched with his own obsessive visions, Heberley is sceptical towards authority, adaptable, practical, and independently minded. He is also instinctively a democrat and thus closer to Ishmael than to Ahab. Worser represents all those characteristics which assert the ability of individuals to subvert the grand designs of the powerful to determine history.

Worser is part of the flotsam of empire, not the vehicle of its explicit designs. He slips through the cracks of official intentions and finds himself 'at home' in New Zealand by virtue of his sense of obligations to the existing inhabitants rather than to the model society in the Antipodes proposed by Edward Gibbon Wakefield. Worser stands subversively towards the version of the nation's destiny as a colonialist Eden containing a new people formed on the pattern of English life. He also explodes the conventional interpretations of the nation's founding by confirming a largely unrecognised feature of early New Zealand social life which the historian Michael King has referred to.

In his biography of Whina Cooper, King describes the Hokianga district in the early 1800s as rivalling the claim of the Bay of Islands to be 'the cradle of modern New Zealand life'. King's description of the way in which the whalers and convicts, the flotsam of empire, were assimilated into existing New Zealand life is significant:

These first foreign residents were runaway sailors, whalers and convicts, and sawyers in pursuit of the district's wealth of kauri spars. Many of them married into local Maori communities, introducing them to European tools, utensils, garments, fruit and vegetables. They were absorbed into Hokianga tribal life and adopted the *mores* of their hosts; far from Europeanising the district, they became to all intents and purposes Maori. And certainly their descendants identified as Maori, whatever the colour of their skin or the vulgar fractions of their genealogy. Such experience was generally harmonious, and typical of the pattern of early Maori-Pakeha relations.[14]

Here lies the basis of the counter-history that Wedde is concerned to elaborate in *Symmes Hole*. Instead of the Wakefieldian model of organised settlement along established English lines, King suggests a haphazard process of arrival and adaptation. The whalers and sawyers may have arrived as a consequence of imperial expansion, but their relation to empire was a contrary one. They did not identify their interests and perspectives with those of official English culture, hence they were readily absorbed into the cultural patterns already established in New Zealand. They were nativised.

In the 'Introduction' to *Symmes Hole* Dr Keehua Roa writes of this same process of assimilation as revealed in such historical sources as the logs of whaling ships and the journals of seamen:

> Many whalers married into local tribes. Some soon sailed away to Hobart Town or the Californian goldfields; but many stayed. They formed what the entrepreneurial colonizer Edward Gibbon Wakefield called 'a new people'. He did not like their newness; he wanted to supply his own 'newness' on a relatively old social model, an English squirearchy.
>
> His brother (W.H.), the 'Colonel', who came out to New Zealand on the *Tory* in 1839 . . . believed that this beach rabble would have to go. They were degenerate; they were 'at home' before that home had been established according to Wakefieldian ideals. They represented an unwelcome interruption to the model history proposed. Consciously or unconsciously, the Wakefields could see that the beach people might drive a subversive wedge between exploitable territory and colonial ideal.
>
> The expendable (in Wakefieldian eyes) 'new people' had meanwhile very often — as in the cases of James Heberley and Jacky Love in *Symmes Hole* — involved themselves staunchly and naturally with the affairs of the people and the place which had become their home. But their history was to go underground before the advancing wave of organized colonization, and, one way or another, the 'new people' seemed to disappear. (pp.7-8)

Symmes Hole is concerned with those who arrived before the approved settlers: the sealers, whalers, and beachcombers who were, in the official view, degenerates and subversives. They offer a point of entry into an alternative mode of cultural exchange. They settle with the Maori and are readily absorbed into tribal life. They make themselves thereby at home, without accepting Wakefield's ideal of home as transplanted England, complete with its class system, stifling, claustrophobic, and polite (just like the well-made poem of English literary culture in the 1970s).

The context of this historical interest is a 1980s one. Wedde reads the past in terms of the preoccupations of the present. The arguments about race, belonging, cultural influence, and language that have been so prominent in New Zealand in the 1980s flow into the book and shape its constructions and deconstructions of history. *Symmes Hole* probes what lies unadmitted beneath the 'official mantlings of history'; it asks how the symbiotic relation that existed between Maori tribes and the flotsam of empire 'developed into something deeper'. That undefined special relationship is of interest at a time when the

Pakeha find themselves obliged by the rhetoric of Maori radicals to defend their claim to 'belong' in New Zealand. For Pakeha liberals that has proved no easy matter. Bill Pearson's anguished question, 'what right have I to claim turangawaewae in this country?',[15] indicated in 1974 an uncertainty among liberal intellectuals about belonging that deepened markedly over the following decade and a half. *Symmes Hole* responds to the liberal Pakeha desire not only to eradicate the imperial legacy (and the guilt that goes with it) but also to validate a new sense of belonging by reexamining the past in terms of that anti-colonialist sentiment. In the unofficial history of Worser Heberley's arrival among the Maori is to be found a means of overcoming Pakeha guilt. Heberley is one of those who came to New Zealand before 1840 and were accepted by the Maori because they didn't seek to displace those already in possession of the land. He acknowledges that the colonial vision of an English lawn and labourers' housing is 'just plain daft' because the land 'didn't belong to anyone' in a way that meant they could turn it into an English pastoralist dream (pp.191-2).

The terms of Worser's occupancy are 'natural' because they are prior and superior to those of the Wakefieldian plan for settlement (p.12). Worser is drawn to New Zealand not by the promise of economic betterment or in the service of some meretricious colonial scheme but by the 'natural' calls and obligations of sexuality and family. For Worser, the phrase, 'woman, house, a home' (ironically reversing the indifference to 'child, and wife, and slave' of the drugged mariners in Tennyson's 'The Lotos-Eaters') serves as a recurrent theme, reminding him of the sense of connection he lacks and desires (p.103). Worser 'comes home' when he accepts ungrudgingly the ties of loyalty and obligation that connect him to the relatives of his Maori wife. His rules for survival as a 'New Zealander' include talking 'fair and square' with his father-in-law and keeping in mind the probationary nature of his residence in the country (p.192).

Moreover, he has the capacity to respond to images of foreign worlds in their own terms, not by reference to familiar ones. There is a crucial moment as his ship makes its way into Wellington harbour when two sets of images contend in his mind: the conventional image of Victorian womanhood and the images of female sexuality he has encountered as a sailor. The latter are involved in his mind with brutal images of the whaling industry, but they are more convincing, sharp, and present to him than the consoling image of a distant feminine ideal. A white girl 'like a little dressed up china doll in a bonnet' looks down in the maelstrom of blood and lust that he views: the black prostitute from the Caribbean, the Aboriginal girl he sees copulating in Australia. The china doll is lost as images crowd into his mind of Smithfield gutters, sharks following the whaling ships, tattooed faces, and the fat-smeared bodies of native women (pp.90-91).

Heberley's chief means of distancing himself from England as 'home' is linguistic. Lost in the Australian hinterland, he lies at night looking at the sky which is 'the colour of ripe mulberries'. The word 'mulberries' triggers a set of associations: 'Dorset mulberries, Weymouth mulberries. *Mother'* (p.27). The suggestions of mother and home precipitate an agitated sense of the craziness of his actual location. Everything is inverted, 'arsey-varsey', wrong. At this point Heberley does not know where he is, but realises that he 'will never be back again' in England. He will have to learn everything anew, in the upside-down world in which he finds himself.

Heberley jumps ship in New Zealand initially because he believes he smells pigeon pie from the land. Among all the mingled rancid smells, the nostalgic odour of squab pie seduces him. Ironically, the bird he smells is a weka, but the process by which the antipodean world has become familiar in its own terms rather than by reference to English assocations has already begun. The incident with the weka supplies Herberley with a name that combines English and Maori in a distinctive and joint form. Worser Heberley's Christian name is a whaler-Maori corruption of the Maori tangata whata: '. . . *tongeter water, worser?. . .* they must be calling me, that's what they're calling me, wonder what it means . . . — Hey Worser come an' have some breakfast — Ta very much don't mind if I do. . . .' (p.138).

Thus Wedde sees the determining energies of New Zealand-English coming from those on the margins, like sailors. Partly, he simply likes the inventive irreverence of their language use: 'you might as well go down singing with a cunty fishtail wrapped under your arse. . . . Me, I'm wiping mustard on my sausage' (p.23). Here obscenity and tall tales provide an obsessive contrast to standard middle-class speech. But more than this, he is interested in the way in which their language reflects those subtle accommodations and shifts of understanding by which those who are the victims of history rather than its disposers and organisers are insinuated into new political, social, and national forms. Worser begins the process by which he becomes a native New Zealander as he begins to use and to bring into existence New Zealand-English speech. He stands at the outset of that evolution described by Elizabeth Gordon: '[i]n the years since the first European settlement in New Zealand, we can trace the development of the English language in New Zealand from its firm roots in Britain into something which is now distinctively New Zealand'.[16]

New Zealand-English springs from the interactions between sailors and Maori, not from standard English. This point of contact is where its most distinctive uses are derived. This unofficial history of the language is opposed to the English of public schoolboy adventure. Colonel Wakefield, who is responsible for the burning of a whole mountainside of virgin forest to see what a really big fire looked like, represents this linguistic and social dead-end (p.79). In the world of 'bourgeois educated vandals like Jerningham Wakefield, you were part of an Adventure . . . whacko, ripping! . . .' (p.84).

In his introduction to *The Penguin Book of New Zealand Verse*, Wedde reads New Zealand literary history as the process by which the colonists have accommodated themselves to the colonised world by way of the 'growth of the [English] language into its location' (p.23). Thus, Wedde seeks to make the English language in New Zealand appear to be a native growth. For Wedde, the Pakeha cease to be colonists and become New Zealanders by announcing their linguistic independence, by making the English language 'at home' in New Zealand. The consequence of this adjustment of the inherited language to its location is the recovery of those qualities of originality and purity associated with the indigenous oral culture.[17] The history of the adjustment of Pakeha writing to its New Zealand location, according to Wedde, 'has been coeval with the growth of language into its centring ganglia of relationships, to the point where we can feel ourselves to be its original poets, its consummators'.[18] Hence, Pakeha poetry has at last reached the point where it can be set alongside the Maori poetry whose originality has never been in doubt.

Wedde's fiction, with its emphasis on the demotic, the used language of the place, shows the same desire to announce its 'originality'. When Wedde writes in *The Penguin Book of New Zealand Verse* that only by a shift towards the demotic 'could a locally original culture' emerge in New Zealand, he means that his anthology marks the establishment of a distinctive and 'original' Pakeha culture after so much time spent longing for the lost colonial 'home' and the hieratic forms of its poetic discourse; his fiction is intended to convey the same impression.[19]

These attitudes flow into and energise the stock of New Zealand-English Wedde employs in *Symmes Hole*. New Zealand, for Wedde, is as much as anything a set of linguistic possibilities. In this he looks back to Sargeson. Although Sargeson is often seen as a realist and a nationalist, the issue of language was always for him more crucial than either geography or social forms. The founding of a national literature, for Sargeson, was a function of the attention paid by writers to the distinctively New Zealand form of the English language. Sargeson's early stories were as strikingly New Zealand as *Huckleberry Finn* was American and Lawson's stories Australian, because, like theirs, his prose is totally immersed in the colloquial forms of 'native' speech (of nativised Europeans, that is). Dan Davin recognised this in the North African desert in 1942 when he first read Sargeson. 'I saw . . . that the special quality of the language lay not only in bold colloquial tropes or an occasional local usage but informed every intonation and every element of the spoken idiom. Here in Sargeson were the same characters to be met around one every day in the desert and using the same terms, the same patterns of thought and speech. "If you'd used your block," I could accuse myself in their idiom, "and listened to the jokers you used to play football with you'd have spotted it long ago".'[20]

For Wedde, the current state of New Zealand-English is the result of a history of assimilation, adaptation, and evolution of which Sargeson's fiction is itself a part. His linguistic and social range is broader than Sargeson's. Nevertheless, like Sargeson, he turns to a male outsider, Heberley, to embody the drive towards national linguistic identity. Wedde lacks Sargeson's objectionable prejudices (in Sargeson's stories women speak English and men speak New Zealand-English) and, unlike Sargeson, he allows a rich linguistic identity to female characters like Kate in both *Dick Seddon* and in *Survival Arts*, where she reappears. New Zealand-English, for Wedde, includes the enormous variety of energies that have arrived, been used, and been changed. Its development as a language is dependent on an interchange between imported English forms and words and the truly 'native' language, Maori. But the generating centre of New Zealand-English is found in the working man, Heberley — the first Pakeha in the process of becoming a New Zealander by turning away from the linguistic and social forms of England to the antipodean 'home'.

In an important sense Heberley is qualified to become a New Zealander because he is 'riffraff' (p.196). He willingly embraces the epithet hurled at the 'beach scum' of runaways, drunks, convicts, and mutineers by the authorities. This is the same epithet that Maori radical Atareta Poananga hurled at resentful white New Zealanders in the late 1980s. Poananga mocked the Pakeha for their pretensions to superior origins (they were not, after all, descended from criminals like the Australians) and accused them of having sprung from the floating scum of empire. Wedde mocks the same pretensions to genteel origins, but he announces the riffraffery of the first Pakeha not, like Poananga, to contest the claim of the Pakeha to belong in Aotearoa but to affirm that claim.

Heberley finds himself at home in New Zealand once he has embraced the name Worser, an amalgamation of the two races claiming to belong:

Worser as he now inescapably was to remain for the rest of his life, stood there in a new world and breathed an original atmosphere through his gaping mouth . . . an inspiration that when he breathed out again with a long groan of awe would be his first message to a place in which he would now be able to see great chiefs and a woman he loved with his life, and their children, where the likes of Colonel Wakefield would only see savages — he would see great captains where the Company and the administration after that would see no one but a broken shore whaler like Jacky Love — he would see an earthly paradise, a home, where the men in white flannel would see a licentious Golgotha or an untenanted exploitable resource. . . . (p.220)

Jonathan Lamb sees Wedde as offering Pakeha New Zealanders a 'homecoming' in Aotearoa by appropriating the qualities of originality and naturalness associated with the 'native' culture. There is some truth in this but the bare statement fails to allow for the complexity with which Wedde approaches the whole knotty problem of culture and language in New Zealand. Wedde's writing is an enormously fluent and inclusive instrument. It embraces contradictions. The affirmations it offers are at best muted and qualified. Above all, it provides a tolerant and relaxed context in which the opposed tendencies and jealously dominant figures of the local literary past — Sargeson and Mansfield — can exist.

Mansfield, in fact, turns up in *Symmes Hole* at a book launch at Parliament Buildings in the early 1980s. She is for the narrator a figure of erotic desire as well as sickness and unattainability:

155

... and here comes Kathleen, with her white clavicles and her dark eyes and her smile that enters your heart like a sentence so perfect it has no sound, no more than the deadly soft click of a pearl-handled pistol being primed in a dark ambuscade: your blood freezes, and then you hear the breath of her laugh, you see maybe a dim gleam of slick on teeth or lipstick or eyeball, hear a rustle of clothing, somehow the lights are up again and you can smell the charnel byre and piss-straw of her rotting lungs' breath. ... (p.278)

Mansfield makes what Alex Calder calls an 'unhomely return' in *Symmes Hole*.[21] She is not the Mansfield of myth, the beloved national icon, but the woman dying of tuberculosis at Fontainebleau. Yet she leaves behind her perfect sentences and phrases. One, 'a little steamer all hung with bright beads', floats through the novel, among a myriad of other snatches and phrases of writing. Wedde is not deferential towards Mansfield. Nor does he distort her, as Ihimaera does in his elaborate act of literary homage, *Dear Miss Mansfield*. But she is not merely 'a peripheral figure' in *Symmes Hole*, as Linda Hardy maintains.[22] Her presence, if 'ghostly', is unexorcised.

Wedde is always alert to the now and the here, yet aware of all that flows into his writing from the past and from elsewhere, as in this passage from *Symmes Hole*:

And he's thinking, I could still make that trip. Keep the mind easy in its gimbals. Plan to break your fast with that pair, those omoos combing the beaches of paradise for ideas ... subtle shells, nacre, cowrie-money ... it all dried dull, and someone will have to answer for that, as well as for the coprolitic 'present' in which he's drifting, thinking: *Who's going to answer for it?* ... drifting out ... the dark surface of the Pacific lit here and there with a skin of phosphorescent whale-food ... the winter whale-season coming on ... putrefying cathedrals of sunk Right whales drifting up, lit with phantom fire ... clean-picked skulls of mariners flicked overboard (you can hear their screams that cease abruptly like cinema FX) by a loop in the smoking harpoon-line, rising to the surface like white long-line floats ... that brilliant common chord, the triad of Saturn, Jupiter and Mars, so clear in the cool autumn sky ... right out of sight of 'the little steamer all hung with bright beads' plying back and forth between the arseholes of 'the present' ... on and out ... gone, lost. ... (p.19)

This writing plies deftly between the linguistic present of pop culture, films, space parlours, McDonalds, and the past: the closing image from Mansfield, the nautical term 'gimbals' (not from 'Jabberwocky'), the echoes of Melville. The prose ripples with lines, phrases, rhythms from Wedde's poetry since the late 1960s, yet it is never prose

trying to be 'poetic', in the word-spinning or falsely inflated sense.
Compare it to the following passage from Ihimaera:

> *The sea scintillates with the sweetness of the kai karanga. . . . Illuminated*
> *jellyfish explode silvered starbursts through the dark depths. Far below, a river*
> *of phosphorescence lends lambent light to the abyss like a moonlit tide. The ocean*
> *is alive with noises: dolphin chatter, krill hiss, squid thresh, shark swirl, shrimp*
> *click and, ever present, the strong swelling chords, of the sea's constant rise and*
> *fall.*[23]

It is true that *Symmes Hole* contains passages which are strikingly
similar in theme: the Humpback whales are said to have their own
'exquisite songs' (p.170). But we do not find in Wedde's novel the
inflated, word-spinning, excited, purple prose we find here. In the
fiction of Hulme and Ihimaera, particularly of the latter, there is a
confused jumbling of non-realistic elements, fantasy writing, and
above all romantic versions of oral literature. The prose is characterised by striving after inflated dignity. It is writing trying to sound
'oral', like *Ossian*, the eighteenth-century verse epic which James
Macpherson claimed to have translated from ancient Gaelic originals.
It strives self-consciously to capture the incantatory rythms and elevated discourse of a heroic culture, in touch with nature and with
world of the spirit. Yet it is a prose cluttered with abstractions: the sea,
the land, the natural world — not observed particulars but elevated
generalities in an organicist and self-consciously primitive world
view.

If we compare sentences by Ihimaera in the passage above to
characteristic sentences from Wedde, we see the differences both in
intention and result. Firstly, here is Ihimaera: 'Illuminated jellyfish
explode silvered starbursts through the dark depths. Far below, a
river of phosphorescence lends lambent light to the abyss like a
moonlit tide.' This writing is straining after a 'poetic' prose style. The
long vowels and alliterations recall Tennyson at his most plangent.
The writing is directed towards creating atmosphere: a sinuous tone,
a phantasmagoria of colours and sounds that might sweep the reader
into the whale-world. Words like 'lambent', 'abyss', 'moonlit tide'
serve no purpose but to suggest a mood. In other words, the writing
is overcharged with effects and undercharged with meaning. Now
here is Wedde: 'In the mulberry sky the stars were thick as grey
mullet. He'd had to learn all *them* again, everything was arsey-varsey,

trees that dropped their bark, kingfishers with heads like coal-scuttles' (p.28). Wedde's diction is various, exact, and surprising. The colloquialism 'arsey-varsey' places the language user neatly in his class and period. The mullet are a nicely mundane counterpoint to the stars they metaphor. Wedde's prose suffers from excess of sense, not absence.

Wedde wants his reader to work, to read reflectively and against the grain. He loads his sentences with allusion and implication. He seeks to subvert the reader's easy patterns of receiving prose. Like Sargeson, he wants the reader to meet him half way in making the novel's meaning. Ihimaera wants to soothe his reader, to lead him or her down below the difficulties of too active a reading process. (Significantly, when he writes negatively against the reader, as in the anti-Pakeha sections of *The Matriarch*, he uses rhetoric, which again requires no *active* involvement by the reader in discerning the direction of the novel's criticism of society.) He invites us where the sounds of the words lull the senses and establish a mood of responsiveness that bypasses our natural scepticism. Ihimaera encourages a passive reading because he wants to win his reader over to a fantasy world where nature is charged with spiritual presences and whales talk.

Symmes Hole is extraordinarily rich in recycled material from literature, popular culture, and from Wedde's own prior texts. There are phrases, snatches, echoes in the book of a range of sources from Ray Kroc and Eddie Rabbit to Sylvia Plath and Tennyson. Wedde has not sought to disguise the extent of the borrowings in his writing. His list of acknowledgements at the back of the book is headed: 'A far from complete list of books that helped me, and to which I helped myself, would have to include . . .' (p.323).

Wedde's debts are not predominantly high-cultural, as Stead's are. Wedde draws on comics, pop songs, advertising, the classics, contemporary literature — everything imaginable. Stead introduces the refrain of a song by The Clash in 'Yes, T.S.', but the quotation is *placed* in the work, as the passage from 'Mrs Porter and her Daughter' is placed in *The Waste Land*. It is held at a distance by the high-cultural context into which it is inserted. Stead's poem, like Eliot's, implies a hierarchy of traditional sources in which the echoes from the great tradition of Europe are superior to those of popular songs. Snatches of pop songs from the sixties, abstruse references to *Moby Dick*, records of oral cultural forms, historical material — all these cohabit in Wedde's texts in a democratic, if not entirely harmonious, fashion.

Yet Wedde expects a highly literate and alert reader, one thoroughly familiar with modern American poetry when reading 'Pathway to the Sea', with Melville when reading *Symmes Hole*, with both 1960s pop songs and Virgil's *Georgics* when reading *Georgicon*. His own relation as author to the material he works into the fiction and the poetry is always complex, distant, ironic, playful. That is not to say that he is merely sending up his sources in popular or high culture. He makes use of them — echoes, models, forms, kinds, styles, repetitions — to confront the restless interpenetration of writing by other writing, of the individual subject as author and all he or she produces by the linguistic varieties of culture.

The problem was how to hold such disparate material together. Wedde faces here the same kind of problem that Ihimaera faced in *The Matriarch* and Hulme in *the bone people*. All are writing national epics that reinterpret the country's history and destiny, describe its origins, and project desirable futures. There is an understandable tendency for such ambitious undertakings to fall into incoherence because they attempt to contain so much incongruous material. Hulme and Ihimaera use myth to unify their novels, transcending the contentions of actual history. They abandon realism where it suits their purposes, to offer the nation a version of its future possibilities to be discovered in its pre-historical past.

Wedde's solution to the problem of making his epic cohere is one that owes as much to Thomas Pynchon as to Melville: he focuses the narrative through a paranoid character. The researcher 'gets totally lost between the shifting faces of history, reality and "reality"' (pp.10-11). 'Fiction and paranoia' are almost interchangeable for him. His obsession takes him close to true madness: 'He had to be almost mad, in fact—in order to have this notion of an alternative history a touch of paranoia does no harm at all'.[24]

The paranoia of the researcher in *Symmes Hole* is not merely a reflection of the author's personality, although as Wedde himself has admitted, 'a breakdown of that needed space between me and the pronoun' occurred in the writing of the novel.[25] It is integral to the novel's design, a way of responding to the disjointedness, deceptiveness, and apparent meaninglessness of post-colonial history in a work of fiction. Wedde's method in *Symmes Hole* confers a kind of meaning on what T. S. Eliot called the 'futility and anarchy' of contemporary history, but only by allowing a paranoid character to do the conferring. The researcher's paranoia revolves around his determination to find Ray Kroc's fast food empire behind an enormous mass of apparently unrelated material. His paranoia does not control this material, but it provides a key, a means of connecting it in a single historical plot. The researcher, like Captain Ahab, discovers a purpose behind events which to others seem motiveless. Behind the whale's actions Ahab discovers a malevolent intention; behind the proliferation of McDonalds' golden arches Wedde's researcher uncovers a tentacular historical plot, a single web of interest and malice.

The Pacific world in *Moby Dick* is represented as a map of conquest and the expansion of American global economic, technological, and military power. In *Symmes Hole* the process of American expansion across the Pacific is complete, but the vehicle of that power is not the whaling ships, the most advanced technology of the mid nineteenth century, but Ray Kroc's McDonalds hamburger empire. Behind both the whaling and fast food industries lie the same ideas that encourage the human subjugation of matter. This historical plot allows Wedde's researcher to connect Moby Dick's retaliations against the *Pequod* with the actions of modern terrorists against US imperialism in the Pacific (pp.167-8).

Wedde himself does not take the novel's paranoia for truth. Paranoia is a convenient myth the novelist employs. It is thematised as Symmes Hole itself: the paranoid theory that there is a route to the centre of the earth. Significantly, the Symmes Hole idea includes among its adherents Adolf Hitler and Jeremiah Reynolds, the advocate of American naval power in the Pacific. It is a right-wing way of making sense of unrelated events, and thus of controlling history. The right-wing version of history leads to utter rigidity, the mapping and control of space, the alienation of humans from the material world. Opposed to this is not the 'left-wing' version of history, which has its own tendencies to paranoia and dogma, but the subversive version, which centres on the discovery of submerged histories. It opens up explanations of social experience denied by official history. It complicates and deepens our sense of the past by suggesting other ways of seeing events and assigning meanings than those approved by 'the "history" written down in books, the selective necessities of "recorded fact"' (p.169).

In a sense, official history is a form of the well-made poem that Wedde rebelled against as a young man. Counter-history corresponds to the American writing to which he responded so enthusiastically, to the openness and colloquial energies of the Beat generation of the fifties and of the postmodern writers of the sixties. Claustro-phobic tidiness is opposed by energetic openness. In his favourite constructions of history, as in his literary preferences, Wedde charac-teristically seeks to unseat the anxious bourgeois ego and relax.

Wedde himself stands back from the myths of which he avails himself in the novel, including the paranoid ones. Paranoia allows Wedde to represent a chaotic world without neatly tying the loose ends together to make a satisfyingly resolved plot. But the novelist does not endorse the chaos he shows. The world uncovered by the researcher's paranoia is a manichaean one. It is rigidly controlled by a materialist destiny which produces disorder as a byproduct of its activities. But the novel simultaneously shows the ways in which humans continually resist the historical, economic, and political plots that engulf them. They make their own shapes that are provisional and open, hence human. They have it in their power to redirect history, although they are so often defeated by it. The novel is an Augustinian novel about a manichaean universe, as it is a modernist novel about postmodernist culture.

This is another way of saying that *Symmes Hole* is a novel which suffers from hubris. Wedde's ambition is on a Melvillean scale, but he cannot make his novel's criticism work simultaneously on a number of levels — economic, social, metaphysical — as Melville does in *Moby Dick*. Nor can he hold together the prodigious amount of material the novel includes as fluently as Melville does. *Symmes Hole* is fecund and engaging, large in scope and impressive in its par-ticulars, but it is also unwieldy. It has the playfulness and some of the anger of *Moby Dick*, but it lacks those 'short quick probings at the very axis of reality' at which Melville is adept.[26] It is less taxing to read than *Moby Dick* and less troubling in its overall effect.

It is a mistake to categorise Wedde within the descriptions post-modernism, modernism, post-colonialism. He belongs wholly to none of them, although each is present in his writing. At times, impelled by his strong antipathy to Eurocentricism and to metropoli-tan elites, he even displays a tendency towards parochialism. Wedde's antagonism towards the cultural elitism of high modernism aligns him with an anti-modernist like the Australian poet, Les Murray. In Murray's words, modernism was 'a disaster. It was an elite takeover'. Murray goes on to condemn 'the dreadful tyranny where only certain privileged places are regarded as the centre and the rest are provincial and nothing good can be expected to come out of them'. This antagonism to the notion of cultural centres and to the courtier art that centres generate is shared by Wedde. When Murray asserts that 'the centre is everywhere', he merely restates Chink's view in *Dick Seddon* that 'there is no centre'.[27]

Yet Wedde is not a nationalist, as Murray is. He both satirises nationalism as part of his general assault on current manners (among the four ships which brought the first settlers to Canterbury in his poem 'The Relocation of Hut 49' are *Bad Karma* and *Gaga in Toto*) and sets about reformulating a new kind of nationalism as part of the overall effort of decolonising New Zealand's culture. But Wedde's writing steers deftly between the Scylla and Charybdis of post-colonialism and nationalism. His sense of the internal complexities of the local writing scene, of the bearing of international influences on local writing, his attentiveness to the particular resonances of the local idiom, his respect for counter-traditions, and his desire to acknowledge them — all these involve a complex and problematic sense of the concept 'nation'.

Decolonisation for Wedde does not mean the attempt to extirpate from consciousness the sources of knowledge that are judged to be contaminated by their origin in a colonial power. Far from seeking to cut off any sources of knowledge, Wedde is eager to admit the richness and diversity of all which has been brought into the national culture and continues to be brought, as well as of all that lies to hand. What is at stake here is a more encompassing and dialectical understanding of the nation as the locus of contending forces as against a narrowing of focus that goes with the rhetorics of post-colonialism or nationalism.

Symmes Hole is Wedde's major novel to date, a large, chaotic, brilliantly eccentric historical novel which is again a linguistic exploration and mapping of our complex condition as New Zealanders: part of the post-colonial world yet with our distinctive atavisms, usages, and nostalgias. Wedde's 1988 novel, *Survival Arts*, is much less ambitious in its scope than its predecessor. Read in the same terms, it is a disappointing novel, frustratingly difficult to read, disjointed, wilfully obscure, seemingly determined *not* to make sense. *Survival Arts* needs to be read in its own terms. At the centre of the novel's attention are the sense-making activities of fiction itself. The novel deliberately thwarts the reader's expectations about how a novel produces meaning, shapes events.

Survival Arts is described on the back cover as 'a hairy dog story'. It is so in the sense that it adopts a mocking attitude towards the reader's expectations of how a novel should generate meaning, organise its plot line, and present characters. Even by Wedde's standards, the dialogue is unusually staccato, the sentences broken, almost to the point of incomprehensibility. The characters are bizarre and marginal: a Vietnam veteran trying to sell a war-surplus M24 tank in Wellington, two lesbians who want to start a sperm bank in a second-hand freezer, a beautiful, Porsche-driving woman who administers katipo venom to her Polynesian lover in car-washes, and three workers in an auction mart. The plot is hectic, involved, ridiculous, and incomplete. The ending leaves the reader hanging with nothing resolved. The action, with its car chases and set pieces with the M24 tank, seems to be spoofing itself.

The reader is continually being set up by the wayward narrative. Even the opening epigraphs contain a false scent. The third epigraph is attributed to To Huu, apparently a Vietnamese poet. The quotation sounds suitably oriental and inscrutable: 'Burning thirst of a hundred years constantly waiting,/and today joy arrives as though in a dream./The sky so calm, unbelievably blue,/the face of the earth peaceful with the sleep of children'.[28] But who is this To Huu? Presumably it is Wedde himself in oriental disguise, as he was in academic disguise in the 'Introduction' to *Symmes Hole*. Again, Wedde's relation to the writing is a slippery and duplicitous one. He makes up voices so as to fool the gullible reader who expects the voice behind the words he reads in non-dramatic prose to be that of the author. Wedde's habit of inventing personae in contexts like this calls into question even the apparently 'sincere' introduction to *The Penguin Book of New Zealand Verse*. Where *exactly* does Wedde himself stand in relation to its circumlocutions and obfuscations?

As far as *Survival Arts* is concerned, it would seem that Wedde is enjoying himself — playing elaborate games, mocking his own narrative, and leading the reader into endless mazes — but not deeply committed to the book. The familiar Wedde themes are present: the earthly paradise, illusion, apocalypse. There is a madcap send-up of Heberley's confusion between pigeons and wekas in *Symmes Hole* when a Huntley and Palmer cream cracker is used to trap a weka for the pot. The fads of the seventies — rebirthing, encounter groups — are exposed to a light irony. The traditional themes of New Zealand literature — the Man Alone, 1930s work camps, escape to nature — are similarly ironically introduced into the novel. But none of this rescues the novel from the ennui it induces.

Perhaps the most notable feature of the novel is the humane tone it adopts towards those of its characters normal enough to be recognisable as vaguely social beings. Salvation, the Vietnam veteran, is not normal in this sense. Snag and Ike, the physically mismatched and reluctant lovers who work in the auction mart, are sufficiently normal, however marginal, and they are presented with a humanity that continually just prevents them from becoming slapstick figures. The two lesbians, Kate and BJ, are similarly saved from becoming ludicrous, for all the craziness of their preoccupations. Kate, in fact, is the Kate from Wedde's first novel, *Dick Seddon*, a decade and a half later, isolate, emotionally ravaged, strange, but with her queer dignity intact. The long rap session where she throws into speech the content of her mind's brooding on so many years of loneliness is curiously powerful. Compared to the lesbians in Stead's *The Death of the Body*, Kate and BJ are impressively rounded characters.

But the overall impression of the book is that the author's intelligence has not been fully engaged in its writing. It is a book of compelling bits and pieces.

*   *   *

In an essay on cultural identity in New Zealand, David Novitz remarks that '[t]he history of European settlement in New Zealand can properly be understood as a lengthy struggle between the indigenous and the imported'.[29] This is another way of saying that the efforts of the Pakeha in New Zealand to establish a distinctive national culture have been characterised by a profound uncertainty about location. The longstanding habit of referring to England as 'home' indicated the extent of that sense of exile as colonials, what Peter Simpson calls the 'provincial' sense of 'permanent banishment from the centre'.[30]

As Simpson also points out in the same article, a line of opposition to the provincial attitude goes back to the early 1950s. James K. Baxter departed from the Curnow stresses on distance and isolation in 1951 by encouraging and siding with the group of young poets who became known as 'the Wellington Group'.

Since he began publishing poetry in the late 1960s, Wedde, more directly and consciously than any other contemporary New Zealand writer, has placed this struggle at the centre of his attention as a writer. Wedde's whole effort as poet, anthologist, novelist, critic (these separate functions merge disconcertingly at times in his practice as a writer) has been directed at finding a way of allowing indigenous and imported elements into his writing without their being continually at war. For Wedde, the contending elements meet above all in the English language as it has developed in New Zealand since the first contact between English sailors and Maori inhabitants. As he has observed, 'The history of a literature with colonial origins is involuntarily written *by* the language, not just in it'.[31]

In New Zealand the problem of power — cultural, economic and political—is increasingly bound up with the problem of language. For Maori nationalists like Donna Awatere, the colonists and their descendants share not only in the benefits of the alienation of Maori land but also in those of 'the imposition of the English language'.[32] The view that English is a 'foreign' language in New Zealand is both an obvious truth and a simplification. A language that has been the tongue of majority usage for a century and half, that has produced a distinctive and in many cases distinguished body of literary texts by Maori as well as Pakeha writers, that is the dominant language of our institutions, our interactions, our commerce, and our cultural expressions (both high and low), can scarcely be said to be 'foreign'. Moreover, it has taken some of its word stock from Maori. The two cultures can no longer be neatly disentangled, although they remain markedly distinct.

It is true, as Alan Riach points out, that 'English as an international language cuts itself off from wherever it is used. As the language of domination and exploitation it is the most pervasive symbol of the colonial process. It is everywhere a foreigner.'[33] But here we must distinguish between 'English' English, the tongue of the colonisers, and the various relatively autonomous forms of the language that have taken root and matured throughout the colonised world. As Wedde argues in his introduction to *The Penguin Book*, the English language, after 150 years of adaption, can be felt by its New Zealand users 'to be original *where it is*'.[34] Terry Sturm has pointedly asked what Wedde *means* by statements like this which 'celebrate . . . the growth of the coloniser's language "into its location"'.[35] Put simply,

Wedde means that there is such a thing as 'New Zealand English', a form of the international English language which has its own peculiar habits and usages.

Wedde's writing considered as a whole, rather than in terms of specific attitudes that can be abstracted from it, offers a compelling plea for the English language in New Zealand as a confluence of the conflicting elements that have been part of the history of colonisation. The writing in its richness of sources celebrates the assimilative tendencies of English and denies no part of the polyglot heritage it encompasses. Even despised dialects, such as the public schoolboy adventure slang of Colonel Wakefield, are allowed a place in the complex balance of registers the writing maintains. The differences Wedde recognises in the culture are not resolved, healed, or synthesised in his fiction. They remain intractably present. This is the source of their energy and their value. By way of the language and its accommodations the descendants of the settlers and the 'riffraff' who came with empire have made a home for themselves in New Zealand. Jonathan Lamb has criticised Wedde for thus exonerating the Pakeha from their guilty sense of the past and from that sense of riffraffery that haunts and terrifies them. But the homecoming Wedde offers the Pakeha is an insecure one. It allows for a considerable degree of that 'displacement, decentering and discontinuity' that other settler cultures, according to Lamb, are learning 'to love'.[36]

Wedde is concerned with the ways in which in the late twentieth century amid the collapse of so many cultural authorities and traditions, people find themselves between cultures rather than securely inside a particular culture. For Wedde, to be without culture is to be dead, and he conceives that it is possible to be in this condition. In a review of *Coolie Odyssey* by the Guyanese poet, David Dabydeen, he describes the poor whites of Brixton. These people are at the dead end of a culture that has become utterly exhausted; they exist in a twilight world of living death. The myth of white supremacy that had sustained their culture has collapsed and they are unable to fasten on to new myths.[37]

They have reached this condition because the coherent culture with an authoritative centre which once sustained them has been consigned to history. London is a post-imperial world in which the original inhabitants find themselves surrounded by the ghosts of their former imperial subjects. All have lost contact with their 'roots'. All suffer from some degree of inauthenticity. They inhabit a de-centred and ungrounded world in which cultures have been displaced, moved around the globe, left to rub against one another. Yet it is possible to be in this condition without being merely lost. The old white myth is dying, dead, but new myths are in the process of being formed.

None of these new myths will be able to enclose humans as the old ones did before the whole process of uprooting and transplantation began. But they will serve. To talk about tradition in such a context is to miss the point. The instability that surrounds our sense of cultural belonging is caused by the homogenisation of culture which is an artificial consequence of so much encounter and assimilation. The English writing of Italian or Greek immigrant communities in Toronto or Sydney has necessarily been contaminated by the alien cultural context, its link to a specific tradition interrupted. This is both loss and liberation. What is lost is the nurturing and defining character of a specific cultural continuity. What is gained is the possibility of the endless exploration of difference itself. Where Stead stands for the white myth, Wedde stands for something more complex. Essentially, his stance involves living among the cultural myths that abound in post-colonial societies without grounding one's being in any of them.

Vincent O'Sullivan has described Katherine Mansfield's 'sense of discomposure *anywhere*'.[38] Mansfield inhabited a world after 1918 in which there were no more unambiguous homecomings, to New Zealand or to Europe. Like V. S. Naipaul and Derek Walcott, who fled their provincial origins in the West Indies into a permanent exile, a homelessness that makes displacement the subject of all their subsequent work, Mansfield achieved an exemplary freedom as an exile.

Sargeson occupied the minds of New Zealand writers for so long partly because of the force of his refusal to be an international writer. He believed that New Zealand literature could only come to self-awareness and maturity as a nationalist and provincial tradition. The New Zealand writer must eschew the international audience Mansfield captured for her writing because it could only be gained at the expense of the demand for expression of the so-far-inarticulate country.

Frame chose to return to New Zealand when the option of remaining in Europe was open to her. Like Sargeson, she elected to work in a 'new' country, helping to give birth to its literature. But her writing is not provincial in the sense that Sargeson's is. Frame is always attentive to the features of a general human dilemma discernible behind the particular forms of New Zealand social life and her writing appeals to an international audience. Frame thus manages to be both a provincial and an international novelist. In this sense she found a compromise between the opposed understandings of how it was possible to be a 'New Zealand writer' presented by her two most significant precursors. Nevertheless, the choice she felt obliged to make was a traumatic one.

For Wedde, the choice between being provincial and being international was no longer crucial or even especially troublesome when he began writing in the late 1960s. For Wedde, to be in New Zealand does not condemn the writer to provincialism; to leave does not visit upon him or her an unbearable sense of displacement. Wedde is a New Zealand writer, but without strain. For Allen Curnow, the writer's native country is, as George Santayana put it, 'a kind of second body'; however much the spirit may wish to be housed elsewhere, it has a responsibility to accept its fallen condition.[39] In Curnow's poetry New Zealand is the inescapable 'reality' which the New Zealand writer must go in search of, but it lacks the fullness of lost realities elsewhere. In Wedde's writing, the spirit is endlessly seeking to immerse itself in the momentary, the actual, but in a sense of exuberant celebration, not of loss. New Zealand is the world to hand, as much a potential earthly paradise or industrial slum as any other part of the world.

Wedde does not feel obliged to help bring into existence a tradition waiting to be born. He is attentive to the 'realities' of landscape and society in New Zealand and to the particular uses of the English language in New Zealand. But he takes the existence of that idiom as an established fact for granted. His fiction shows a fully international sense of current formal and linguistic practice in the novel *and* an easy and wide-ranging familiarity with the current speech forms and literary-historical record of New Zealand-English.

It is this ease that is important. Wedde feels free to draw on an enormous number of sources and to weave those writings into his own work. His fiction reflects a prodigious range of interests and sources. But whatever he includes, he turns to his own purposes. The American influence is not merely 'the *identical article*, manufactured under licence, as it were, out of local materials by local industry'.[40] He *relocates* those influences in the context of an ambitious endeavour as a novelist, poet, and anthologist that is grounded in the current state and possibilities of the English language in New Zealand.

CHAPTER 6

Maurice Gee:
Mistakes and Miracles

'Did God make a mistake?' I asked.
'He doesn't make mistakes.'
'But you said it was one of His miracles. And the cow died.'
                    MAURICE GEE, *In My Father's Den*[1]

LAWRENCE JONES concludes a short treatment of Maurice Gee's trilogy, *Plumb, Meg,* and *Sole Survivor,* on a note that is less affirmative than it sounds: 'he has used his craft to present us with such living people and to challenge us to stretch our moral imaginations and widen our judgements'.[2] By placing Gee as a humanist realist novelist, Jones imposes a limit on the kinds of reading his work can be subjected to. There is no doubt that Gee is primarily a realist writer and that his fiction is minutely detailed, historically informed, psychologically acute, and above all humane. It criticises the repressions and inhumanities of the dominant society. But, as Jones's own study points out, developments in fictional practice in this country over the last fifteen years have shown that novels and stories can provide other kinds of satisfactions than these. Moreover, in the last decade linguistically self-conscious kinds of writing that do not aim to 'stretch our moral imaginations' have gained precedence over traditional realist and moralist ones.

Bill Manhire notes in his book on Gee the apparent absence of 'metafictional' tendencies in his writing:

He does not seem to be greatly interested in parody, collage, game-playing transactions between fiction and actuality. When he published *Plumb,* he appended a note which acknowledged the book's roots in his own family history, but only as a means of insisting that he had written a piece of *fiction*: 'My uncles and aunts are not to accuse me of putting them in a novel'.[3]

The missing features to which Manhire alludes here have become more and more important in the period since the publication of *Plumb* (1978). To say that the virtues of Gee's fiction exclude those which have been so prominent in the fiction of the period under consideration is to call into question the literary-historical value of his work. Although Manhire's book is thoroughly respectful towards Gee's writing, the omission he notes in that work of a quality strongly marked in his own writing leaves a question about its range and relevance that will not go away.

This question was first asked by Russell Haley, reviewing Gee's *Games of Choice* in the literary broadsheet *Spleen* in the mid 1970s:

> What worries me about Gee is precisely his care, his exactness, his craft. . . . It is clever, crafty, careful but we are still being *told* about the characters — they are not being revealed. The craft lies in the way in which Gee retains the kind of aphoristic statement about character which is the hallmark of the omniscient, naturalistic author but we are picking up some of the special resonances, the disguised interior monologue, of the single point-of-view.[4]

The chief problem for Haley is that Gee's narrative strategies proceed from naturalistic genre conventions that the author never questions or examines. The texture of the prose is too immaculate in its smooth representation of life. The reader is not sufficiently active in the reading process. The author's presence is overweening, nudging the reader towards the appropriate responses. In spite of the title of the book under review, *Games of Choice*, there is no real 'play' in the book because all the choices have already been made by the author. Above all, Haley finds his own response to the fiction inhibited because the rules of naturalistic representation are so rigidly adhered to: 'the straight and narrow path to the goal of reality is naturalism'.[5] This naturalistic tidiness oppresses Haley. He finds the book closed and confined.

If Gee had remained thus enclosed within naturalistic genre conventions, the limits of his fiction would inevitably have become more and more pronounced over the last decade. But there is another potential in Gee's writing which works against the dominant naturalism. It is present, if thwarted, even in *Games of Choice*. Haley points to it thus:

> . . . under the bland careful, referential prose, I can feel that there is a lurking obsessive poet in Gee. It is a poetry that wants to break the surface

tension of the prose but we can only glimpse this obsession with a kind of sideways glance.[6]

Here Haley points to something fundamental about other major New Zealand fiction. He offers a hint about alternative ways in which the fiction of Sargeson and Duggan as well as Gee can be read. The problem with Gee's fiction, if we follow this hint, is not simply that it exists inside limits imposed by the straitjacket of naturalism, but also that its buried subversive tendencies have not been sufficiently acknowledged. The problem, then, is not only the ways in which New Zealand masculine realist fiction has been written but also the ways in which it has been read. The other quality is there, waiting only to be dragged into the light by readers attentive to the dark undercurrents in the writing:

> . . . in the best of our writers, and I include Gee here, we can feel something bulging the surface of the prose. Often it is a hidden sexual charge — the strange tittering deviance in Sargeson is an example, the presence of death in Duggan's final marvellous works which makes his language as charged as Camus' and as grotesquely funny as Beckett's — but in Gee it is an overwhelming sense that he can reach something numinous and atavistic when he deals imaginatively with place.[7]

Haley is referring here to a story, 'Right-Hand Man', which shows exactly the extent of Gee's debt to Sargeson and points up the direction of Gee's development of the Sargeson line. The story is in a sense an elaboration of 'Conversation with My Uncle', Sargeson's very early moral fable which sketched the method he was to develop so richly. In 'Conversation' the world of bureaucracy and respectability is exposed by a naive and talkative narrator who describes the spiritual deadness of his uncle. In tone, the story is rather like D. H. Lawrence's famous poem, 'How Beastly the Bourgeois Is', written after the First World War:

> How beastly the bourgeois is
> especially the male of the species.

But Sargeson's bourgeois figure is shabbier and less confident than Lawrence's. The Depression has put a shine on his suit. Lawrence's bourgeois has had the stuffing knocked out of him by the War and the collapse of the rhetorical and moral power of the high Victorian bourgeoisie, but he keeps up appearances. Sargeson's 'uncle' is lower-middle rather than upper-middle class. Yet he too stands for the dominant class — that which controls business and morality in society as a whole. In New Zealand that dominant class was always a notch lower than in England. Above all, like Lawrence's bourgeois male, the uncle has no inner self, he is a hollow man.

Gee's Vincent Brown, like Sargeson's Uncle, has power and self-confidence. In fact, he has more authority in the period of post-war affluence than his forebear did in the Depression period. His chief difference from the uncle is that he is presented from within. We do not have to read his inner emptiness in terms of Sargeson's narrator's deceptively naive chatter or that objective correlative to his state of soul, the hard knocker. We move inwards into Vincent Brown's motives and emotions, inside the whole internal order of a world view that is complete, self-enclosed, and utterly repellent. We inhabit his twisted, destructive, and oddly knowing mind.

In other words, Gee has moved from Sargeson's expressive realism towards a richly detailed and extensive psychological realism. But the same moral criticism of society's repressive codes is mounted in the story. What has gone is Sargeson's revealing/concealing narrator, who stands apart from the object of the story's savage criticism and focuses it. Even in the later stories, where Sargeson employs narrators beyond the range of the marginal, poor, inarticulate, and uncomprehending speakers in the early stories, there are significant differences from Gee in the way the stories work and in the way in which they are organised.

Sargeson's 'City and Suburban' (1965) is focused through the consciousness of an accountant: suburban, married, heterosexual, the antithesis of Sargeson's early narrators. But as if to compensate for having to work through such a despised narrative consciousness, a Sargesonian horror is included. The accountant's family discover on the beach a finger which is briefly mistaken by the sexually harried husband for a severed penis, a similarly placed husband's method of escaping connubial duties. In his fiction up to the late 1970s, Gee is capable of including violences quite as horrifying as Sargeson's (the killing of the horse in 'The Losers', for example) but nowhere does he make them unreal or deliberately bizarre, as Sargeson does. Nor does he introduce outrageously anti-realistic touches like the names of the children — Happy and Glad — in 'City and Suburban'. (In the later fiction he makes a point of dwelling on the obscene pun in R. Sole's name and even names a minor character in *Prowlers*, the director of a research institute, Manifold.)

The characteristic indirection of the Sargesonian method is also absent in Gee. The felling of the trees at the end of 'Right-Hand Man' is an act of brutality which expresses the puritan antipathy to life embedded in the culture. But in Sargeson's 'Sale Day' the forces are channelled through an uncomprehending victim/victimiser, the narcissistic, possibly homosexual, Victor, who drops the randy tom-cat into the fire (cats have a hard time in New Zealand literature, as Bill Manhire has noted).[8] In 'Right-Hand Man' the narrative focus, Vincent Brown, acts explicitly on behalf of those forces. He expresses the most life-denying forces in society.

In Gee's story the realism is more seamless and detailed than in Sargeson. Gee achieves greater psychological resonance. He traces minutely within the opened-out selves of his characters the whole complexity of the relations between culture and consciousness. The prose is less pared, the social range is greater. Vincent Brown is not a mere straw man as is Sargeson's Uncle, a representative figure of social narrowness and repressions, to be knocked down by the narrator. He is the focus of a banality and capacity for evil that is particularised and complete. We enter into the world of his mind and discover not a monster, but a familiar human consciousness, one which is distinguished by its ordinariness. Vincent Brown is even alert enough to recognise the 'mental stratagems' by which he has avoided full self-knowledge in the past.[9]

Yet what has not gone is Sargeson's ability to allow into his stories dramatic moments and sly undertones which act against the prevailing naturalism. Haley senses this in Gee as the possibility of poetic apocalypse lurking just under surface. For Haley, Gee's private places — the grove, den, room, thicket — operate 'against the naturalistic tidiness in the stories'. More important, they provide an 'unconscious metaphor for the role of the writer/observer'.[10] According to Haley, this is where the real imagination is functioning.

In 'Right-Hand Man' Vincent Brown's apocalypse occurs in the patch of bush which he is determined to destroy on the grounds that it encourages 'perverts' and stands in the way of the orderly progress of suburban development. Entering the trees, his own inner darkness is coaxed to the surface by the surrounding gloom. He discovers a complicity with the perverts:

> The trees moved close to his sides. His knowledge of how the pervert must feel was a kind of sympathy. The red uniforms of the schoolgirls beckoned, and the sunlit grass. For a moment he saw how the act would explode one into light and power.[11]

What Vincent Brown discovers here is a darkness within the human mind — a concentration of desire and power — over which the codes and rules of organised social behaviour have little control. The urge to clear the bush, to make every area of human life neat and tidy, rises from the denial of that darkness and power and at the same time expresses it. Here Gee recalls that pervasive and disturbing concentration on violence in Sargeson's stories, the sudden eruptions into the texts of a rage against the constraints which society has imposed on nature, twisting and distorting the shapes of individual desire. But in Gee the violence springs from a level of the human mind that precedes the construction of social order. For Sargeson, the violence in humans proceeds ultimately from society. For Gee, there is an ineradicable terror that lies at the basis of being itself.

Haley suggests that the imagery of privacy and seclusion in Gee provides metaphors for the role of the artist/observer. He means that there is a buried poetic and obsessive quality in Gee's writing which only manifests itself occasionally and obliquely. In Gee's fiction of the 1980s this quality moves progressively into the foreground. Moreover, it becomes associated with an apocalyptic sense of violence, terror, and darkness that lies under the formal orders which literature and society impose upon chaos and emptiness.

It might be said that the obsessive imagery of voyeurism in Gee's fiction is more telling as a metaphor for the role of the artist in relation to his material than is the imagery of seclusion. In *Prowlers* this material comes into the open, as it were, and is more explicitly linked to the role of the writer/observer. But this does not necessarily mean a gain in power in the writing, although it involves a move away from naturalistic genre conventions. The voyeurism in Gee's earlier fiction has a special charge attached to it, a frisson, that relies upon the unconsciousness of the preoccupation. A disturbing power is present precisely because the implications of the motif are not fully acknowledged.

Haley presumptuously tells the author what he should do to rescue him as reader from the boredoms Gee's fiction subjects him to. He advises Gee to allow the organic imagination working below the levels of character, action, and event freer rein. Thus, he urges, Gee might become more than the patient meticulous journeyman who both impresses and irritates Haley. Gee himself has not responded directly to criticism of his work, though courteous towards critics. Reluctant to give interviews, he seems anxious to protect the organic sources of his creativity from direct probing. He has steadfastly resisted any form of engagement with the discussion about the theory of novel writing that became fashionable in the 1980s.

Yet, for all this, Gee has moved progressively since the late 1970s away from the naturalism that Haley dislikes. Certainly, he has remained the meticulous craftsman, and certainly he has avoided the flamboyantly self-conscious gestures of postmodernism. But a fundamental shift has occurred in the underlying attitudes on which his characters, his sense of history, and the formal properties of his fictions are built. That shift occurs at the close of the last book in his Plumb trilogy, *Sole Survivor*. Gee's work from the late seventies into the eighties calls into question the organising assumptions of the earlier work and seeks some adequate formal response to the collapse of meaning, the disappearance of depth, and the general aimlessness of contemporary life.

Towards the end of *Sole Survivor* Raymond Sole, the novel's narrator, recalls entering his grandfather's study. There he finds the intact record of that humanist tradition of 'great' works which had sustained his grandfather's intellectual and moral questing as a young man. Ovid, Wordsworth, *The History of Pantheism* — there is not even a hint of bathos in the last entry. Ideas — spiritual and philosophical — had governed the old man's life, shaped and directed his energies, his passions, and his decisions about how to conduct his life. But then the old man was part of a world, now vanished, in which intellectual enthusiasms had currency among rich and poor, in which people changed religions amid soul searching and rigorous inquiry into the conflicting claims of the various faiths. Matters of doctrine counted. In other words, the world had depth and significance. Problems of meaning surrounded and affected individual lives.

Raymond Sole pats his grandfather's Buddha and takes some mock golf shots with a walking stick. Then he walks off oppressed by a sense of his own limitations. He cannot answer the ancient banal question about identity — what constitutes this person myself? —

that preyed upon the old man. Nor does the question affect him more than momentarily. Cynical, wisecracking—Raymond Sole confronts the emptiness within that his forebears had so painstakingly filled with the anxieties and illuminations of their terrible obsession with meaning.

This condition is not peculiar to Ray Sole: it is the condition of his time. Gestures no longer relate to any shared meanings. His cousin Duggie Plumb, the machiavellian politician, is not merely an aberration, he is representative. Ray, who has seen himself as morally superior to Duggie, discovers himself as merely a dispersed collection of conventional roles and attributes. Centreless, drifting — he occupies the ungrounded space that is the late twentieth century.

Ray opens the glory box left him by his grandmother. Earlier in his life it has stood as a repository of rich unspecified meanings. The details of family life were made numinous and significant by their part in the passage of the generations, the passing down not merely of cloths and china but of meanings and continuities. These significances rub momentarily against the edges of Raymond's consciousness, then lapse:

The sight of them was — moving? — touching? — sad? I felt threatened with speculations about 'meaning', and I closed the lid and shrugged and said, 'What am I going to do with these bloody things?' The sensible thing was to sell them to a junk shop. . . .[12]

Sole Survivor ends amid the exhaustion of the energies that had been so remarkably present at the beginning of the Plumb trilogy. More than this, it marks the end of the historical and ideological framework that had generated Gee's earlier fiction. Here Gee moves reluctantly but surely beyond the sense of history as a meaningful progression of related events, beyond character as the persistence of personality over time, beyond subjecthood as the experience of depth of self—beyond the universe of shared assumptions that made possible humane values. The novel enters a world of banal repetition, parody, emptiness, shallowness. It proliferates with signs that point to no substantial meanings.

Raymond Sole, who has seen himself as a moral being unlike his cousin Duggie, as one standing for positive values in society, finds that the socialism that had shored up his values and sense of identity as a younger man has dissipated. Moreover, 'it had never had any real existence' (p.161). His grandfather's socialism, he concludes, had been sentimental; his own was 'insubstantial as a shadow'. This is not mere loss of meaning but the discovery that meaning had all along been a pose, a front behind which lay a great hollowness.

Raymond has been a political journalist, a savage critic of the lies and shoddinesses of the rulers and disposers. But the vantage point from which that savage indignation had struck has been eroded over time, leaving him, like all those among whom he has mixed, with his inner being unrefined by experience. He has 'passed through no cleansing fire; no fire of thought, experience, language' (p.161). He faces himself at last as a loose collection of attitudes and postures — unshaped, ungrounded, inwardly dead.

For Raymond this is a linguistic as well as a moral loss. As a journalist, he has associated truth with nouns and pronouns. 'Adjectives blur things, adverbs too; and verbs can falsify. Glenda. That's the truth. Glenda died — less true. Glenda drowned herself. That can't be said in three words' (p.169). The old order had preserved the pure connection between words and things. Truth was a mere matter of naming things that existed in a solid world before words became caught up in the general decay, became slippery and unreliable. Language at last becomes unable to point beyond itself to familiar realities, becomes self-enclosed and empty.

Ray's sense of language literally delimits his world, and this is a cultural as well as a personal loss. The old themes and preoccupations of his grandfather's time return in the late 1970s as repetition and parody. His own son, Gregory, becomes a born-again Christian preaching on the streets, his brain addled by drugs and drink. His daughter echoes her great-grandfather's Emersonian interest in Eastern mysticism by entering an ashram in Auckland and then setting off for India to 'conquer Self' (p.173). This is neither 'the curve of tragic action' which leads to self-discovery nor that of comedy which leads to self-exposure (p.170). It is merely dispersion of energy and degeneration of idea.

The children are drifting. They are flotsam, decked out in the proliferating and meaningless signs of 1970s counter-culture: swastikas, temple bells, skulls, Christianity. All these signs have become undifferentiated and unconnected to the meanings they once stood for. The past has been 'blotted out' for the children (p.175). They are lost.

By the close of *Sole Survivor*, in fact, history itself has disappeared as a meaningful shaping of selfhood or national identity. The structuring core of values and continuities that had made history and self possible have been obliterated by the prevailing shapelessness of experience. Ray's dealings with Alaric Gibbs, Duggie's murderer, delineate the chaos he has entered.

Gibbs, like Ray, is a writer. Seeking the opinion of a successful author, he sends Ray his autobiography, which has been rejected by the publisher to whom he first offered it. Ray himself is engaged in writing a biography of Depression prime minister and national icon, Michael Joseph Savage, and does not want to be distracted. But he is unable to 'put . . . together' the pieces of the Savage biography he has collected (p.177). The thing will not cohere. The gaps will not be filled. The problem is not simply how to give shape to a man's life, how to dispose its elements so as to suggest a coherent personality; it involves relating the outward life, the set of explicit meanings it generated, to the private, essentially chaotic experience of self. Here Alaric Gibbs provides a necessary counterpoint to Ray himself.

Gibbs is little interested in the external 'facts' or the myths which surround public figures. He is interested in 'what goes on underneath' (p.180). His own daughter has been seduced and destroyed by Ray's cousin, Duggie Plumb, and Gibbs suggests to Ray a means of giving shape to the vacancy of the recorded lives of public figures. Listening to Gibbs, Ray's sense of Duggie takes shape and he acknowledges parts of himself that had previously been unknown (p.181). Ray completes his picture of what it is to be human by uncovering the squalid, animal struggle for survival and mastery that lies beneath the orders of humane social organisation. Language itself, the hitherto unexamined enabling condition of his humanism, has become treacherous. For Ray, it now partakes of the jungle. It offers weapons in the ceaseless struggle for dominance.

Here Gee moves into a terrain of the modern that Haley is apparently unaware of. The novel is written from the viewpoint of a reluctant modernism which acknowledges the collapse of its governing principles. Like Patrick White, Gee writes in apparently traditional forms — the realist novel, the family chronicle, the historical novel — while allowing into his fiction the full subversive force of the historical and cultural conditions that make such modes of writing anachronistic. Gee's trilogy is a historical novel which moves towards the negation of history, a family novel which traces the breakdown of family in the triumph of futile egotisms. It is a vast, intricate linguistic order which uncovers a tangle of violence and emptiness behind language itself. It describes the historical decline which undermined the basis of liberal humanism. Ray's grandfather, in his own words, 'knew the powers of evil. They were demonic. You could front up to them like a wrestler. And you fought them with reason and right behaviour. In the cause of man.' That humanism has given way to Duggie's world where evil is nihilistic: 'A vast emptiness. You fight that with a raging in the ego' (p.184).

But Ray has no fight left. He is part of what he records. He sits at home watching soap operas on television. His mistresses discover an emptiness where they had assumed a depth (p.200). Ray is untroubled by his own inner vacancy. He lives almost beyond effect. He hears his own name with its silly obscene pun echoing: 'R. Sole'. He observes Duggie's politics as the ceaseless manipulation of signs with no meaning behind them (p.207). He sees the collapse of parliamentary government as the dawning of the 'age of power'. But power here is pursued for no purpose other than its own possession.

Ray has nothing left within himself with which to oppose Duggie's ruthless, irresistible drive to absolute power. Nor can he resist his utter lack of ideology. When Ray urges the value of the human, the private, the inward, Duggie simply laughs at him (p.208). Duggie exists in a world of pure absence—pastless, guiltless, amoral but endlessly, energetically engaged in the here and now. Ray has glimmerings of the deeps and terrors left over from his humanism and from his old guilt. But he will not enter those terrors and darknesses, seeking a realm of experience and knowledge other than the barren one he inhabits.

Alaric Gibbs, on the other hand, dwells in that darkness and terror. His daughter has been made mad by Duggie, who has destroyed her simply out of boredom or for pleasure. She has been forced by Duggie to engage in sexual practices that 'twist[] her in her soul' (p.215). Of course, in the 'liberated', sexually adventurous 1970s such intimacies were supposedly unrelated to guilt. When Meg spies on her daughter and boyfriend in the earlier novel that bears her name, she voyeuristically anticipates the sin she no longer really believes in. To the daughter, Meg's action is merely 'some barb from another time'.[13] Ray witnesses his own granddaughter Jilly having oral sex in the river at the beginning of the novel and notes only the beauty of the act. His own grandfather would have driven the perpetrators out from Eden as he drove his homosexual son, Alfred. But Jenny Gibbs, a freak with a residual puritan conscience, is driven mad by what has become commonplace.

Reluctantly Gee moves his fiction into the postmodern world. He does so without Wedde's exuberance, without Stead's playfulness, without Frame's extreme linguistic self-consciousness. He moves into it looking over his shoulder to the world of values and meanings it replaces. But move into it he does. In the 1980s, without breaking explicitly with the realist historical novel, Gee moves progressively away from the humanist and realist assumptions that sustained his early fiction.

There is a fairly long gap between the close of the Plumb trilogy and Gee's next novel, *Prowlers* (1987), much longer than that between the novels within the trilogy. In part this hiatus may no doubt be explained by Gee's involvement with other kinds of writing. In this period he wrote the children's books, *The Priests of Ferris* (1984), *Motherstone* (1985), and *The Fire Raiser* (1986), the last of which has strong links to *Prowlers*. But the gap is a telling one. At the close of *Sole Survivor* Gee undercuts the basis of the realist and humanist method he had perfected in his earlier work. Yet he does so without embracing the explicitly postmodern strategies and tendencies that have replaced traditional realism for a number of important writers in the late 1970s and '80s. In a sense, turning to children's literature allowed Gee to write novels that were not realist or humanist, that delighted in lexical play, but did not require him to make a conscious and deliberate break with the perspectives that shaped his early work.

In terms of those formal strategies that shape his fiction Gee characteristically works unconsciously. He does not sit down and read the latest theoretical pronouncements about the state of the novel and the death of the author. He moves slowly, nervously, hesitantly in these matters. But the movements he does make correspond to profound shifts in the cultural and historical attitudes that influence and perhaps generate literary forms. By 1987, after a four-year period in which no adult novels appeared, what was different about Gee's fiction?

As Brian Boyd has noted, *Prowlers* develops Gee's command of his craft by its concentration of experience. Gee, Boyd observes, 'has learned to amplify one central character's life by making it interact with innumerable other lives and times. . . . A white dwarf of a book, it manages to compress an astonishing amount of fictional matter into the densest space and still make it glow.'[14] That is to say, Gee's novel deftly spins a complex web of reference and motif and draws together a vast sweep of historical and family material with extraordinary economy of means. The novel is historical without ever becoming mere factual record. The historical material is focused through a particular consciousness that is selective, partial yet compellingly actualised. There are no clumsy authorial intrusions into the narrative. The characters live as vivid portraits in the realist mode.

Yet the important development in *Prowlers* is not merely a refinement of Gee's technical means as a realist novelist. It consists rather in the pervasive scepticism which the novel directs at language as a reliable means of representing the 'truth' of things. Certainly, the novel still offers that credibility of character and action which are the hallmarks of naturalism and of Gee's fiction. But at the same time the novel slyly calls into question its own use of mimesis. The complicated narrative form of the novel shows how far Gee has moved from the assumption that 'the straight and narrow path to the goal of reality is naturalism'.

Prowlers is narrated by an old man, a scientist named Noel Papps, in the form of a diary to his grand-niece and unofficial nurse, Kate Adams. Kate herself is engaged sporadically in writing a biography of his sister, Labour politician Kitty. The novel, then, is constructed around a complex and interlocking web of writings. All these writings are at one remove at least from the events they describe. They are focused through a consciousness dwelling on its past, casting it into written record for another character who is herself engaged in a different kind of written account. In short, the novel is less concerned with the literariness of life than with the literariness of literature. We are ushered into a self-enclosed and self-reflexive world of words. For all the detail of the novel, its reaching out towards a substantial world, that world is experienced by the narrator as well as the reader as one slipping inexorably into language. The novel still wants to hold its mirror up to nature, but nature continually eludes the novel's narrator and us, who read over his shoulder.

Noel Papps himself, a scientist and seemingly a good positivist, is educated over the course of his life in the intricate ways in which subjectivity always gets caught up in what we observe. As a young man, he regards language as a transparent means of describing external reality. The topologies of science allow him to 'control' external nature which he does not 'trust' to any degree.[15] He desires

181

above all to know the names of things, to establish boundaries, to categorise and analyse. In a remarkable passage he establishes his credo:

To know the name of things is my desire; our only proper knowing is through names. Circles are completed in the noun, margins and boundaries are clear, and we are free from vagueness, free from fear, with every object known from every other. The name, the name, is the single proper epithet.
  And having said that, what about the verb? Isn't breaking down and building up the thing that chemistry is all about? For I'm a chemist. Nouns create a landscape without movement or sound. Nothing happens. Verbs bring activity and change. Yes, I agree with that argument. But I see pre-dication as closer naming. Noun and verb unite in my craft or science. (p.9)

Yet the scientist is betrayed by his own language, which ironically echoes a usage John Locke would certainly have considered fanciful. The last phrase of the quotation recalls a Dylan Thomas poem, 'In My Craft or Sullen Art', where it is the lovers, 'their arms round the griefs of the ages', who unite, while the poet apart exercises his craft or art alone. *Prowlers* is a richly *literary* novel, one the postmodernists would call 'intertextual'. James K. Baxter's poem, 'Wild Bees', is echoed in the storming of the hive/city (p.82). Allen Curnow's refrain from 'Canst Thou Draw Out Leviathan With An Hook?' is echoed in Kate's exclamation facing the nest, 'A big one' (p.78). Edgar Le Grice might have leapt out of Ronald Hugh Morrieson's gothic imagina-tion. Noel's remembered vignette of his sister, Kitty, her skirt hitched up, wading in the river, recalls the famous epiphany of Stephen Dedalus in *A Portrait of the Artist As a Young Man*, watching the wading girl. When Noel writes of his lover Ruth he picks up snatches of T. S. Eliot as he goes along: 'I try to put her down in dry small words. I measure Ruth out in micrograms' (p.174).

Noel Papps comes close to the artist's sense of reality with his awareness of the 'nasty things' as well as the beauty that lie under surfaces, the rich ambiguous life beneath the skin. Moreover, there is nothing positivist (or naturalistic) about his understanding of human personality. He conceives of character as fragmentation rather than consistency: 'I've flown apart. There are bits of me floating off as I spin and spin' (p.3). This is curiously close to the instructions given by postmodernist playwright Sam Shepard to actors of his play, *Angel City*, as to how they are to think of character: '[i]nstead of the idea of a "whole character" with logical motives behind his behaviour. . . he should consider instead a fractured whole with bits and pieces of characters flying off the central theme'.[16] For Noel, individual being 'rests on lawlessness' (p.6). Nature's processes are violent and chaotic. Only the abstract analytic intellect of the scientist manages to control the dark forces of reality. He wants to 'look *straight* at the *single* thing' (p.14). Yet he is obliged to see round corners, to view 'through mirrors cunningly placed' (p.14). There is no escape from obliquity, because the relations between subjects and objects are always governed by opaque and distracting media, in particular, by language.

The business of writing leads Noel to acts that are reprehensible for the scientist. He embellishes, he invents. He dresses up the past in the bright, distorting colours of memory. His description of Edgar Le Grice lighting the fire is closer to expressionism with its wild colours and deliberate distortions than to the sober, denotative style which Locke advocated:

> Edgar Le Grice strikes a match. His red balaclava blooms like a rose. He pulls a piece of rag from his pocket and sets it alight and his hand is on fire; but he doesn't feel, he looks as if he means to eat the flame. Then he leans down and touches sacks and they spring alive, he's printed on the ground of his fire. (p.21)

Noel, like Ray Sole, is both terrified by and preoccupied with emptiness. Like Ray, he is a pattern-maker, one committed to objectivity and rationality. Yet he senses under the skin, behind the structures of things, a mere vacancy that mocks the mind's orders. He pokes his fingers into the science-room skeleton the schoolboys name Miss Montez, 'feeling the hollowness inside' (p.48). This is the form all his acts of possession take.

Like Ray also, he inhabits the late twentieth century reluctantly. Its enthusiams — feminism, consumerism, gay rights, Jesus — appal him. The problem is that all the ideas that once had force in the society — Christianity, for instance — have been turned into commodities. Jesus is advertised on car window stickers like beer (p.69). Whether milk should come in bottles or cartons is a *political* issue. Postmodernity is a world he despises, through which he sees himself as passing 'to somewhere else' (p.69).

But where? There is a moment, contemplating the wasp hole which Kate is about to attack, when Noel discloses a Frameian sense of reality as a bright picture stretched over nothing. It is Kate herself who pictures the black hole in the ground 'going down to nothing', but the vision is just as much the old man's. Noel sees both the beauty and the terror beneath appearances, and he knows that their source is within the human mind itself. Listening to Irene play the piano, he finds that the music 'penetrates dark places in my mind' (p.90). Yet he cannot see anything but confusion of purpose and poverty of execution in her brother's paintings. Royce, like Noel, knows there are depths beneath appearances. Noel acknowledges this later, considering another of his paintings which Royce offers him as a gift, but which he refuses to accept: 'He [Royce] has always been good at things lying underneath; shapes within; shadows under surfaces' (p.223). Royce is bolder in pursuing these deeps than Noel. He wants to 'lift the skin and see large shapes' (p.103). Noel wants to keep what control he has. He knows the deeps, but will not follow them down.

Noel, in his own words, is 'shallow, shifty, a kind of Aral Sea in [his] emotions' (p.94). Faced with any deep emotion, his self threatens to dissolve altogether, to open up a space so great, to thin his being to such a degree, that he fears he might go mad. Unwillingly and in spite of his fetishistic need to exert control, he has entered the postmodern world in which *all* the old certitudes — not only those of science and positivism but also those of language and signification — have given way to a free-floating relativism, a lack of depth, a radical barrenness of being. He has lost contact with 'all that solid, all that real old stuff' of scientific research represented by his schoolboy mentor, Tupp Ogier (p.99). Tupp himself has stared into space terrified by the immeasurable distances that neither mathematics nor instruments can reduce to the human scale. But watching Halley's comet advance 'out of deeps beyond comprehension', he regains his sense of his own being by pure assertion of will (p.99). This is beyond Noel. He is too weightless, featureless. He drifts.

Noel Papps exists in a world of which the moral base has entirely disintegrated. He refuses to judge his friend, Phil Dockery, for forcing an abortion on one of his mistresses, because he is 'no more interested in that than I am in my death' (p.121). He declines to visit Dachau because he does not want to 'face up to Man' (p.131). His vision of the material world is abstract and uncharged by the imagination. It is like Blake's version of Newton's universe of the five senses: 'it's atom and void, a multitude of bodies rolling about and damaging each other when they come close' (p.133). Reality, for Noel, lacks plenitude: it allows no human contact; it has no depth; it discloses no significance.

Why, then, has Gee placed at the centre of his novel a narrator who is himself, as a kind of writer, a counterweight to the novelist? Noel

Papps in his account refuses to allow himself to 'invent' or 'imagine' too much (p.155). He dismisses the urge to shape or structure his narrative as a game, one which he does not deign to indulge in: 'All I'm doing is remembering and putting down. What does it matter how it's shaped?' (p.156). As a writer, he is not one to enter that favourite Gee territory, the 'hard privateness' in the human mind (p.160). The mind in question here belongs to Royce Lomax. To Noel, viewing his paintings, Royce has made no progress as an artist because he has moved away from strict mimesis. He notices only the awkwardness in the work, the distortions, the distance from fact; he misses the expressivity and the power that springs from a mind able to confront its own darknesses and desires and thus meet those which are common to all humans. Noel cannot face visiting the concentration camps because they might confront him not with something alien and inhuman, but with something merely human—with himself.

Yet Noel finds that the exercise of writing his account in itself widens the gap between words and the things and events they are supposed to name. A sly literary self-consciousness creeps into the narrative. Words themselves 'breed words' (p.182). Writing the record he knows will be read by Kate, Noel asks coyly, 'Who is my reader, anyway?' (p.182). Confronted by his own lack of interest as a subject for a narrative, Noel finds almost irresistible the urge to embellish, to play games, to dress up the bare facts, to disguise, to invent. This playfulness is a sign of defeat in the face of his own inadequacies before the past. There is a lack of proportion between the events themselves and their echoes in his mind when he attempts to set them down. The past he dredges up for his story seems 'potent with meaning, ripe with extensions, but always failing to *signify*' (p.192). The deeps in history or in the self are too terrifying and too large in scale for him, so he makes do with games, gestures.

That past — personal and historical — is evoked in a passage when Noel remembers walking with Kitty to the top of a hill and looking down on an unreclaimed stretch of swamp, away from the profitable pastures with fat lambs Noel himself has helped to make. In two brief paragraphs Gee here encapsulates the whole process of colonisation — claiming and reclaiming — that has 'turn[ed] this South Pacific wilderness into the giant dairy farm and sheep run and slaughter-house of today':

First the settlers and soldiers, raw encounter, gaining and getting, then

185

politicians rationalizing theft, then men like me with our improvements. I'm not ashamed, I'm not proud either. That is the way it was. Who comes after? I can't identify them properly. The entrepreneurs and the urban peasants. Kate and Shane come from a different world, I know that much. Big city world, city apprehensions. They don't have much of the loot but they understand it. I never will, and don't want to.

Phil Dockery understands. It's a world he helped to make and lives in happily. That putting up, money and buildings both, 'developing'; and that ripping down, and 'ripping off', as Kate would say. We have gangsters, and Wall Street men, smart-money men, and footpads, hunting packs, and there are fights in the streets, with real knives. And the original owners are acting up. They want back what was theirs and I don't blame them. (pp.204-5)

This is Noel Papps's synopsis of that whole process of nation-making which became so ambiguous in the late 1980s. For Noel the exercise is irreversible. Once begun, the business of 'developing' the 'unreconstructed' world that existed before European habitation has a mechanical inevitability. He has been a part of it and feels no regrets. But he does not see it as heroic. Behind it lies not destiny but greed. And whatever rationale, beyond the mere urge to accumulate, it may once have had has given way in the post-war period to shoddy replication of the crimes of commercial and urbanised societies everywhere. For Noel, it is a process which serves to hold the attention of those immersed in it away from the utter meaningless-ness that governs their lives.

Behind the outward New Zealand — a busy, greedy, meretricious, manufactured paradise — is not merely the swamp of unreclaimed nature but also the void of unreclaimable reality. Noel and Kitty walk through a beech forest to Harkin's Hole. They sit, Noel feeling 'the pull of gravity; of desire'. He wants 'that fall and dark and oblivion; terror, peace. Terror, then nothing, which lies beyond peace and cannot be imagined or spoken of' (p.205). This is a vision oddly close to Janet Frame's familiar one of a terrifying absence behind the furious efforts of New Zealanders to improve the world as it is.

It has been remarked that the structure of the Plumb trilogy is modelled on Joyce Cary's trilogy from the 1940s, *Herself Surprised, To Be a Pilgrim*, and *The Horse's Mouth*.[17] *Prowlers*, though not to the same extent and perhaps not consciously, seems to have been loosely modelled on Patrick White's 1973 novel, *The Eye of the Storm*.

White's novel explores the consciousness of a dying old woman, a society belle left over from the Edwardian period, attended by a young nurse. The old woman stands for inwardness and sensibility, the young woman for extroverted sensuality. By focusing the novel's action through the old woman, White manages to suggest the historical sweep from Edwardian certainties to contemporary hedonism and anomie. His novel embodies that Whitean sense of the twentieth century as a progressive decline into a levelling and rancorous democracy. The old forms and hierarchies break against the materialism and vulgarity of contemporary Australia. At the same time White has placed at the centre of his novel the old woman's experience, while trapped on an island during a hurricane, of a core of self that separates the essential woman from the picture of her which detractors hold. She is redeemed by her vision of a mystery and power at the centre of life.

Prowlers is focused through the consciousness of an old man whose life spans much the same historical period. He is attended by a young woman who stands for 'the modern woman': assertive, feminist, unabashedly pleasure-seeking. Noel Papps is a scientist, a rationalist. He has no mystical experiences. But he has a Whitean sense of the refraction of experience. The image of the crystal in *Prowlers* which conveys Noel's sense of the structure of his narrative and of the self is very like White's favourite motif of the chandelier as an image of the complex ways in which the individual's perception of reality is refracted through the multiple aspects of subjectivity (p.48). Like all White's major characters also, he is preoccupied with the terror and mystery that lie under surfaces. Gee differs from White in the residual force of his humanism. Noel Papps avoids Dachau, which is at the centre of White's anti-humanism. For White, the concentration camps pitched human life in the late twentieth century against the metaphysical. They reinvented good and evil as absolutes that mock rationalism. For Gee, they merely render human life flat and meaningless. The scale of moral possibility has been diminished, but the desire remains for the world in which such judgements were possible, in which the human personality could become caught up in enthusiasms about meaning.

Gee's need — conscious or unconscious — to refer his novels to some prior work is significant. It has nothing to do with any nervousness about his own powers as a writer. But it does suggest the consequences of Gee's unwillingness to confront directly those fundamental assumptions about form that determine how a novelist will proceed. Gee evidently feels a need to protect from too deliberate a scrutiny the intuitional and organic bases of his creativity. Yet at a deep level he has already addressed the criticism which Haley directed at him in the mid 1970s, before the appearance of the Plumb trilogy. At the end of *Sole Survivor* he enacts the historical collapse of those assumptions about subjecthood, meaning, history itself which his earlier fiction had rested on. *Prowlers* inhabits the postmodern world, although the novelist is always looking back to the world that has disappeared and which he clearly prefers. Hence he shows the emptiness behind language, but avoids pure self-reflexivity. Hence he shows the lapse of the self from the assurance and centrality it had assumed in the pre-modern world, but mourns the loss of that depth and the significance it conferred on individual being. Hence he shows history lapsing into incoherence, but continues to tell the story of history as a shaped continuity. In this precarious balancing between worlds lies Gee's achievement as a novelist.

Gee's pictures of New Zealand life are exact and comprehensive. His novels are extraordinarily rich in both social and psychological observation. His historical range is extensive and minutely detailed. In Gee's early work a prodigious authorial effort is directed at concealing the work of fabrication that has gone into the making of the picture. His fictions up to the end of the 1970s are the least self-conscious, the most self-effacing we have. One enters them and walks around, dazed by the precision and scope of the world he has made.

In the extensiveness and detail of its realism, Gee's fiction is the most impressive discussed in this book. He is a more gifted novelist than any of the others in terms of his ability to represent what seems to be not a world, but *the* world, seemingly to lift up a portion of the actual world and hold it before our eyes as readers. Yet this effort of transparent representation, the characteristic expression of Gee's particular talent as a novelist, thwarted the full fictional potential of his work once the historical conditions that had supported realism had passed. In his later novels Gee doesn't altogether abandon realism, but he slyly undercuts it. To some extent he subverts the structures of the novels themselves, though he does so discreetly. In moving beyond realism, without embracing the gameplaying of postmodernism, Gee finds his own ground as a novelist. If, as Frank Kermode suggests, 'research into form' is the essentially modernist means of discovery, then Gee, albeit reluctantly and to some extent unconsciously, is inescapably modern.[18]

Certainly, Gee's novels are never embedded in or enslaved to fact in the way Stevan Eldred-Grigg's *Oracles and Miracles* is. Eldred-

Grigg himself has encouraged this stress on the novel's grounding in fact by making clear its genesis in oral historical record.[19] If readers assumed that *Oracles and Miracles* offered them a direct transcription of the real and wrote letters to the author telling him they recognised their own lives in his novel (which is like writing letters to Coronation Street, in Simon During's memorable phrase),[20] the fault was partly the author's, who chose the historian's (though not the journalist's) subservience to factual record over the novelist's limitless scope as 'maker'. Gee's truth is pre-eminently that of the novelist, the maker of fictions, even where his novels are least flamboyant. This is a sign both of modesty and of force.

CONCLUSION

Violent Dualities

He often asked her what she was thinking about, but it was impossible to tell. (Once, he complained that the blurb on the back of a book of women's fiction said, 'What women are writing *about*' (his italics). 'It should say 'What women are writing,''' he said.) She said, 'I am not thinking about anything, I am just thinking.'
ANNE KENNEDY, 'An Angel Entertains Theatricals'[1]

IN 1972 a new edition of *The Art of Australia* by art critic Robert Hughes appeared. It was a time when the market for Australian painting was aggressively bullish. A new, wealthy, art-consuming bourgeoisie had appeared in Sydney and Melbourne whose eagerness to advance themselves socially by the acquisition of 'culture' accompanied an unabashed nationalism. By placing local artists' works on their walls they were announcing the repudiation of the cultural cringe by the Australian middle class. No longer was it socially expedient to disguise an Australian accent, defer to English taste and standards, or deck the lounge wall with reproduction Constables in mock-gilt frames. 'An ebullient bourgeois society', observed Hughes, 'which loves culture as a badge, but lacks discrimination, has developed a taste for a homogeneous and self-contained — that is, purely Australian — art.'[2]

As Hughes went on to say, 'It gets what it wants; but to speak of an Australian cultural explosion, for no reason but that a lot of Australians are painting, is meaningless. Australia also has a knitting explosion and a cooking explosion, equally to be accounted for in terms of the abundance of Australian wool and steak.' In other words, increases in quantity (or art-auction prices) do not automatically denote increases in quality.

The New Zealand fiction scene in the middle-to-late 1980s looked very much like the Australian art scene in the late 1960s and early '70s. More New Zealand books were being produced and sold. The longstanding domination of the market by mainstream English titles marketed by the local distribution agents of the English publishing houses was no longer as pronounced as it had been until the early 1980s. The New Zealand branches of Penguin, Heinemann, and Hodder and Stoughton eagerly sought out local titles and marketed them aggressively and successfully. Increasingly, New Zealand novels in expensive hardback editions were appearing in suburban bookshelves where *Readers' Digests, National Geographics* (and perhaps *An Encyclopaedia of New Zealand*) used to hold sole sway.

Belatedly, New Zealand was witnessing the rise of a self-conscious, culture-consuming, nationalistic middle class, just as Canada did under Trudeau in the late 1960s and Australia under Whitlam in the early 1970s. That is no bad thing, of course. A substantial market for local literature is the necessary condition of a developed national literary culture with a variety of literary and critical journals, decent reviewing organs, a body of substantial texts that might make possible a reliable system of discriminations. Yet we should be cautious about the extravagant claims that are sometimes made about local writing. The emergence of a substantial middle-class reading public with an appetite for 'purely' New Zealand fiction will no doubt aid the development of the New Zealand novel, but it is no guarantee that better novels and short stories will be produced in the 1990s than were produced in the 1930s and '40s when the reading public was much smaller. It is certainly premature to be discovering 'renaissances' in our writing on the grounds of what we have to hand.

*   *   *

In 1983, when Peter Simpson surveyed fiction published in the years 1981-82 for the first number of the *Journal of New Zealand Literature*, he noted that there had been few new novels of substance over recent years 'but collections of short stories [had] been fairly numerous'.[3] In the two years under survey, in fact, no fewer than fifteen collections of stories had been published, while only half a dozen novels worthy of notice had appeared. Part of the explanation for this, according to Simpson, was that 'a vigorous national tradition of short story writing' sustained the story writer, while the novelist had little 'in the way of a usable tradition to guide and ease his progress'.[4] Story writers had the overwhelming fact of the Sargesonian tradition which they could continue, modify, or react against. Novelists were obliged to proceed as solitary practitioners, struggling to bring into existence a tradition not yet born.

By 1988 the case was very different indeed. In that year there were sixteen novels and two collections of short stories submitted by their publishers to contest the New Zealand Book Awards. It is true that in the following year the balance swung back partially towards the story. In 1989 nine collections of stories were submitted for the fiction award. But the novel was still the preferred form, with eighteen submissions.[5] The dominant literary form in New Zealand in the late 1980s was the novel, and this marked a significant departure from the longstanding preference for the short story. Moreover, in number of publications, range of subject, and quality of production the end of the decade offered a considerably more lively fiction scene than the beginning. The question was, did that increase in activity represent an increase in quality? Had some significant breakthrough been achieved in local fiction? Had the blinkered 'masculine realist' viewpoint of the Sargeson tradition been abandoned for a new diversity of representations and modes of writing?

The important differences between 1983 and 1988 derive not so much from the forging of a specific tradition in the novel as in the discovery that a substantial market existed for novels. The short story had remained pre-eminent for so long not only because of the continued force of the Sargeson tradition but also because of the smallness and homogeneity of the reading public, a reading public brought into existence in large part by Sargeson himself. While Mansfield had had to leave New Zealand to gain an audience sympathetic to international modernism, Sargeson had returned after his time in Europe to write against the limits and prejudices of the available readership. That effort itself nurtured a small audience that shared the writer's own sense of alienation from the culture.

From the 1950s onwards (in spite of a period in the late 1950s and early '60s when the novel gained ground against the short story),[6] this readership was largely satisfied by the short story form as Sargeson had established it: that is, as a means of mounting a critique of the dominant culture and as a fairly strictly observed set of formal conventions. Stories were published in *Landfall*, the *Listener* and, after 1972, *Islands*, then collected and published in book form after an appropriate space of time. Thus a reading public for serious local literature which probably numbered a few hundred at most was satisfied by a form particularly suited to its needs, dimensions, and tastes. The stories circulated inside a small, familiar world that shared common assumptions about and aversions towards the larger culture. By the late 1980s the market for short stories had not diminished but it had changed significantly.

The extent of that change was shown by the variety of kinds of stories included in *The Penguin Book of Contemporary New Zealand Short Stories*, edited by Susan Davis and Russell Haley, which appeared in 1989. In the 1950s, '60s and '70s the popular Oxford series of anthologies of New Zealand short stories, edited first by Dan Davin, then by C. K. Stead, and then by Vincent O'Sullivan, had reflected a general homogeneity of taste and style in the relative sameness of the stories included and in the confident tone adopted by the successive editors. Lydia Wevers's fourth series of Oxford short stories, published in 1984, showed the breakup of this homogeneity by the tensions in its introduction and in the selections themselves.[7] By 1989 Davis and Haley evidently felt easy about allowing the different trends, kinds, and constituencies represented in their anthology to live together.

The three main trends represented in *The Penguin Book of Contemporary New Zealand Short Stories* were the experimental, the traditional, and the socially critical. But these three kinds of story writing were not grouped into different sections. They were tendencies or dispositions to be found with different degrees of emphasis and preference throughout the stories in the anthology; they overlapped. Two other important trends need to be mentioned which had emerged as story writers adjusted to a changing readership. Essentially, the writers sought either to hold on to an existing audience or to reach potential audiences.

Firstly, there was the emergence of the story written for the glossy magazines. Since the 1970s a number of large circulation monthly magazines like *Metro, More*, and *North and South* had appeared, in addition to the two weekly magazines which had traditionally dominated the entire New Zealand market: the *Listener* and the *New Zealand Women's Weekly*. These new journals catered to more specialised readerships than the weeklies without aiming at the readers of the literary journals. They wanted stories by 'name' authors that were more sophisticated than the popular romances of the *Women's Weekly* and less earnest than the usual *Listener* or *Landfall* stories. They wanted well-written, entertaining stories and were prepared to pay up to ten times more than the established literary journals. Hence they attracted a substantial body of writers ranging from Rosie Scott, Lauris Edmond, and Graeme Lay to Vincent O'Sullivan, Kevin Ireland, and C. K. Stead. Most of these, of course, had traditionally written for literary journals and continued to do so. The effect of the well-paying glossies was to develop a particular kind of story — accessible but undemanding, competently crafted but formally unadventurous — which could regularly be issued in bumper Christmas numbers of *Metro* or in the anthologies, *Metro Fiction*.

Secondly, writing anti-realist short fiction became a less marginal activity during the 1980s. In a review of Michael Morrissey's *The New Fiction*, Stead characterises most postmodern fiction in the anthology as 'minor offshoots from the major stem of fiction'.[8] But this criticism is based on too confident an assumption about where exactly that 'major stem' is to be found. It involves a sense of tradition that too readily defines orthodoxies and heresies. Certainly, Morrissey lays himself open to such criticism by his apocalyptic understanding of literary history, by looking for sudden leaps into new kinds of writing rather than continuities with established kinds. But as Stead's own fiction shows, by the mid 1980s anti-realistic strategies had become the stock in trade of established and avowedly traditional writers as well as of the experimental writers clustered round the little magazines and English department cliques. By 1989 *The Penguin Book of Contemporary New Zealand Short Stories* was able to represent the formal 'edge' of short story writing as found not only in surrealists and postmodernists but also in established and traditional writers.

The short story in the late 1980s showed little sign of exhaustion. Writers like Vincent O'Sullivan, Owen Marshall, and Damien Wilkins continued to produce stories as a development of a longstanding preference for the form in New Zealand writing. For these, the short story is a form in its own right, with particular strengths arising from its compression and its history of distinguished practitioners in this country, not a kind of lesser novel. Barbara Anderson's *I Think We Should Go Into the Jungle* (1988) showed that the story form is still attracting practitioners attentive to craft, drawing on their precursors while cautiously extending and updating linguistic and formal possibilities.

A number of writers continued to use the story form as the vehicle of social observation and critique. The stories of Patricia Grace, whose *Electric City and Other Stories* appeared in 1987, address racial issues in New Zealand. Others responded to a substantial market for well-written stories that offer recognisable portraits of contemporary New Zealand life. Fiona Kidman, whose *Unsuitable Friends* was published in 1988, and Marilyn Duckworth, whose *Explosions in the Sun* appeared in 1989, write assured and observant studies of contemporary middle-class lifestyles, the latter with more comic panache than the former. Their subjects are the family, sexual relations, infidelity. Albert Wendt's stories manage to be both fabulist in form and politically engaged in content.

Nevertheless, in the late 1980s the short story was no longer the prestigious or the dominant form as it had been in the 1940s, '50s and '60s. The energies of New Zealand's most inventive and prominent fiction writers had moved towards the novel to meet the demands of a substantial and heterogeneous readership for that form. Publishers had become noticeably more receptive to novels and eager to persuade short-story writers to write novels instead.

The increased interest in the novel as a form in the late 1980s reflected the breakup of the familiar world of readers that had waited for the next number of *Landfall* or *Islands* and a new batch of stories by Sargeson, Gaskell, Duggan, Stead, O'Sullivan. The novels of Gee had substantially enlarged that world; *the bone people*'s success indicated that a new kind of reading public had emerged, one receptive to sprawling novels which ignored the decorums of Sargesonian good writing and one which adopted a different stance towards the dominant culture. The aversion towards the repressions of lower-middle-class Pakeha culture had not disappeared; but those holding that aversion were no longer a clique of disgruntled intellectuals. Anti-puritanism had become a dominant social attitude.

The old church-going, respectable, puritan culture of red-roofed suburbia had finally been swamped by the hedonist bourgeois culture that had begun to emerge in the early post-war period. Bill Pearson had remarked on the trend in 1952, predicting, as Lawrence Jones notes, that 'if the old puritanism died it would be replaced, "not by a more liberal, humanist spirit, but by a shallow and sneering hedonism"'.[9] In the mid 1980s there was a rapid extension of wealth to an arriviste middle class which wore its nationalism 'as a badge'. Middle-class suburbia prospered and found both its consumerist aspirations and its cultural anxieties expressed in *Metro*. In the inner city suburbs of Auckland yuppies were moving in on the aging hippies, art students, and unemployed of the Ponsonby demi-monde.

The old homogeneous reading public was inevitably and irreversibly breaking up into discrete groups.

For the newly rich of the middle eighties a distinctive national culture was as desirable a sign of having arrived as a deregulated finance sector, a thriving wine industry, and chic restaurants. Even the commercial middle class, from which Sargeson to his lasting horror had sprung, had become more conspicuously pleasure-seeking than sin-bound. Puritanism still figured in the culture, of course, but it was now more likely to be encountered among feminists than among suburban citizens. As jokes in *Metro* about the temperance-dominated suburb Mt Roskill indicated, the church-going lower-middle-class had shrunk in extent and in influence. It was no longer the oppressive norm but the object of glib ridicule. Henceforth, the artist as Man Alone, standing apart and aloof from the dominant culture, would be obliged to adopt a conservative rather than a liberal stance. Certainly, Keri Hulme, for all the rhetorical antagonism her novel directs at Pakeha 'monoculture', is not *outside* Pakeha culture as Mulgan, Hyde, Sargeson, Gaskell, and Hilliard were. Her criticism was assimilated remarkably swiftly and her book appeared on university English courses within three years of publication.

The bone people was difficult in both manner and subject matter; yet it sold as no New Zealand novelist's work had since the yarns of Barry Crump became popular in the early sixties. Its criticism of middle-class, Pakeha culture seemed to continue that of Hilliard and Finlayson, those Pakeha writers who found in the Maori an irresistible compensating image for New Zealand suburban values. The difference was that while Hilliard and Finlayson had addressed a liberal Pakeha audience — the school teachers, civil servants, and librarians who read *Landfall* and the book pages of the *Listener* — Hulme's novel was addressed to the nation *as a whole* and called for a general change of cultural bearings, a reformulation of the nation itself. In 1984-85 — the extended honeymoon period of the new Labour Government — a substantial section of the populace felt a broad sympathy for this call.

It is true that *the bone people* sold so spectacularly well in New Zealand because it appealed to middle-class white people. That accounts for the sheer numbers of copies sold. Stories of the book's being sought in tiny, isolated Maori communities are exaggerated in terms of their effect on the book's overall sales. They serve the myth that the novel sprang out of the earth of Aotearoa and thus made a signal and exemplary break with the male, white, middle-class, and 'monocultural' tradition of fiction derived from Sargeson. The novel's impressive sales figures did not depend on its interest among sections of the population previously ignored by the publishing industry — women and Maori, in particular — but on its confirmation of a core of attitudes which were at the centre of a widespread nationalistic mood: anti-cosmopolitanism, anti-colonialism, the desire for gods to replace the puritan ones the populace had ceased to worship.

Nevertheless, the appeal of *the bone people* cut across the traditional class and to some extent racial lines of the New Zealand fiction-reading public. Hulme's book rapidly became a cultural icon. While in large measure its success was owed to the desire among many middle-class Pakeha (male as well as female) to redefine their own identity in terms that were confidently local, special, and indigenous, such desires were not confined to this group. The important change in readership signalled by *the bone people*'s success was not that it was bought and read by people other than middle-class Pakeha novel-readers, but that its readers no longer saw themelves as belonging to a circle of humane intellectuals surrounded by hordes of wowsers.

After *the bone people*'s singular success, the publishing houses overcompensated for prior caution by building up local fiction titles as quickly as possible and by getting books into print to capitalise on the newly discovered extent of the market. Books were published that should have been rejected, apparently simply because they were there, like the films that were frantically produced in the period of grace given by Sir Robert Muldoon in the early 1980s to the tax dodgers who had backed the local film industry. As Anne French, managing editor of Oxford University Press, has written of Rachel McAlpine's 1986 novel *The Limits of Green*, the 'quite remarkable' enthusiasm shown by publishers for fiction had some decidedly 'unfortunate' results.[10] Such lack of discrimination by publishers serves the interests of neither writers nor readers. Certainly, there was a notable slump in fiction standards during the eighteen months after the publication of *the bone people*.

The year 1984 saw the publication of *the bone people* and *All Visitors Ashore*, which prompted Lawrence Jones to compare it to 1957-8, an *annus mirabilis* when *Owls Do Cry* and Ian Cross's *The God Boy* both appeared.[11] In 1985 a number of minor novels were published — Don Binney's *Long Lives the King*, Ian Middleton's *Sunflower*, Heather Marshall's *A Nest of Cuckoos* — none of which bore what Curnow has called 'the marks of permanence'.[12] Some major novels appeared from 1986 on — Stead, Wedde, Frame, Ihimaera all brought out important new works. In 1986 Shadbolt's *Season of the Jew* and Grace's *Potiki* appeared. Gee's *Prowlers* appeared in 1987. Some lively new novelists appeared in the late eighties: Elizabeth Knox, Lloyd Jones, Rosie Scott, Gregory O'Brien, and Nick Hyde, among others.

But how many of them, in the words of the blurb writer for Mike Johnson's *Anti Body Positive* (1988), 're-draw the parameters of New Zealand's literary tradition'?[13] Much of the criticism of contemporary New Zealand fiction has been concerned to break with established traditions, to find ruptures with existing patterns, or to extend persistent thematic dualities from the past into the present scene. Michael Morrissey sees a postmodernist breakthrough occurring in New Zealand fiction in the 1980s.[14] Lydia Wevers sees a sharp break with the ruling Sargeson line towards a new diversity of representations and styles. Lawrence Jones sees a continuation of the two separate lines derived from Mansfield and Sargeson. Heather Roberts sees a continuation and culmination of a counter-tradition of women's writing running from Edith Grossmann to Keri Hulme. The literature, it would seem, serves as a mirror which conveniently reflects the preoccupations of the critic, and in the 1980s critics have tended to be preoccupied with downgrading the formerly pre-eminent 'masculine realist' tradition, some because it is masculine, some because it is realist.

To invoke the idea of tradition is to insist — not dogmatically or in a spirit of nationalist assertion — that the accumulation of writing in a given place over time exerts a shaping influence on succeeding generations of writers. The important question, if we wish to determine what it means to talk of a *New Zealand* tradition in fiction, is how do *these* writers revise, extend, modify, react against their significant local precursors? It is by the forcefulness of their engagements with earlier writers that contemporary writers signal where the significant developments are taking place.

How many of the novels published in the late eighties genuinely 'redrew' that tradition? How many even engaged with, far less reshaped, it? The year 1988 was representative. Five years after the publication of *the bone people* more novels were being published. Novels were generally better presented and better marketed than they had been in the early eighties. The novel seemed to be flourishing as a form and 1988 was as notable for its minor works as for its successes. In fact, only one major new novel appeared, *The Carpathi-ans*. But in the same year novels appeared by Lloyd Jones, Rosie Scott, Mike Johnson, Michael Jackson, Noel Virtue, and Anne Kennedy which showed, in spite of flaws in execution, the various energies of the fiction scene, the discontents with old habits and forms, and the unsteady attempts to fashion new kinds of writing.

Lloyd Jones's second novel, *Splinter*, is illustrative. It is an ambi-tious novel that shows plentiful evidence of the author's wide and intelligent reading. He knows his local precursors, but is unawed by them and is capable of witty references to Morrieson, Sargeson, and Mansfield. He has also learned from Salman Rushdie, Peter Carey, and other international novelists the strategies of magic realism which he experiments with in his own fiction. Jones *imagines* New Zealand history and does not bully his readers by projecting on to the past contemporary views of history's crimes and errors. The school-yard enactment of the Land Wars in *Splinter* is both hilarious and accusatory because it is so exuberantly and self-consciously playful; it is history fictionalised rather than turned into rhetoric. His novels so far have been attempts to develop a kind of realism that is tolerant of exaggeration and distortion without indulging in the gothic ex-cesses of Morrieson or the fantasy of Hulme, McAlpine, and Ihimaera.

Jones inventively confronts a problem that is a longstanding one for New Zealand fiction writers. It is the problem Robert Chapman alludes to in his essay, 'Fiction and the Social Pattern', first published in *Landfall* in 1953. As Chapman puts it: 'Place New Zealand society behind the hierarchical time-cut fretwork of English society and its lower middle class would nearly cover all our variety'.[15] In other words, in a country whose population has been characteristically small-town or suburban, how is the writer to render its history and forms of social life interesting in a novel? Sargeson's solution was partly a narrative one — he focused his stories through marginalised figures — and partly stylistic — he affected an elaborately vernacular prose style whose seeming realism is richly concentrated and self-consciously mannered. Jones's solution is to 'distort and heighten the ordinariness of New Zealand life without turning it into outrageous fantasy'.[16] If the method remains to be fully achieved in the fiction, it offers a promising way of coping with an old problem.

Michael Jackson's finely written first novel *Rainshadow* is as pol-ished as the poems for which he is better known. *Rainshadow* is deft in its handling of character and states of mind, assured in its evocation of atmosphere. But its strategies for coping with the old problem of the lack of range of New Zealand life are less successful than Jones's are. The narrative rests on an element of cultural wish fulfilment that makes the conclusion of the novel unsatisfactory. Jackson takes up the familiar theme of identity, and seems to avoid the essentialist bias which colours its treatment in Hulme's fiction. The hero's struggle towards self-understanding and self-definition is presented as an ongoing process rather than as a preliminary to the discovery of some pre-existing identity imposed by birth or race. As one of the characters puts it, 'Who we are isn't something inherent. There's no fixed identity . . . something we can go and dig up or discover readymade. Surely we've all got to give birth to ourselves.'[17]

Yet Jackson falls into the trap of echoing a prevalent cultural wish to discover authentic belonging in New Zealand by identification with the indigenous. Jackson's hero, raised a Pakeha, discovers the secret of his Maori maternity. This discovery confers on him an authenticity lacking in the hectoring interest taken in things Maori by his Lawrentian poet friend, Jonathan Bogsanyi. The novel thus enacts that dream of the Pakeha to which Janet Frame refers in *A State of Siege*: the desire to 'disown' parents and imagine oneself 'adopted', hence new , exciting, redefined.[18] This is an inverted 'post-colonial' version of the Victorian fantasy of the lost child, raised in poverty, who turns out to have concealed parents and an inheritance that has been denied him.

Mike Johnson's *Anti Body Positive* employs a range of styles, from straightforward realism to Kafkaesque fantasy and science fiction. Yet all this, apparently 'postmodern' pastiche, has none of the troubled sense of the lack of depth of contemporary social forms that we find in Thomas Pynchon's frenetic, complicated novels of the 1960s and '70s. Postmodernism in the work of Pynchon or Wedde or the playwright Sam Shepard is not a mere reflection of the meaninglessness and superficiality of contemporary social forms; it contains a criticism of that lack of depth, a yearning for the fuller kinds of experience that were available in previous, less image-saturated, cultures. For this anguished looking backwards Johnson substitutes pop philosophising about the death of Western culture. Cobbled together from apocalypticism, sexual fantasy, and AIDS paranoia, *Anti Body Positive* lacks intellectual or literary force.

Rosie Scott's *Glory Days* breaks with the Sargeson tradition by trading its understated realism for a hectic naturalism. Her prose has a racy toughness, edged with sentimentalism, that recalls at times Damon Runyon. Yet her novel has much in common with Sargeson's fiction in terms of its concentration on marginal characters, its bohemian-criminal-deviant milieu. Her scenes are crowded with low-life types and extravagant events. *Glory Days* has been described as 'That Summer' updated.[19] One notes also the re-emergence in the book of the anti-domesticity theme, apparently ingrained in New Zealand fiction, masculine or feminine.

A 'tradition' is not 'redrawn' merely because some contemporary writers find its weight oppressive and decide to break with it, either by representing kinds of social experience it has excluded or by employing kinds of writing it has avoided. It is redrawn where a writer uses it *consciously* as a background to his or her own writing without merely writing in a dated style. If *Glory Days* shows that a tradition is present even in writing that seems removed from its ancestors within that tradition, Noel Virtue's *The Redemption of Elsdon Bird* shows that tradition is not reaffirmed by the mere effort of repeating its habitual forms. *Elsdon Bird,* a popular and critically well-received 1988 novel, returns to a central motif of the Sargeson tradition with its story of a sensitive young boy's upbringing in a life-denying puritan household. The action of the novel, with the murder of fundamentalist parents by another boy who fears the effect their fierce religion will have on his younger siblings, crosses familiar Sargeson territory. The prose style in its harsh simplicity is that of classic Sargeson. The theme of the artist's necessary alienation from the puritan culture is also Sargesonian. Even the blowfly in Jack's anecdote in 'The Hole That Jack Dug' turns up in Virtue's book, and Elsdon, like the young Frank, has a sympathetic homosexual uncle. Virtue is 'traditional' in the sense that he writes in the manner of some previous writer or period style. He writes as though nothing significant had occurred in literary historical terms since 1950; and this is not to place him in the Sargesonian line.

Tradition in its full sense means writing out of a sense of the past — of what that past has left us that is significant now — without losing that historical sense that recognises how the habits and manners and styles of the past are continually being reformulated in the present. Of the novels published in 1988 Janet Frame's *The Carpathians* most strongly engages with previous New Zealand fiction as though it constitutes a respected, acknowledged, continual presence. But something of the force of that engagement with a literary ancestry is evident, in spite of uncertainties, in a first novel by Anne Kennedy, *100 Traditional Smiles*.

Kennedy's most important debt is to Frame herself. She shares Frame's intense engagement with the word, and her writing is characterised by a Framean linguistic playfulness. Kennedy's method is to penetrate the endless possibilities of the word itself, to explore the bizarre and humorous collocations and dislocations made possible by words. She is more interested in extending the linguistic and formal range of New Zealand fiction than in expanding the material of 'real life' on which fiction supposedly draws. Even a very early story, 'Jewel's Darl', which was adapted for television and was widely read as a direct transcription of life, is utterly steeped in *literature*. The title itself shows how far removed is her work from the naturalism which usually goes with the subject of the story: the harrowing lives of transvestites. Jewel and Darl are two characters in William Faulkner's novel, *As I Lay Dying*.

When Kennedy writes in *100 Traditional Smiles* that her narrator envies the graphic artist's ability 'to disappear without the obligatory puff of smoke', she recalls the disappearance of Tommy in *Living in the Maniototo*. [20] When she writes of how the New York power blackout of 1966 'made the language of electrical appliances including blanketings of snow quite useless', she draws directly on Mavis Halleton's reflection in *Living in the Maniototo* on the way in which agriculture determines linguistic imagery in New Zealand and automobiles give rise to the predominant imagery in California.[21]

Frame's influence on Kennedy's novel is lopsided. She mines the rich lode in Frame which looks at the ways in which language governs the production of imagery in a culture and thus shapes reality itself and leaves as dross Frame's story-telling powers. *100 Traditional Smiles* is an apprentice book whose engagement with language and representation needs to be tempered by those skills at narrative and characterisation Frame herself so abundantly possesses. Kennedy has divided her attentions, writing 'stories' for television and 'art' for the little magazines. In time, no doubt, she will learn to join the separate strengths, as they are so richly joined in Frame's own fiction. What is most promising here is the directness of Kennedy's engagement with a major writer she seeks not to emulate but to assimilate. In such an engagement one would expect the influence in a first novel to be prominent. It takes time for so strong an influence to be subdued and worked into the total achievement. Kennedy promises much because she seeks to extend the formal and linguistic possibilities of fiction, not simply the amount and variety of life it can contain. Her attention is always on the word as well as the world.

Clearly, there are more diverse kinds of fiction being written than was the case a decade ago. A new range of representations of New Zealand social life is being offered. There are signs of a new and more sophisticated appetite for local works among the fiction-reading public. Moreover, as Margaret Mahy points out in a review of Gregory O'Brien's *Diesel Mystic* (1989), although '[e]stablished novelistic forms are still in evidence . . . the novel is also mutating into challenging shapes and making unexpected demands on the intuition of a reader'.[22] But, the continuities with earlier New Zealand writers are as striking as the departures taken. Mansfield is glimpsed in *Symmes Hole* and Sargeson stalks through *All Visitors Ashore*. It is premature to claim that a leap beyond the tradition of New Zealand fiction exemplified by Sargeson has been achieved, when writers as various as Frame, Marshall, and Stead continue to draw on Sargeson and when young writers like Kennedy continue to draw on Frame. Here are to be found the enriching attentions to earlier writers that over a period of time make a literature 'something different, something/Nobody counted on'.[23] It is by this concentration on form and language, not by any sudden leaps to other kinds of experience or modes of representation, that influence passes from one writer to another. Where it is is not present, the writers all too often return blindly to the themes and procedures of a previous generation.

In *Where Did She Come From? New Zealand Women Novelists, 1862–1987* Heather Roberts observes that in the work of most of the historical novelists of the 1930s 'the use of history was an escape'.[24] In the late 1980s novelists showed a determination to confront the problems of New Zealand history. Wedde, Ihimaera, and Shadbolt all produced historical novels which examine the originating events of New Zealand as a society born out of the conflict of vastly different interests, races, and cultures. Stevan Eldred-Grigg's very popular *Oracles and Miracles* (1987) extends and updates this historical theme and interest by working in the period from the 1930s to the present. But this concern to dramatise and reinterpret the past went with a moralising tendency that produced a contemporary version of the historical romance (or romanticised history) in *The Matriarch* and *the bone people.* In the thirties fiction tended to fall into simple binary oppositions: romances and historical novels. In the late eighties the two tendencies could be found in the same text.

The historical trend in the novel reinforced a general interest in reevaluating New Zealand's past in anti-colonialist terms that found expression in a number of crucial texts in the late eighties. Claudia Orange's *The Treaty of Waitangi* (1987) and James Belich's *The New Zealand Wars and the Victorian Interpretation of Racial Conflict* (1986) are the most significant efforts to redefine New Zealand identity since 1959-60 when, respectively, Keith Sinclair's *A History of New Zealand* and W. H. Oliver's *The Story of New Zealand* appeared. While Orange and Belich concentrate on the importance of racial conflict in the formation of a New Zealand identity, Jock Phillips in *A Man's Country? The Image of the Pakeha Male, a History* (1987) focuses on gender as well as race. A number of anthology introductions, notably Wedde's introduction to *The Penguin Book of New Zealand Verse* and Lydia Wevers's introduction to *Yellow Pencils: an Anthology of Poetry by Women,* and essay collections with titles such as *Culture and Identity in New Zealand* (1989) and *Te Whenua, te Iwi: The Land and the People* (1987) extended the general effort to re-examine the nationalist interpretation of New Zealand identity formulated by an earlier generation of Pakeha historians and cultural commentators in the 1950s.

In the 1980s each of the major cultural authorities who came to prominence in the post-war period was criticised by politicised younger writers. While the years 1957-60 saw the consolidation of a generation of literary nationalists, with the appearance of crucial essays, anthologies, histories and novels, the years around 1985 saw the emergence of a new generation of fretful sons and daughters, eager to speak for the groups the fathers had omitted. Curnow's 1960 *Penguin Book of New Zealand Verse* is revised on bicultural lines by Wedde's and McQueen's 1985 anthology. *An Introduction to New Zealand Painting, 1839-1967* (1969), by Gordon H. Brown and Hamish Keith, is opposed by Francis Pound's anti-nationalist *Frames on the Land: Early Landscape Painting in New Zealand* (1983). Sinclair is subject to attack by Eldred-Grigg on the grounds that his *History*'s nationalism suppresses a host of differences within New Zealand — differences of region, class, race, and gender. Moreover, Eldred-Grigg's attacks on Sinclair are published in *Landfall,* founded by

Brasch in 1947 to promote New Zealand literature and establish a high cultural 'tradition'.[25]

In other words, approaching the sesquicentenary, the culture was as interested in its history as it had been in the years around the centenary. Its novelists responded to this interest by and large without offering merely flattering images of the country. They explored the nation's anxieties about the cultural and racial problems of the present by dramatising them in terms of the crucial conflicts and encounters of the past. Nevertheless, reading through the fiction of the late 1980s, it is difficult to avoid the conclusion that the nation was let off lightly. By way of comparison, the writers of the late 1930s and '40s saw the writer's role in terms expressed by James K. Baxter: 'to purge themselves "of a lie commonly held to be the truth and begin to speak meaningfully" by voicing the unpalatable truth "that we now live in an Unjust City"'.[26] As Lawrence Jones observes, the response to the centennial celebrations of 1940 by writers like Glover, Curnow, and Sargeson was strongly antagonistic. Viewing the Pakeha cultural identity and their relation to it in a critical way, they saw the centennial not as the occasion for the 'literary self-congratulation' occasioned by Queen Victoria's Jubilee in 1890 but as a time to focus on the country's failures.[27] The works these writers offered to the nation around the centennial year — Curnow's 'Island and Time', Sargeson's *A Man and his Wife*, Glover's 'Centennial' — all contributed to what Curnow was later to call 'the anti-myth about New Zealand which a few of us poets — and almost nobody else — were so busy making in those years'.[28]

Only Stead and Frame in the late eighties criticise the Pakeha in their fiction as directly and forcefully as did the writers of 1940, and they do so in much the same terms. They mount a critique of the prevailing myths of the Pakeha. Wedde, Hulme, and Ihimaera criticise the Pakeha also, but they do so in terms acceptable to many Pakeha. Wedde's *Penguin Book of New Zealand Verse* has proved very popular in schools. Hulme and Ihimaera are revered as Glover, Curnow, and Sargeson were (and are) not. Moreover, there has been no concerted effort among writers in the late 1980s to create what Curnow calls an 'anti-myth'. In *the bone people* we see the typical Pakeha (there are surprisingly few Pakeha in the novel) in terms that the generation of the 1930s would have substantially agreed with: racist, conformist, and dull, if not puritan. But in the same novel we also see a revival of the myth that the earlier generation so trenchantly opposed, the myth or dream of New Zealand as a South Seas paradise. Near the end of *the bone people* Kerewin has a dream in which she returns to her ruined tower:

She touched the threshold, and the building sprang straight and rebuilt, and other buildings flowed out of it in a bewildering colonization. They fit onto the land as sweet and natural as though they'd grown there.
The karangatia grows wilder, stronger.
The light bursts into the bright blue daylight, and the people mill round, strangely clad people, with golden eyes, brown skin, all welcoming her.
They touch and caress with excited yet gentle hands and she feels herself dissolving piece by piece with each touch. She diminishes to bones, and the bones sink into the earth which cries 'Haere mai!' and the movement ceases.
The land is clothed in beauty and the people sing. (p.446)

Here the process of colonisation is reversed as Kerewin comes 'home' to her people and to the spiritualised land of Aotearoa. The old Pakeha myth of Eden has been transposed to the pre-European Maori world, which opens up to include those Pakeha who have refashioned themselves in Maori terms. The criticism of the Pakeha remains, but it has been subsumed into a myth that underlies the nation's foundation. The novel, seeming to oppose the Pakeha, affirms the myth of perfectability that has sustained their nationalism. As the decade closed this myth was resurrected and reformulated for the sesquicentennial celebrations.

What is most surprising in the late 1980s is the absence of satire in fiction. There are exceptions such as the brilliant, scatological *Kisses in the Nederends* (1987) by Tongan novelist, Epeli Hau'ofa, where the satire is only incidentally directed at New Zealand. There are also paler attempts by Keith Ovenden and Marilyn Duckworth. Yet it is difficult to think of a period in New Zealand social history when the age has offered richer fare to the satirist. The period of the Lange Government was marked by mass addiction to bizarre economic fads, sudden reversals of public policy, radical shifts in taste, the spectacular rise and fall of a new class, and, above all, by a massive gap between political language and the reality it purported to describe. Yet the absurdities and injustices of the late eighties gave rise to no substantial satire. New Zealand's literary culture threw up no Salman Rushdies possessed of a fierce indignation against the nation's follies and blindnesses, without illusions about its myths of the past or present, excoriating its political deceptions, yet able to meet the political mythmakers on their own ground. When politicians and those who market their policies learn so relentlessly and efficiently to prise apart signifiers and their signifieds in television campaigns for government measures, writers cannot afford to be less enterprising. What is needed in the last decade of the century is a more alert sense of the novel as a form that confronts by its inventive fictions the reckless proliferation of political images and rhetoric that disguise what they represent.

In their treatments of the past, the writers of the eighties, no doubt reflecting a general cultural ambivalence, failed to find a satisfactory balance between romance and history. While novels like *Oracles and Miracles* stress historical authenticity at the expense of imagination, novels like *The Matriarch* at crucial points surrender the historical to the fantastic. Few found that desirable ground for the novelist which lies where the imagination, informed by the senses both of play and of responsibility, engages with history. Here is the most fertile territory of the novel as form. The novel has always depended not on its truth to experience as such but on its truth to *imaginative* experience, and this is as true of Dickens and Hardy as it is of Patrick White and Rushdie. This is not to assert that the novel's value is purely aesthetic, a matter of its form and style rather than its content of ideas, or that its social and political significance is merely the freight which literary history will discard. The point is that the novel most richly engages with history when it is most vigorously imagined. This is what distinguishes it from journalism, factual reportage, or propaganda or, indeed, from history as a discipline. This is what Sargeson meant when he observed at the end of *Once Is Enough*, the first of his memoirs, that it was the imagination, not 'dull documentation', which had transformed his uncle's farm, judged by the official record to be, like New Zealand itself, 'third-class country'.[29]

In the period since the last war there has been a progressive, radical, and international shift in the genre of the novel towards the fictive and the fantastic at the expense of the mimetic and the sober, and this has been mirrored by fiction in this country. Yet this movement has been prompted not by the desire among novelists to dispense with historical experience but to engage with it more fully. In spite of the extreme claims of some postmodernists for the autonomy of the fictional orders of language from those of external reality, the major novelists in the post-war period — Lowry, White, Marquez,

Kundera, Pynchon, Rushdie, Lhosa — all work in that territory where history and myth, fantasy and reality, enmesh.

We have only one name to set securely in such company, that of Janet Frame. Frame's fiction continues both to draw on and to extend not only the general tradition of the novel in the post-war period as an international genre but also that New Zealand tradition glibly referred to on the cover of Johnson's *Anti Body Positive*.

Yet Wedde, Stead, Hulme, and Ihimaera, like Frame, are all as novelists active in a task which Rushdie sees as at the heart of the contemporary novelist's responsibility: the business of representing the world in terms of alternative kinds of truth to those of the politicians and the newspapers. As Rushdie puts it, 'If writers leave the business of making pictures of the world to politicians, it will be one of history's greatest and most abject abdications'.[30] The writer's ultimate responsibility is to language; there is nothing escapist about that. Language is the medium in which conflicting interpretations of the real do battle. If more fantasy has crept into fiction in the last twenty years, that merely reflects the determination of so many writers, particularly those who have lived under repressive political regimes, to match the extreme and bizarre deeds of those in power. The outrageous narrative events in *Midnight's Children* or *The Satanic Verses* — Shandean elongations of bodily organs, miraculous survivals of air accidents, transformations into mythical demons and angels — all these are no more 'fantastic' than the acts carried out by the Pakistani or Bengali generals Rushdie condemns so fiercely: the killings that cannot be named, the use of torture, and the corruption. They are merely more humane. They defend the right of the novelist to imagine realities other than those of the murderers and betrayers who hold power. In Frame's words, they enable alternative interpretations of the 'hierogylphic commonplace'.[31]

There are, of course, important differences in the way the six New Zealand novelists who are the subject of this book see their responsibility towards the competing claims of fiction and fact. For Frame, narrative 'mischief[s]' are a means of allowing into the novel that sense of the extraordinary quality of material reality itself which she inherited from her mother.[32] The world, the word, the extension of the body — all these are signs of both limit and wondrous possibility for Frame. It is in the novel, where word and world are transformed utterly by the imagination ('the magical technology'), that an adequate picture of the possibilities of life is discoverable. Her imagined worlds, seemingly bizarre and ruptured by a quirky playfulness, are at once criticisms of the actual world and versions of its possible forms.

For Stead, history occurs not in the records of the doings of the great but in the ways in which external events reverberate in the minds of ordinary individuals. He sees history in the larger sense as the constant fabrication of reality by politicians and moulders of opinion for their own purposes. History is mendacity and deception. It is experience badly written. Stead's views on the relations between the maker of fictions and the historian echo those of Sir Philip Sidney in his *Defense of Poesy* (1583).[33] The novelist is distinguished from the historian by his 'wit' or imagination, which gives him scope to invent, that is, to 'lie' in the interests of a higher truth. The novel itself, for Stead, is a more truthful form than the factual records of the historians or the fantastic duplicities of the politicians because it is playful *and* serious, open to fantasy *and* attentive to reality, able to offer mirror-like representations *and* willing to enter the playgrounds of language.

Wedde, Ihimaera, Hulme — all find their different balances between fiction and fact, history and the imagination, yet all depart from realism wherever it suits their purposes. Of all these novelists, Maurice Gee offers the least deliberately distorted pictures of the real. Reading his fiction up till the 1980s, we are left with the impression of a fictional world fully achieved, rich, teeming, and realised in every particular, but one in which the very seamlessness of the picture of life rendered becomes an impediment to the full display of the novelist's powers. Into the novels since *Meg* (1981), however, Gee slyly insinuates a quality which disrupts the purity of his naturalism. The novels do not overtly announce their own status as literary artifacts; they are not flagrantly metafictional. Nevertheless, they confess the unbridgable gap between the orders of literature and the world those orders seek to reflect.

In the end it is not enough for the novelist to update his or her pictures of the real, to make them contemporary by the addition of current mores, fashions, technologies. The writer must update the form itself in which the representation occurs. Otherwise, in spite of the addition of space parlours or current medical phobias or ecological or feminist concerns, the novels produced will seem more and more to belong to a kind of writing that is passing, or has passed. Gee's fiction since 1980 reluctantly but discernibly begins to address those underlying shifts in cultural meanings that influence, perhaps generate, literary forms.

Among the fiction published in this country during the 1970s and '80s, Gee's is certain to remain of lasting value if only because it is so consistently well written. Frank Sargeson once remarked that if he were writing to Gee, he would like to say 'it is nice to read someone who knows how to write a sentence'.[34] One doubts that he would have felt as warmly towards much of the writing that was fashionable in the late 1980s, particularly that in the historical fantasy style.

Fiction by Hulme, Ihimaera and others in the eighties fits into that concerted effort called for by educationists and social scientists to shift the cultural emphasis in this country away from the inherited tradition of Europe to Pacific themes and stresses. Brasch and Curnow in the 1940s and '50s strove to avoid provincialism. In a 1947 *Landfall* editorial Brasch urged local writers to make 'the European tradition . . . take root and grow' here. 'Every province', he said, 'can be a centre in its own right — provided that it does not imagine it can be self-sufficient'.[35] By 'self-sufficient' he meant inward-looking. Brasch was not unsympathetic to, merely dimly aware of, the Maori tradition. It did not occur to him that local writers might build a New Zealand literary tradition by attending to the indigenous culture *at the expense of* the inherited one, any more than it occurred to Fairburn who stridently condemned the European gaze of Pakeha New Zealanders. In the 1980s Hulme and Ihimaera sought to make a new tradition, in which the chief sources would be indigenous rather than imported.

In the 1980s a kind of writing appeared which set out self-consciously to break with imported writing styles. It presented itself as new kind of writing, attentive to the Pacific location of New Zealand, redolent of the Maori sense of the natural world, imbued with spirituality, ecologically aware. The old high-cultural bias had gone. The writing spoke through a voice that identified itself with spiritual presences of the country, not with the alienated distaste of the Man Alone.

This style had significant differences from the dominant trends in contemporary prose fiction in the English language. It is true that *the bone people* enjoyed considerable success internationally. It won the Booker Prize for 1986 and was soon being discussed in learned journals dealing with post-colonial literature.[36] The danger is that the kind of validation this success confers on the book in the metropolitan centres is the literary equivalent of ethnic food 'fads', while in New Zealand itself the old provincial cringe is repeated: the book is major because it has been approved of in London. In the fiction of Carey or Rushdie we find a style that is both local and confidently international. Their writing is steeped in the myths, fables and tall stories of the places the authors come from, yet is fully aware of the formal developments in the genre as a whole.

The divergence of *the bone people* and *The Matriarch* from the dominant international style was itself a significant departure in New Zealand fiction. New Zealand fiction has tended to follow pretty closely the ruling English-language style. Even in the 1930s when there was a concerted effort to forge a distinctive national literature, the ruling style in fiction was very similar to the style represented by Christopher Isherwood and George Orwell which drew on Hemingway. The stress on realism, the preference for short sentences, proletarian characters, and colloquial diction, the objectivity, even the masculine tone of the writing are international characteristics as much as reflections of nationalist priorities.

It is true, however, that international styles tend to arrive in New Zealand belatedly and to take on particular shapes and forms when they do arrive. They are assimilated to the existing literary scene and combined with literary preferences already established. In spite of Maurice Duggan's efforts, it wasn't until the 1970s that modernism emerged as a forceful presence in New Zealand fiction (Dan Davin's debts to Joyce were to the naturalism and Irishness of *Dubliners* not to the modernism of *Ulysses*). When it did become established in the 1980s, it was already outdated in literary-historical terms and tended to take impure forms. In Wedde it gets mixed up with the postmodern and post-colonial enthusiasms of the period. In Hulme's work the stylistic backlog of modernism (chiefly registered as Joycean word-plays like 'lightswarm', reminiscent of Duggan's 'Light lovely and fannygold' in 'Along Rideout Road That Summer')[37] is fastened to a romantic primitivism. Even in Stead's fiction, where we find most clearly a stylistic debt to the concision and hard particularity of Imagism and that hatred of cliché and love of 'the composed phrase' that Cyril Connolly identifies as essentially modernist,[38] modernism has to co-exist with elements of traditional realism and postmodernist flourishes. Stead's stylistic debt to modernism is, in fact, less important than his debt to the ideological assumptions of high modernism. When he locates himself within the great tradition of European high culture he asserts the continued force and centrality of modernism in his thinking.

In the late 1980s Stead's insistence on his debts to the 'Great Tradition' of English literature is judged 'Eurocentric' and reactionary, while Hulme's denial of her debts to prior Pakeha writing is greeted as an exemplary break with the dead weight of a redundant tradition. Such violent dualities run through the literary culture in the eighties. They are reflected in the title of Lawrence Jones's study of New Zealand prose fiction, *Barbed Wire and Mirrors*, in the separatist anthologies, *Yellow Pencils* and *Into the World of Light*. They are also reflected in the stark choice offered New Zealanders by some cultural commentators between defining themselves as colonial or postcolonial, European or Pacific. The starkness of this choice was exemplified when Bruce Stewart spoke on a *Frontline* television programme against Stead's role in purchasing an apartment in Bloomsbury for New Zealand writers.[39]

The same choice is presented in simplistic and romantic terms by feminist Joce Brown, writing in the radical broadsheet, *The Republican*, where she urges Pakeha to abandon entirely their remaining links to Europe and to their own colonialist past:

We have to deliberately forget what happened before the boats came here. We were created when our families landed. We have to reject the monarchy, Government House, Garden parties, Kings and Dio, Deb balls, hunt balls — the whole paraphanalia [*sic*] of our colonial heritage.[40]

Thus European New Zealanders are offered the prospect of remaking themselves by deliberately forgetting their own history. For Brown, speaking for a significant number of radicalised Pakeha, New Zealanders decolonise themselves by rejecting at least the outward trappings of what Stead sees as at the heart of their inheritance: the debt to Europe.

Perhaps, as Lamb puts it in a Maori proverb that ought to exist but doesn't, Maori people would do well to 'beware of Pakeha baring guilts'. For Lamb, there always was 'an unfortunate, unconscious immodesty in the history of Pakeha guilt'.[41] Its secret purpose all along was to bring the Pakeha to the satisfied sense of not being elsewhere, scattered, cut off from origins, blown about the world. The desire for home, in such a reading, is a version of the desire for God, for an authority set outside the whole disintegrating system, keeping everything in its rightful place, holding in check the terrifying centrifugal tendencies of history. The other possibility for the anxious descendants of the immigrants to New Zealand, one which Lamb urges on them, is to learn to accept their displacement and cease their obsession with purity of origins (the Pakeha are almost as conspicuously concerned with genealogy as the Maori). To wish for more — for plenitude, connection to location, authentic belonging — is to perpetuate the act of expropriation in the very moment of decrying it. As unashamed riffraff, the Pakeha might come at last to rejoice in the brokenness of their cultural situation.

One would like to find a middle ground between the options presented by Brown and Lamb. European New Zealanders have surely reached a point where they can put behind them their sense of England as 'home'. In fact, to a considerable extent they have done so in the last fifty years. To assert the need to break with the colonial source culture in the late 1980s is merely to parody efforts that were made in the 1930s and '40s. To assert that they can only do so by repudiating their European literary, linguistic, and cultural inheritance, by remaking themselves as a Pacific people, is both wrongheaded and appropriative. It is patronising to the Maori people who are thereby made to serve the decolonising interests of their dispossessors as they were once made to serve their colonising interests.

What we need now is a sense of history since colonisation as a rich and complex layering of various cultural traditions, different yet related, capable of maintaining their integrity as separate cultural elements yet mutually respectful. A precondition to that is no doubt the resolution of some outstanding *political* grievances among Maori. If Maori culture is to assert itself independently and self-confidently in New Zealand after so many years of denigration, then issues of land and law must be fairly settled. Similarly, Maori may be more tolerant of the assimilation of Maori words into English once they feel confident of their own language as a language of daily use and prestige.

At the end of that process we may be able to talk about a genuine cultural diversity. But it needs to be said that that process will not be advanced by Pakeha denigration of their own culture nor by a compulsive attachment to the romanticised values of Maori culture by Pakeha (or by Maori). Even if we accept the view that colonisation is not a process confined to the past but is a continuing effect of the Pakeha presence, of institutional repression and cultural hegemony, we must accept that presence after a century and half in the country as a massive and irreversible fact. That means accepting that the colonising culture itself, which undoubtedly has presented itself in monolithic and absolutist terms at times, and still does in some respects, is an inescapable presence in the country, with positive as well as negative associations. It means, moreover, that the efforts by so many New Zealand writers to find a way of writing in English appropriate to New Zealand experience and speech are a source of richness not of shame.

For Wedde, the tradition which the Pakeha writer in this country inevitably encounters in the act of writing is above all that of the history of the growth of English since settlement towards a distinctive national form. Wedde does not oversimplify the complexities of the cultural situation of the Pakeha. His own writing remains open to an enormous range of influence from everywhere imaginable, local and foreign, native and exotic. At the same time he retains a quick sense of the peculiar shapes and stresses of the English language in this country, the way in which over a century and a half it has become, if not nativised, then localised by usage. For Wedde, language is culture itself that wraps around its users in dense layers. It is inescapable, as fundamental as life itself:

> To be without culture — to be cut off from that which speaks and writes for us, which transcribes our myths, conveys the dialect of inconsistencies and contradictions with which we adjust our sense of value, exchange, power and knowledge, and authority — is to be dead. It is to be without language, even if, as individuals, we have one to speak.[42]

By comparison with this historically alert understanding of culture, Stead's determination to maintain the 'Great Tradition' is over-zealous. No doubt also, his habit of defending literary hierarchies and authorities is elitist (although Brasch would have regarded his defense of cultural elites as unremarkable and sensible). Moreover, Stead's determination to define a 'mainstream' does not take enough account of that dispersion of literary energies away from the centres, canons, and authorities that has marked English-language writing since the war. The centre, as Les Murray observes, 'is everywhere',[43] which doesn't mean that the old centres — linguistic, literary, cultural — no longer have power; it means rather that it is hard to find any secure vantage point from which canonical judgements can be made.

Nevertheless, the continuities Stead insistently affirms are valuable and inescapable. There *is* such a thing as 'New Zealand Literature', a body of existing texts which modifies the practice of contemporary New Zealand writers. And behind that particular tradition lie

214

larger and older ones, which also continue to exert a shaping influence. New Zealand literature is not a fixed body of canonical texts. It is not a single authoritative tradition. It is a whole that continually accommodates new influences and directions as the various energies of contemporary writing are assimilated into a given writing scene and shaped by the habits, practices, and stresses of previous writers in that place.

Erecting counter canons, as Roberts does with her feminine tradition of New Zealand fiction, merely reinforces the error it opposes. The binary habits of New Zealand criticism have not allowed us to see our literature as a 'complex wholeness' made up of conflicting elements.[44] Lines of force and influence run through it. The myths that it throws up are historically conditioned and need periodically to be reformulated and revised. It is continually being transformed. Its existing order of works is continually being revalued by new works. But the whole exists as an evolving form of the English language, to which various linguistic communities have contributed.

The history of European presence in this country is undeniably an ambiguous one, marked by crimes and errors as well as good intentions and genuine, if unsuccessful, attempts at creating a just society. One of its chief strengths is surely the form of the English language it has developed over time, drawing on the original stock of settler dialects, modified by borrowings from Maori, taking in a rich welter of influences from Europe, America, Australia, evolving its own idiosyncratic habits and forms — above all, building up a body of literature expressing and extending that idiom. The existence of 'New Zealand-English', a language enriched by its everyday use in this country as well as by all it draws on, from here and from elsewhere, is surely cause for celebration. Neither nostalgic for its lost home nor jealous of Maori originality, New Zealand-English could coexist with the indigenous tongue and give rise to a literature less blinded by its yearning to belong than much of what it currently produces. As Tom Paulin, writing on the situation of English in modern Ireland, puts it, '[a] language that lives lithely on the tongue ought to be capable of becoming the flexible written instrument of a complete cultural idea'.[45]

Both Maori and New Zealand English would be nourished by the achievement of an independence which cherished difference yet which connected the currently antagonistic parts of the cultural picture into a complex wholeness, distinctive and rich.

215

Notes

INTRODUCTION

1. Frank Sargeson, *Once Is Enough: A Memoir.* Wellington, A. H. & A. W. Reed, 1973, p.41.
2. C.K. Stead, rev. of *The Penguin Book of New Zealand Verse,* ed. Ian Wedde & Harvey McQueen, *Landfall,* 155, Sept. 1985; reprinted as 'At Home with the Poets' in *Answering to the Language: Essays on Modern Writers.* Auckland, Auckland University Press, 1989, pp.141-2.
3. See Jonathan Lamb, 'Problems of Originality: Or, Beware of Pakeha Baring Guilts', *Landfall,* 159, Sept. 1986, pp.352-8.
4. Stead, *Answering to the Language,* p.144.
5. Wole Soyinka, *Six Plays.* London, Methuen, 1984, p.vi.
6. Allen Curnow, 'Introduction' to *A Book of New Zealand Verse 1923-45.* Christchurch, Caxton, 1945; reprinted in *Look Back Harder: Critical Writings, 1935-1984,* ed. Peter Simpson, Auckland, Auckland University Press, 1987, p.67.
7. *Kowhai Gold: An Anthology of Contemporary New Zealand Verse,* ed. Quentin Pope. London, Dent, 1930, p.vii.
8. Simon During, 'Postmodernism or Postcolonialism?', *Landfall,* 155, Sept. 1985, p.369.
9. Jonathan Lamb, 'The Status of Originality in Some New Zealand Literary Criticism'. Talk given to the Sociology Department, Univ. of Auckland, 3 Oct. 1985, n.p. A revised version of this talk appeared in *Landfall* as 'Problems of Originality', see above, note 3.
10. During, 'Postmodernism or Postcolo-
nialism?', p.380.
11. Lydia Wevers, 'Changing Directions: The Short Story in New Zealand', *Meanjin,* v.44 no. 3, Sept. 1985, p.353.
12. Bill Pearson, 'The Maori and Literature 1938-1965', in *The Maori People in the Nineteen-Sixties: A Symposium,* ed. Erik Schwimmer Auckland, B. & J. Paul, 1969; reprinted in *Essays on New Zealand Literature,* ed. Wystan Curnow, Auckland, Heinemann Educational, 1973, p.137.
13. Pearson, 'The Maori and Literature', pp.137-8.
14. See A. A. Phillips, *The Australian Tradition: Studies in a Colonial Culture.* Melbourne, F. W. Cheshire, 1958, pp.89-95.
15. This is a point made by C. K. Stead in his review of *The Penguin Book, Answering to the Language,* p.142. Trixie Te Arama Menzies in a subsequent article in *Landfall* on the Kowhai Gold theme (*Landfall,* 165, March 1988, p.19.) claims that Stead is here arguing against the inclusion of Maori poetry itself. But Stead's objection is in fact to the way in which Maori poetry is represented, not to the fact that it is represented. Essentially he is criticising contemporary Pakeha liberal ideology for blindness to its own motivations.
16. Trixie Te Arama Menzies, rev. of *Dalwurra* by Colin Johnson Mudrooroo Narogin, *Landfall,* 169, March 1989, p.109.
17. Joy Cowley, rev. of *the bone people, New Zealand Listener,* 12 May 1984, p.60.

18. Radio talk first broadcast on 28 July 1948, printed in Frank Sargeson, *Conversation in a Train and Other Critical Writing*, ed. Kevin Cunningham. Auckland, Auckland University Press/Oxford University Press, 1983, p.29. Quoted in Lawrence Jones, *Barbed Wire and Mirrors: Essays on New Zealand Prose*. Dunedin, University of Otago Press, 1987, p.7.

19. Sargeson, *Conversation*, p.32.

20. Sargeson, *Conversation*, quoted by Jones, *Barbed Wire*, p.7.

21. See, for instance, Peter Alcock who has stated that Mansfield's 'position vis-à-vis a local fiction has distinct affinities with that of *Kowhai Gold* for our poetry', 'Correspondence', *Landfall*, 82, June 1967, p.219. For Alcock, as Lawrence Jones puts it, 'the true indigenous progenitor of New Zealand fiction [is] "a man called Sargeson"', Jones, *Barbed Wire*, p.7.

22. Janet Frame, *Living in the Maniototo*. New York, George Braziller, 1979, p.58. All further references to this work appear in the text.

23. Wevers, 'Changing Directions', p.356.

24. Ian Wedde, *Survival Arts*. Auckland, Penguin, 1988, p.93.

25. Frank Sargeson, 'The Hole that Jack Dug', *The Stories of Frank Sargeson*. Auckland, Longman Paul, 1975, pp. 244-5.

26. Ian Wedde & Harvey McQueen, eds. *The Penguin Book of New Zealand Verse*. Auckland, Penguin, 1985, p.23. All further references to this work are indicated in the text.

27. John Hovell notes that Joe falls into the landscape in an unpublished Masters essay for the University of Waikato, 1987.

28. C.K. Stead, 'Keri Hulme's *the bone people* and the Pegasus Award for Maori Literature', *Ariel*, v.16 no.4, 1985; reprinted in *Answering to the Language*, pp.182-3.

29. See Simon During, 'Towards a Revision of Local Critical Habits', *And/1*, Oct. 1983, pp.75-92.

30. Peter Simpson, 'Recent Fiction and the Sargeson Tradition', *Journal of New Zealand Literature*, 1, 1983, p. 19.

31. Frank Sargeson, *The Hangover & Joy of the Worm*. Auckland, Penguin, 1984, p.71.

32. C.K. Stead, *All Visitors Ashore*. London, Harvill, 1984, p.87. All further references to this work are indicated in the text.

33. C.K. Stead, 'On the Margins', *Islands*, 37, August 1986; reprinted as 'A New New Zealand Fiction?', *Answering to the Language*, p.238.

34. Stead, *Answering to the Language*, p.238.

35. Stead, *Answering to the Language*, p.182.

36. Witi Ihimaera, *The Matriarch*. Auckland, Heinemann, 1986, p.192. All further references to this work are indicated in the text.

37. Arthur O. Lovejoy, 'On the Discriminations of Romanticism', *Essays in the History of Ideas*. Baltimore, Johns Hopkins Press, 1948, pp.228-53.

38. Sargeson, *Conversation*, p.61.

39. See Joost Daalder, 'Violence in the Stories of Frank Sargeson', *Journal of New Zealand Literature*, 4, 1986, pp.56-80.

40. Sargeson, *Conversation*, p.57.

1: JANET FRAME

1. Janet Frame, *To the Is-Land: An Autobiography*. London, Women's Press, 1983, p.12.

2. Frame, *To the Is-Land*, p.15.

3. Frame, *To the Is-Land*, p.15.

4. Frame, *To the Is-Land*, p.123.

5. *Milton's Prose Writings*, intro. by K.M. Burton. London, Dent, 1958, p.124.

6. Frame, *To the Is-land*, p.66.

7. William Blake, *The Marriage of Heaven and Hell*, in *Blake: Complete Writings*, ed. Geoffrey Keynes. London, Oxford University Press, 1969, p.154.

8. Frame, *To the Is-Land*, p.67.

9. Frame, *To the Is-Land*, p.100.

10. P. D. Evans, *Janet Frame*. Boston, Twayne, 1977, p.19.

11. Janet Frame, *Faces in the Water*. 1961; reprinted London, Women's Press, 1984, p.11.

12. Alan Sheridan, *Michel Foucault: The Will to Truth*, London, Tavistock, 1980,

p.7.

13. Richard Ellmann, *James Joyce*. New York, Oxford University Press, 1959, p.692.

14. Joan Stevens, *The New Zealand Novel, 1860-1965*. Wellington, A. H. & A. W. Reed, 1966, p.127.

15. In the typescript version of the novel held in the Hocken Library Istina commits suicide. I am grateful to Susan Ash for alerting me to this version.

16. Frame, *An Angel at my Table*. Auckland, Hutchinson, 1985, p.99.

17. Frame, *Faces in the Water*, p.251.

18. Janet Frame, *A State of Siege*. New York, Braziller, 1966, p.122. All further references to this work are indicated in the text.

19. Alex Calder, 'The Closure of Sense: Janet Frame, Language, and the Body', *Antic*/3, Nov. 1987, pp.94-95.

20. This phrase was coined by Roger Horrocks in 'Readings of *A State of Siege* (1967) and *A State of Siege* (1978)', *And*/3, Oct. 1984, pp.131ff.

21. Calder, 'The Closure of Sense', p.96.

22. There are precedents for this kind of eruption of 'nonsense' into a novel in Edgar Allen Poe's *Narrative of Arthur Gordon Pym*, where the hero enters a cave on an isolated island and discovers indecipherable hieroglyphs scrawled on the walls, and in Patrick White's *The Vivisector* where the hero, the painter Hurtle Duffield, suffers a stroke as the novel concludes and emits a species of poetic interior monologue very similar to Malfred's in *A State of Siege*. In both cases the linguistic disruptions are entirely *conscious* authorial ploys. Poe, like his contemporaries was deeply impressed by the Egyptian hieroglyphs to which no key then existed. He wanted to suggest that sense they conveyed of forms of language that seem to mean something but which we find ourselves unable to penetrate. White, like Frame, wants to fracture and recombine bits and pieces of words in order to catch something of the jumbled complexity with which

the dying painter's mind snatches a kind of transcendent lucidity out of the pieces of his life as they flash before him.

23. Calder, 'The Closure of Sense', p.103.

24. *New Zealand Herald*, 11 July 1963. See also *When Art Hits the Headlines: The Study of Controversial Art in New Zealand* by Jim and Mary Barr. Wellington, National Art Gallery /*Evening Post*, 1987, pp.25-28.

25. Frame, *Angel at my Table*, p.182.

26. Patrick White, 'The Prodigal Son', *Australian Letters*, 1, no.3, 1958, p.39.

27. Keri Hulme, *the bone people*. Wellington, Spiral, 1983, p.374. All further references to this work are indicated in the text.

28. Frame, *Angel at my Table*, p.76.

29. During, 'Postmodernism or Postcolonialism?', p.373.

30. During, 'Postmodernism or Postcolonialism?', p.367.

31. Mavis here suggests that humans thus discover that they themselves 'have been shaped and patterned not by a shadow of light but an original' (p.118). The 'original' is here described in terms of Pythagorean mathematics as 'the sum of all equals and unequals and cubes and squares; the shaping inclusion; the hypoteneuse of the entire manifold'. This means, I take it, that the manifold can be likened to a rectangular shape on one of whose sides an equilateral triangle may be inscribed. The universe thus hangs, in another of Mavis's images, beneath the form of God as bags of seed hang beneath the bodies of some insects (p.117). All this is suggestive of the metaphors whereby Mavis seeks to understand the process of writing itself rather than Frameian essays on pure metaphysics. Notably Mavis who is here obsessed with the lack of Yeats's poetry among the Garretts' well-stocked bookshelves, picks up an echo of Yeats's 'For love has pitched his mansion in/the place of excrement' in the following line: 'so God has pitched his worlds'.

32. P.D. Evans, rev. of *The Carpathians*,

New Zealand Listener, 24 Sept. 1988, p.71.

33. Stead, *Answering to the Language*, p.142.

34. Frame, *Angel at my Table*, p.62.

2: C. K. STEAD

1. Janet Frame, *Faces in the Water*, p.[6].

2. Sargeson, *Once Is Enough* p.9.

3. See Gregory O'Brien, *Moments of Invention: Portraits of 21 New Zealand Writers*. Auckland, Heinemann/Reed, 1988, p.76.

4. Alex Calder, rev. of *The Matriarch*, *Landfall*, 161, March 1987, p.80.

5. C. K. Stead, 'Affirmative Injustice', Letter to the Editor, *New Zealand Listener*, 16 April 1988, p.12.

6. C. K. Stead, 'The New Victorians', *Answering to the Language*, p.285.

7. C. K. Stead, ed. *The Letters and Journals of Katherine Mansfield: A Selection*. London, Allen Lane, 1977, p.26.

8. Sargeson, *The Stories of Frank Sargeson*, p.198.

9. See Kai Jensen, 'Holes, Wholeness and Holiness in Frank Sargeson's Writing', paper delivered at the AULLA congress XXV, Sydney, February 1989; reprinted *Landfall* 173, March 1990, pp.32-44.

10. *James K. Baxter as Critic*, ed. Frank McKay. Auckland, Heinemann Educational, 1978, p.172.

11. Ian Cross, 'Salad Days', rev. of *All Visitors Ashore*, *New Zealand Listener*, 10 Nov. 1984, p.46.

12. John Mulgan, *Man Alone*. Auckland, Longman Paul, 1980, pp.7-8.

13. See Baxter, *James K. Baxter as Critic*, p.195. See also Vincent O'Sullivan, Introduction to the *Oxford Anthology of Twentieth Century New Zealand Poetry*, 3rd ed., Auckland, Oxford, 1987, p.xxv.

14. John Osborne, *Look Back in Anger*. New York, Criterion, 1957, p.17.

15. C. K. Stead, *Answering to the Language*, p.278.

16. K.K. Ruthven, rev. of *Pound, Eliot, Yeats and the Modernist Movement*, by C. K. Stead, *Landfall*, 160, December 1986, pp.509-13.

17. Frank Sargeson, *More Than Enough: A Memoir*. Wellington, A. H. & A. W. Reed, 1975, p.71.

18. C.K. Stead, *The Death of the Body*. London, Collins, 1986, p.7. All further references to this work are indicated in the text.

19. See Jonathan Lamb, 'The Uncanny in Auckland', *And/4*, Oct. 1985, pp.32-45.

20. C.K. Stead, *Smith's Dream*. Auckland, Longman Paul, 1971, p.11.

21. W.H. Auden, 'In Memory of W.B. Yeats', *W. H. Auden, Collected Shorter Poems, 1927-1957*, London, Faber & Faber, 1966, p.142.

22. Lawrence Jones, 'Versions of the Dream', in *Culture and Identity in New Zealand*, ed. David Novitz & Bill Willmott. Wellington, Government Printing Office, 1989, p.201.

23. The 1973 Longman Paul paperback edition of the novel has a rewritten ending with the appended 'excuse' that the new ending was the one originally intended by the author.

24. Kate Fullbrook, *Katherine Mansfield*. London, Harvester, 1986, pp.16-17.

25. Lamb, 'The Uncanny in Auckland', p.32, *et seq.*

26. Stead, *Answering to the Language*, pp.279-80.

27. The issue of *Craccum*, the students' newspaper in which this charge occurred, appears to have disappeared from the University of Auckland library holdings and from those of the Students' Association. I have checked my own memory of the passage with other members of the Department.

28. C.K. Stead, 'From Wystan to Carlos: Modern and Modernism in Recent New Zealand Poetry', *In the Glass Case: Essays on New Zealand Literature*. Auckland, Auckland University Press/Oxford University Press, 1981, p.148.

29. Reginald Berry, 'Stead's Dream', rev. of *The Death of the Body*, *Landfall*, 163, Sept. 1987, p.345.

30. Stead, *Smith's Dream*, p.55.

31. Stead, *Smith's Dream*, p.21.

32. C. K. Stead interviewed by Michael

Harlow, *Landfall*, 148, Dec. 1983, p.464.

33. Stead, *The New Poetic*. London: Hutchinson, 1964, p.134.

34. Stead's 'flow of the tide' corresponds exactly with Eliot's 'main current'. See Stead, 'From Wystan to Carlos, p.145; T. S. Eliot, 'Tradition and the Individual Talent', *Selected Essays*, London, Faber, 1972, p.16.

35. See my 'T. S. Eliot, Tradition and Contemporary New Zealand Poetry', *The Literary Half-Yearly*, v.29 no.2, July 1988, p.152.

36. Quoted in James Bertram, 'A Rakehelly Man', rev. of *The Letters of A. R. D. Fairburn* by Lauris Edmond, *New Zealand Listener*, 6 Feb. 1982, p.19.

37. Curnow, *Look Back Harder*, p.133.

38. Stead, *Answering to the Language*, p.284.

39. Stead, *Answering to the Language*, p.287.

3: KERI HULME

1. See, for instance, Miriama Evans, 'Politics and Maori Literature', *Landfall*, 153, March 1985, p.41; reprinted as 'The Politics of Maori Literature', *Meanjin*, v.44 no.3, Sept. 1985, pp.358-63.

2. See Anne French, rev. of *The Limits of Green* and *Running away from Home* by Rachel McAlpine, *Landfall*, 163, Sept. 1987, p.348.

3. Henry James, *Hawthorne*, intro. by Tony Tanner. London, Macmillan, 1967, p.109.

4. When I first pointed out the novel's debts to such sources in *New Outlook* magazine (Jan./Feb., 1985, p.46), Hulme herself wrote to me agreeing about the novel's literary ancestry, though pointing out that she had never read any Malcolm Lowry, whom I also listed, 'not even *Under the Volcano*'. She went on, however, to assert in opposition to my reading of her novel that the novel 'grew from the breast of Papatuanuku, alright, but there were seeds & seeds, and some of them came lately here'. Letter to the author, 24 Dec. 1984.

5. Samuel Taylor Coleridge, *Biographia Literaria*, ch. 14, *Selected Poetry and Prose of Coleridge*, ed. Donald A. Stauffer. New York, Random House, 1951, p.264.

6. It is interesting to compare Kerewin's, and the novel's, ambivalence towards English as the language of colonial dominance with Epeli Hau'ofa's exuberant celebration of English for its inexhaustible stock of obscene expression, in contrast to some of the other Pacific languages. See Epeli Hau'ofa interviewed by Subramani, *Landfall*, 169, March 1989, pp.35-51.

7. Simon During has noted the heaviness of the debt to Eliot's *The Waste Land* in 'Postcolonialism or Postmodernism?', p.373.

8. Paul Fussell, *Abroad: British Literary Travelling between the Wars*. New York, Oxford University Press, 1975, p.151.

9. Jones, *Barbed Wire*, p.7.

10. Cyril Connolly, *Enemies of Promise*. 1939; reprinted London, Andre Deutsch, 1973, p.47.

11. William Shakespeare, *The Tempest* III.ii.133-4, ed. Frank Kermode. London, Methuen, 1971, p.84.

12. Stead, *Answering to the Language*, pp.182-3.

13. Elsdon Best, *Spiritual and Mental Concepts of the Maori*. Wellington, Government Printer, 1954, p.16.

14. Elsdon Best, *Maori Religion and Mythology*, vol. 2. Wellington, Government Printer, 1982, p.71.

15. Best, *Spiritual and Mental Concepts*, p.34.

16. Best, *Spiritual and Mental Concepts*, p.35.

17. Keri Hulme interviewed by Harry Ricketts, *Talking About Ourselves: Twelve New Zealand Poets in Conversation with Harry Ricketts*. Wellington, Mallinson Rendel, 1986, p.19.

18. John Keats, Letter to George and Thomas Keats, 22 Dec. 1817, *The Letters of John Keats*, ed. Maurice Buxton Foreman. 4th ed., London, Oxford University Press, 1960, p.71.

19. T. S. Eliot, '*Ulysses*, Order and Myth', *The Dial*, 75, July-Dec. 1923, p.483.

20. Robin Hyde, *Nor the Years Condemn*, ed. Phillida Bunkle *et al*. Auckland,

New Women's Press, 1986, p.xxix.
21. Bunkle *et al. Nor the Years Condemn*, p.xxvi.
22. Ricketts, *Talking About Ourselves*, pp.28-29.
23. See Lawrence Jones, 'Stanley Graham and the Several Faces of "Man Alone"', *Journal of Popular Culture*, v.19 no.2, Fall 1986, pp.121-36.
24. Stead, *Answering to the Language*, p.183.
25. Stead, *Answering to the Language*, p.181.
26. Michael Neill, 'Coming Home: Teaching the Post-Colonial Novel', *Islands*, 35, Apr. 1985, p.53.

4: WITI IHIMAERA

1. Alistair Campbell interviewed by Tapu Misa, *New Zealand Herald*, 20 May 1989.
2. Witi Ihimaera, 'Maori Life and Literature: A Sensory Perception', The Turnbull Winter Lectures 1981, *The Turnbull Library Record*, May 1982; reprinted as *New Zealand Through the Arts: Past and Present*. Wellington, Friends of the Turnbull Library, 1982, p.54.
3. Ihimaera, 'Maori Life and Literature', p.48.
4. Ihimaera, 'Maori Life and literature', p.50.
5. Ihimaera, 'Maori Life and Literature', p.50.
6. Roderick Finlayson, 'The Totara Tree', *Some Other Country: New Zealand's Best Short Stories*, ed. Marion McLeod & Bill Manhire. Wellington, Allen & Unwin/Port Nicholson Press, 1984, p.44.
7. Pearson, 'The Maori and Literature', p.100.
8. 'A Game of Cards', *Pounamu, Pounamu*. Auckland, Heinemann, 1972, p.1.
9. See my 'Muscular Aesthete: Malcolm Lowry and 1930s English Literary Culture', *Journal of Commonwealth Literature*, v.24, no.1 (1989), pp.65-87.
10. Kai Jensen observes that Fairburn 'edited the *Compost Magazine*, "the voice of the New Zealand Humic Compost Club", . . . while Sargeson

tells in his autobiography how he dreamt of a community founded on organic farming. "Wholeness" for both men required an organic relationship with the land', 'Holes, Wholeness and Holiness', p.37.
11. Calder, rev. of *The Matriarch*, p.82.
12. Witi Ihimaera, *The New Net Goes Fishing*. Auckland, Heinemann, 1985, p.110.
13. This discussion draws on my 'Literary Recession: New Zealand Fiction, 1985 - mid-1986', *Journal of New Zealand Literature*, 5, 1987, pp.22-26.
14. Witi Ihimaera, *Tangi*. Auckland, Heinemann, 1975, p.37. This expression recalls the Irish-English colloquialism: 'to get a paddy up'.
15. *The New Net*, p.116.
16. Witi Ihimaera, *The Whale Rider*. Auckland, Heinemann, 1987, p.112.
17. Ihimaera, 'Maori Life and Literature', p.48.
18. M.P.K. Sorrenson points out that early Pakeha scholars of Maori beliefs like Edward Tregear, John Macmillan Brown and S. Percy Smith 'found Greek, Celtic and especially Scandanavian models for Polynesian gods', *Maori Origins and Migrations: The Genesis of Some Pakeha Myths and Legends*. Auckland, Auckland University Press/Oxford University Press, 1983, p.26.
19. D.H. Lawrence, *Apocalypse*. 1931; repr. London, Heinemann, 1972, p.25.
20. Ihimaera, 'Maori Life and Literature', p.48.
21. Calder, rev. of *The Matriarch*, p.84.
22. See '*Matriarch* Passages Copied— Historian', by Andrew Johnston, *Dominion Sunday Times*, 26 Nov. 1989.
23. Keith Sorrenson, 'Land Confiscations', *An Encyclopaedia of New Zealand*, v.2, ed. A. H. McLintock. Wellington, Government Books, 1966, p.483.
24. J. H. Mitchell, *Takitimu*. Wellington, A. H. & A. W. Reed, 1973, p.30.
25. Mitchell, p.30.
26. Compare pp.234-6 of *The Matriarch* to pp.216-18 of *Whina: A Biography of Whina Cooper*, by Michael King, Auckland, Hodder & Stoughton, 1983.

27. Ian Wedde, *Symmes Hole*. Auckland, Penguin, 1986, p.14. All further references to this work are indicated in the text.
28. See Dennis McEldowney, rev. of *Between*, by C. K. Stead, *Landfall*, 173, March 1990, pp.106-8.
29. C. K. Stead, *Geographies*. Auckland, Auckland University Press/Oxford University Press, 1982, p.65.
30. Malcolm Lowry, Letter to Albert Erskine, 5 June 1951, *Selected Letters of Malcolm Lowry*, ed. Harvey Breit & Margerie Bonner Lowry. New York, Capricorn, 1965, p.243.
31. Letter to the author, 24 Dec. 1984.
32. *The Letters of Hugh MacDiarmid*, ed. Alan Bold. London, Hamish Hamilton, 1984, p.168.
33. Stead describes Ian Wedde as 'a splendid and original poet', *In the Glass Case*, p.157; cited by Lamb, 'Problems of Originality', p.352.
34. C. K. Stead, 'War Book', rev. of *The Matriarch*, *London Review of Books*, 18 Dec. 1986, p.22.
35. Ihimaera, 'Maori life and Literature', p.48.
36. Ihimaera, 'Maori Life and Literature', p.47.
37. Georg Lukacs, *The Theory of the Novel*, trans. Anna Bostock. Cambridge, Mass., MIT Press, 1977, p.56.

5: IAN WEDDE

1. Ian Wedde, *Dick Seddon's Great Dive*, published as an issue of *Islands*, 16, Nov. 1976, p.171.
2. Ian Wedde, 'Dreaming of a White Myth', *Landfall*, 170, June 1989, p.238.
3. Bill Manhire, 'Breaking the Line: A View of American and New Zealand Poetry', *Islands*, 38, Dec. 1987, p.152.
4. Ian Wedde interviewed by David Dowling, *Landfall*, 154, June 1985, p.163.
5. Wedde interviewed by David Dowling, p.163.
6. Wedde interviewed by David Dowling, p.164.
7. Wystan Curnow, 'Speech Balloons and Conversation Bubbles', *And*/4,
Oct. 1985, p.126.
8. Curnow, 'Speech Balloons', p.126.
9. Wedde interviewed by David Dowling, p.167.
10. James Bertram, 'Ian Wedde's Fiction', *Islands*, 17, March 1977, p.303.
11. Ian Wedde, *The Shirt Factory and Other Stories*. Wellington, Victoria University Press/ Price Milburn, 1981, p.23. All further references to this work are indicated in the text.
12. Wedde interviewed by David Dowling, p.168.
13. See my '"Design of Darkness": The Religious and Political Heresies of Captain Ahab and Johann Voss', *Australasian Journal of American Studies*, v.5, no.1, July 1986, pp.26-40.
14. King, *Whina*, p.22.
15. Bill Pearson, *Fretful Sleepers*. Auckland, Heinemann, 1974, p.161; see also Michael Neill, 'Coming Home: Teaching the Post-Colonial Novel', *Islands*, 35, April 1985, pp 38-53.
16. Novitz & Willmott, *Culture and Identity*, p.78.
17. See Lamb on this point, 'Problems of Originality', p.357.
18. Wedde, *Penguin Book of New Zealand Verse*, p.29.
19. Wedde, *Penguin Book of New Zealand Verse*, p.29.
20. Jensen, 'Holes, Wholeness and Holiness', p.39.
21. Alex Calder, 'My Katherine Mansfield', *Landfall*, 172, Dec. 1989, p.485.
22. Linda Hardy, 'The Ghost of Katherine Mansfield', *Landfall*, 172, Dec. 1989, p.430.
23. Ihimaera, *The Whale Rider*, p.113.
24. Wedde inteviewed by David Dowling, p.168.
25. Wedde interviewed by David Dowling, p.168.
26. Herman Melville, 'Hawthorne & His Mosses', *Moby Dick*, Norton Critical Edition, ed. Harrison Hayford and Hershel Parker. New York, Norton, 1967, p.541.
27. Les Murray interviewed by Iain Sharp, *Landfall*, 166, June 1988, p.160.
28. Ian Wedde, *Survival Arts*. Auckland, Penguin, 1988, p.[7]. All further refer-

ences to this work are indicated in the text.

29. Novitz & Willmott, *Culture and Identity*, p.277.

30. Peter Simpson, 'The Trick of Standing Upright', *World Literature Written in English*, v.26, no.2, p.373.

31. Wedde, *Penguin Book of New Zealand Verse*, p.23.

32. Donna Awatere, *Maori Sovereignty*. Auckland, Broadsheet, 1984, p.35.

33. Alan Riach, 'Stranger Eyes: Charles Olson, "Pacific Man" and Some Aspects of New Zealand Poetry', *Landfall*, 169, March 1989, p.70.

34. Wedde, *Penguin Book of New Zealand Verse*, p.23.

35. Terry Sturm, rev. of *The Penguin Book of New Zealand Verse*, *Listener*, 13 July 1985, p.53.

36. Lamb, 'Problems of Originality', p.358.

37. Wedde, 'Dreaming of a White Myth', pp.237-42.

38. Vincent O'Sullivan, 'Finding the Pattern, Solving the Problem', Victoria University of Wellington Inaugural Addresses, New Series. Wellington, Victoria University Press, 1989, p.5.

39. Allen Curnow, 'New Zealand Literature: The Case for a Working Definition', *Essays on New Zealand Literature*, p.141.

40. Curnow, 'New Zealand Literature', p.141.

6: MAURICE GEE

1. Maurice Gee, *In My Father's Den*. London, Faber & Faber, 1972, p.24.

2. Jones, *Barbed Wire and Mirrors*, p.145.

3. Bill Manhire, *Maurice Gee*. Auckland, Oxford University Press, 1986, p.67.

4. Russell Haley, rev. of *Games of Choice*, *Spleen* 6, Dec. 1976, p.[6].

5. Haley,p.[7].

6. Haley, p.[7].

7. Haley, p.[7].

8. Manhire, *Maurice Gee*, p.26.

9. Maurice Gee, *Collected Stories*. Auckland, Penguin, 1986, p.190.

10. Haley, p.[7].

11. Gee, *Collected Stories*, p.184.

12. Maurice Gee, *Sole Survivor*. Auckland, Penguin, 1984, p.153. All further references to this work are indicated in the text.

13. Maurice Gee, *Meg*. Auckland, Penguin, 1981, p.141. All further references to this work are indicated in the text.

14. Brian Boyd, rev. of *Prowlers*, *Landfall*, 166, June 1988, p.213.

15. Maurice Gee, *Prowlers*. Auckland, Viking, 1987, p.1. All further references to this work are indicated in the text.

16. Sam Shepard, *Seven Plays*, Intro. by Richard Gilman. London, Faber & Faber, 1981, p.xvi.

17. Manhire, *Maurice Gee*, p.62.

18. Frank Kermode, 'The Modern', *Modern Essays*. London, Collins, 1971, p.60. Kermode's distinction between 'paleo-modernism' and 'neo-modernism' corresponds roughly to that between high modernism and postmodernism.

19. Stevan Eldred-Grigg, '*Oracles and Miracles*: Working Class Novel, Okay?', *Sites*, 16, Autumn 1988, pp.111-20; for a critical view see Elizabeth Gordon, '*Oracles and Miracles*: Truth or Fiction?', *Untold*, 9/10, 1988, pp.40-46.

20. During, 'Towards a Revision of Local Critical Habits', p.75.

CONCLUSION

1. Anne Kennedy, 'An Angel Entertains Theatricals', *Landfall*, 172, Dec. 1989, pp.397-8.

2. Robert Hughes, *The Art of Australia*. Harmondsworth, Penguin, 1966; rev. ed. 1970, p.315.

3. Simpson, 'Recent Fiction', p.20.

4. Simpson, 'Recent Fiction', p.20.

5. These figures apply to the end of February 1990. They exclude one book entered in the fiction category which is a biography, *Pawelka* by Des Swain.

6. Simpson, 'Recent Fiction', p.20.

7. See my review of *New Zealand Short Stories: Fourth Series*, ed. Lydia Wevers, *Landfall*, 152, Dec. 1984, pp.504-6.

8. Stead, *Answering to the Language*, p.242.
9. Jones, 'Versions of the Dream', p.202.
10. Anne French, rev. of *The Limits of Green*, p.348.
11. Lawrence Jones, 'Reflections on a Bumper Year in Fiction', *Journal of New Zealand Literature*, 3, 1985, p.17.
12. Allen Curnow interviewed by Harry Ricketts, *Talking About Ourselves*, p.103. On the year 1985 in fiction see my 'Literary Recession', pp.14-27.
13. Mike Johnson, *Anti Body Positive*. Auckland, Hard Echo, 1988.
14. Michael Morrissey, introduction to *The New Fiction*. Auckland, Lindon, 1985, pp.13-74.
15. Robert Chapman, 'Fiction and the Social Pattern', in *Essays on New Zealand Literature*, p.74.
16. Dennis McEldowney, Judges' Report, Ansett New Zealand Book Awards, 1989. Thanks to Dennis McEldowney and the Queen Elizabeth II Arts Council for permission to quote this document.
17. Michael Jackson, *Rainshadow*. Dunedin, John McIndoe, 1988, p.187.
18. Frame, *A State of Siege*, p.125.
19. McEldowney, Judges' Report.
20. Anne Kennedy, *100 Traditional Smiles*. Wellington, Victoria University Press, 1988, section 118.
21. Frame, *Living in the Maniototo*, p.207.
22. Margaret Mahy, rev. of *Diesel Mystic* by Gregory O'Brien. *Landfall*, 173, March 1990, p.76.
23. Allen Curnow, 'The Unhistoric Story', *Collected Poems, 1933-1973*, Wellington: A. H. & A. W. Reed, 1974, pp.79-80.
24. Heather Roberts, *Where Did She Come From?: New Zealand Women Novelists, 1862-1987*. Wellington, Allen & Unwin/Port Nicholson Press, 1989, p.75.
25. Stevan Eldred-Grigg, rev. of *A Destiny Apart: New Zealand's Search for National Identity*, by Keith Sinclair, *Landfall*, 162, June 1987, pp.222-8. See also Stevan Eldred-Grigg, 'A Bourgeois Blue? Nationalism and Letters from the 1920s to the 1950s', *Landfall*, 163, Sept. 1987, pp.293-311.
26. Jones, 'Versions of the Dream', p.196.
27. Jones, 'Versions of the Dream', p.196.
28. Allen Curnow, 'Author's Note', *Collected Poems*, p.xiii. Quoted in Jones, 'Versions of the Dream', p.196.
29. Sargeson, *Once Is Enough*, p.133.
30. Salman Rushdie, quoted by Edward W. Said, 'Dealing With Rushdie's "Complicated Mixture"', *Guardian*, 19 March 1989.
31. Frame, *Faces in the Water*, p.251.
32. Frame, *Living in the Maniototo*, p.120.
33. See Dorothy M. Macardle ed., *Sir Philip Sidney's Defense of Poesy*. London, Macmillan, 1964, pp.4, 12-20.
34. Sargeson, *Conversation*, p.184.
35. Charles Brasch, 'Notes', *Landfall*, March 1947; reprinted as 'Documentary', *Landfall Country: Work from 'Landfall', 1947-61*, chosen by Charles Brasch, Christchurch, Caxton, 1962, p.433.
36. See, for instance, Graham Huggan, 'Opting out of the (Critical) Common Market: Creolization and the Post-Colonial Text', *After Europe: Critical Theory and Post-Colonial Writing*, ed. Steven Slemon & Helen Tiffin, Denmark, Dangaroo, 1989, pp.27-40.
37. Maurice Duggan, 'Along Rideout Road That Summer', *Some Other Country*, p.114.
38. Connolly, *Enemies of Promise*, p.81.
39. *Frontline*, 25 Feb. 1990.
40. Joce Brown, 'Royalty, the Tour and Colonialism', *The Republican*, no. 57, Jan. 1986, p.4.
41. Lamb, 'Problems of Originality', p.356.
42. Wedde, 'Dreaming of a White Myth', p.238.
43. Les Murray interviewed by Iain Sharp, p.160.
44. Wilson Harris, *Explorations*, Denmark, Dangaroo, 1981, p.135.
45. Tom Paulin, 'A New Look at the Language Question', *Ireland's Field Day*. London, Hutchinson, 1985, p.15.

Select Bibliography

Awatere, Donna. *Maori Sovereignty*. Auckland, 1984.

Berry, Reginald. 'Stead's Dream'. Rev. of *The Death of the Body*, *Landfall*, 163, 1987, pp.344-7.

Bertram, James. 'Ian Wedde's Fiction', *Islands*, 17, 1977, pp.302-6.

Best, Elsdon. *Maori Religion and Mythology*, 2v. Wellington, 1982.

——. *Spiritual and Mental Concepts of the Maori*. Wellington,1954.

Brasch, Charles. *Landfall Country: Work from 'Landfall', 1947-61*. Christchurch, 1962.

Calder, Alex. 'My Katherine Mansfield', *Landfall*, 172, 1989, pp.483-99.

——. 'The Closure of Sense: Janet Frame, Language, and the Body', *Antic/3*, 1987, pp.93-104.

——. Rev. of *The Matriarch*, *Landfall*, 161, 1987, pp.79-84.

Connolly, Cyril. *Enemies of Promise*. 1939; repr. London, Andre Deutsch, 1973.

Cowley, Joy, 'We are the bone people', rev. of *the bone people*, *New Zealand Listener*, 12 May 1984, p.60.

Curnow, Allen. *Collected Poems, 1933-1973*. Wellington, 1974.

——. *Look Back Harder: Critical Writings, 1935-1984*, ed. Peter Simpson. Auckland, 1987.

Curnow, Wystan, ed. *Essays on New Zealand Literature*. Auckland, 1973.

——. 'Speech Balloons and Conversation Bubbles', *And/4*, 1985, p.125-48.

Daalder, Joost. 'Violence in the Stories of Frank Sargeson', *Journal of New Zealand Literature*, 4, 1986, pp.56-80.

Deane, Seamus, *et al. Ireland's Field Day*. London, 1985.

During, Simon. 'Postmodernism or Postcolonialism?', *Landfall*, 155, 1985, pp.366-80.

——. 'Towards a Revision of Local Critical Habits', *And/1*, 1983, pp.75-92.

Eldred-Grigg, Stevan. 'A Bourgeois Blue?: Nationalism and Letters from the 1920s to the 1950s', *Landfall*, 163, 1987, pp.293-311.

——. Rev. of *A Destiny Apart: New Zealand's Search for National Identity*, by Keith Sinclair, *Landfall*, 162, 1987, pp.222-8.

——. '*Oracles and Miracles*: Working Class Novel, Okay?', *Sites*, 16, 1988, pp.111-20.

Eliot, T. S. *Selected Essays*. London, 1972.

Evans, Miriama. 'Politics and Maori Literature', *Landfall*, 153, 1985, pp.40-45.

Evans, P. D. *Janet Frame*. Boston, 1977.

——. Rev. of *The Carpathians*, *New Zealand Listener*, 24 Sept. 1988, p.70-73.

Frame, Janet. *An Angel at My Table: An Autobiography*. vol.2. Auckland, 1985.

——. *The Carpathians*. Auckland, 1988.
——. *Faces in the Water*. 1961; repr. London, 1984.
——. *Living in the Maniototo*. New York, 1979.
——. *A State of Siege*. New York, 1966.
——. *To the Is-Land: An Autobiography*. London, 1983.
Fullbrook, Kate. *Katherine Mansfield*. London, 1986.
Fussell, Paul. *Abroad: British Literary Travelling Between the Wars*. New York, 1975.
Gee, Maurice. *Collected Stories*. Auckland, 1986.
——. *In My Father's Den*. London, 1972.
——. *Meg*. Auckland, 1981.
——. *Prowlers*. Auckland, 1987.
——. *Sole Survivor*. Auckland, 1984.
Gordon, Elizabeth. '*Oracles and Miracles*: Truth or Fiction?' *Untold*, 9/10, 1988, pp.40-46.
Haley, Russell. Rev. of *Games of Choice*, *Spleen* 6, Dec. 1976, n. p.
Hardy, Linda. 'The Ghost of Katherine Mansfield', *Landfall*, 172, 1989, pp.416-32.
Harris, Wilson. *Explorations*. Denmark, 1981.
Hau'ofa, Epeli. Interview with Subramani, *Landfall*, 169, 1989, pp.35-51.
Horrocks, Roger. 'Readings of *A State of Siege* (1967) and *A State of Siege* (1978)', *And*/3, 1984, pp.131-45.
Hughes, Robert. *The Art of Australia*. 1966; rev. ed. Harmondsworth, 1970.
Hulme, Keri. *the bone people*. Wellington, 1983.
——. Interview with Harry Ricketts, *Talking About Ourselves: Twelve New Zealand Poets in Conversation with Harry Ricketts*. Wellington, 1986.
Hyde, Robin. *Nor the Years Condemn*, ed. Phillida Bunkle, *et al*. Auckland, 1986.
Ihimaera, Witi. *The Matriarch*. Auckland, 1986.
——. *The New Net Goes Fishing*. Auckland, 1985.
——. *Pounamu, Pounamu*. Auckland, 1972.
——. *Tangi*. Auckland, 1975.
——. *The Whale Rider*. Auckland, 1987.
Jackson, Michael. *Rainshadow*. Dunedin, 1988.
James, Henry. *Hawthorne*, intro. by Tony Tanner. London, 1967.
Jensen, Kai. 'Holes, Wholeness and Holiness in Frank Sargeson's Writing', *Landfall*, 173, 1990, pp.32-44.
Johnson, Mike. *Anti Body Positive*. Auckland, 1988.
Jones, Lawrence. *Barbed Wire and Mirrors: Essays on New Zealand Prose*. Dunedin, 1987.
——. 'Reflections on a Bumper Year in Fiction', *Journal of New Zealand Literature*, 3, 1985, pp.17-34.
——. 'Stanley Graham and the Several Faces of "Man Alone"', *Journal of Popular Culture*, v.19, 1985, pp.121-36.
Kennedy, Anne. 'An Angel Entertains Theatricals', *Landfall*, 172, 1989, pp.397–8.
——. *100 Traditional Smiles*. Wellington, 1988.

Kermode, Frank. *Modern Essays*. London, 1971.

King, Michael. *Whina: A Biography of Whina Cooper*. Auckland, 1983.

Lamb, Jonathan. 'Problems of Originality: Or, Beware of Pakeha Baring Guilts', *Landfall*, 159, 1986, pp.352-8.

——. 'The Uncanny in Auckland', *And*/4, 1985, pp.32-45.

Lawrence, D. H. *Apocalypse*. 1931; repr. London, 1972.

Lukacs, Georg. *The Theory of the Novel*, trans. Anna Bostock. Cambridge, Mass., 1977.

McKay, Frank, ed. *James K. Baxter as Critic*. Auckland, 1978.

McLintock, A. H., ed. *Encyclopaedia of New Zealand*, 2v. Wellington, 1966.

Mahy, Margaret. Rev. of *Diesel Mystic*, by Gregory O'Brien, *Landfall*, 173, 1990, p.76-78.

Manhire, Bill. 'Breaking the Line: A View of American and New Zealand Poetry', *Islands*, 38, 1987, pp.142-54.

——. *Maurice Gee*. Auckland, 1986.

—— and Marion McLeod, eds. *Some Other Country: New Zealand's Best Short Stories*. Wellington, 1984.

Menzies, Trixie Te Arama. 'Kowhai Gold—Skeleton or Scapegoat?' *Landfall*, 165, 1988, pp.19-26.

Mitchell, J. H. *Takitimu*. Wellington, 1973.

Morrissey, Michael. *The New Fiction*. Auckland, 1985.

Mulgan, John. *Man Alone*. [1939]; repr. Auckland, 1980.

Murray, Les. Interview with Iain Sharp, *Landfall*, 166, 1988, pp.150-68.

New Zealand Through the Arts: Past and Present. The Turnbull Winter Lectures 1981. Wellington, 1982.

Neill, Michael. 'Coming Home: Teaching the Post-Colonial Novel', *Islands*, 35, 1985, pp.38-53.

O'Brien, Gregory. *Moments of Invention: Portraits of 21 New Zealand Writers*. Auckland, 1988.

O'Sullivan, Vincent. 'Finding the Pattern, Solving the Problem', Victoria University of Wellington Inaugural Addresses, New Series. Wellington, 1989.

Pearson, Bill. *Fretful Sleepers*. Auckland, 1974.

Phillips, A. A. *The Australian Tradition: Studies in a Colonial Culture*. Melbourne, 1958.

Pope, Quentin, ed. *Kowhai Gold: An Anthology of Contemporary New Zealand Verse*. London, 1930.

Roberts, Heather. *Where Did She Come From? New Zealand Women Novelists, 1862-1987*. Wellington, 1989.

Ruthven, K. K. Rev. of *Pound, Eliot, Yeats and the Modernist Movement*, by C. K. Stead, *Landfall*, 160, 1986, pp.509-13.

Sargeson, Frank. *Conversation in a Train and Other Critical Writing*, ed. Kevin Cunningham. Auckland, 1983.

——. *The Hangover & Joy of the Worm*. Auckland, 1984.

——. *More Than Enough: A Memoir*. Wellington, 1975.

——. *Once Is Enough: A Memoir*. Wellington, 1973.

——. *The Stories of Frank Sargeson*. Auckland, 1975.

Sheridan, Alan. *Michel Foucault: The Will to Truth*. London, 1980.

Simpson, Peter, 'Recent Fiction and the Sargeson Tradition', *Journal of New Zealand Literature*, 1, 1983, pp.17-29.

——. 'The Trick of Standing Upright', *World Literatures Written in English*, v.26, 1986, pp.369-78.

Slemon, Steven and Helen Tiffin, eds. *After Europe: Critical Theory and Post-Colonial Writing*. Denmark, 1989.

Sorrenson, M. P. K. *Maori Origins and Migrations: The Genesis of Some Pakeha Myths and Legends*. Auckland, 1983.

Stead, C. K. *All Visitors Ashore*. London, 1984.

——. *Answering to the Language: Essays on Modern Writers*. Auckland, 1989.

——. *The Death of the Body*. London, 1986.

——. *In the Glass Case: Essays on New Zealand Literature*. Auckland, 1981.

——. Interview with Michael Harlow, *Landfall*, 148, 1983, p.464.

——, ed. *The Letters and Journals of Katherine Mansfield: A Selection*. London, 1977.

——. *The New Poetic*. London, 1964.

——. *Smith's Dream*. Auckland, 1971.

Stevens, Joan. *The New Zealand Novel, 1860-1965*. Wellington, 1966.

Sturm, Terry. 'Shifting the Points', rev. of *The Penguin Book of New Zealand Verse*, *Listener*, 13 July 1985, p.48–53.

Wedde, Ian. *Dick Seddon's Great Dive*. Auckland, 1976.

——. 'Dreaming of a White Myth', *Landfall*, 170, 1989, p.237-42.

——. Interview with David Dowling, *Landfall*, 154, 1985, p.159-81.

—— and Harvey McQueen, eds. *The Penguin Book of New Zealand Verse*. Auckland, 1985.

——. *The Shirt Factory and Other Stories*. Wellington, 1981.

——. *Survival Arts*. Auckland, Penguin, 1988.

——. *Symmes Hole*. Auckland, 1986.

Wevers, Lydia. 'Changing Directions: The Short Story in New Zealand', *Meanjin*, v.44, 1985, p.353-6.

Williams, Mark. '"Discourse More Sweet"? The Politics of Language in New Zealand and Fiji', *Meridian*, v.7, 1988, pp.23-33.

——. 'Literary Recession: New Zealand Fiction, 1985 - mid-1986', *Journal of New Zealand Literature*, 5, 1987, pp.14-28.

——. 'Race and Nationalism: The Novel in New Zealand', *Island*, 36, 1988, pp.31-37.

——. 'T. S. Eliot, Tradition and Contemporary New Zealand Poetry', *The Literary Half-Yearly*, v.29, 1988, pp.148-62.

Willmott, Bill and David Novitz. *Culture and Identity in New Zealand*. Wellington, 1989.

Index